Desk Reference on

AMERICAN
COURTS

BOOKS IN THE DESK REFERENCE SERIES

CQ's Desk Reference on American Courts

CQ's Desk Reference on the States

CQ's Desk Reference on the Federal Budget

CQ's Desk Reference on American Government

CONGRESSIONAL QUARTERLY'S

Desk Reference on
AMERICAN
COURTS

PATRICIA G. BARNES

CQ PRESS

A Division of Congressional Quarterly Inc.

To my first point of reference,

my parents

CQ Press
A Division of Congressional Quarterly Inc.
1414 22nd St. N.W.
Washington, D.C. 20037

(202) 822-1475; (800) 638-1710

http://books.cq.com

Printed in the United States of America

Cover and interior design: Anne Masters Design, Inc., Washington, D.C.

Library of Congress Cataloging-in-Publication Data

Barnes, Patricia G.
    Congressional Quarterly's desk reference on American courts / Patricia G. Barnes.
        p.   cm.
    Includes bibliographical references and index.
    ISBN 1-56802-435-5 (cloth)
    1. Courts—United States—Popular works. 2. Justice, Administration of—
United States—Popular works. I. Congressional Quarterly, inc. II. Title. III. Title:
Desk reference on American courts.
KF8720.B37   1999   99-28730
347.73'1--dc21

CONTENTS

PREFACE

In churning out books, movies, and television shows about the American court system, the popular media portray courtrooms as the coliseums of yore, where modern-day gladiators—armed with words, strategy, and passion—thrust and parry in the pursuit of justice. A taciturn judge cloaked in black sits on high. A jury wrestles with the facts behind locked doors. Justice is done.

Reality, of course, is altogether different from the media's portrayal. The business of the courts typically moves at a glacial pace through massive and seemingly impenetrable bureaucracies. Many courts have overlapping jurisdictions. Civil cases outnumber criminal cases. Most criminal cases are resolved through plea bargains. Jury trials, relatively rare events, often are influenced by external factors, such as the defendant's bank account. Justice, in many cases, is neither swift nor sure.

The *Desk Reference on American Courts* is an invaluable guide to the complexities of the American court system. It presents a plethora of information—gleaned from hundreds of popular, scholarly, and government sources—in an easy-to-understand, question-and-answer format. The book takes readers step by step through the history and law that is the foundation of the system, through the halls of the Supreme Court of the United States and the lower federal courts, to the fifty states, where courts, like speech patterns, vary from state to state and sometimes within each state.

In addition to giving readers information essential to an understanding of the form and function of the courts, the *Desk Reference* provides insight into what goes on behind the scenes. Before a judge takes the bench, for example, he or she is selected through a process that is influenced by political party, gender and race, and, once again, money. The book demystifies this process, as well as the courts' specialized customs and language, in brief, reader-friendly paragraphs. The *Desk Reference* contains concise and clearly written definitions of commonly used legal terms, such as *grand jury, hearsay, nollo contendere,* and *habeas corpus.*

Every effort has been made to present the most up-to-date and accurate information on how courts decide the 90 million civil and criminal cases that come before them each year. Until now, information about their day-to-day operations was found primarily in obscure government reports that circulate mainly to major libraries, government bureaucracies, and universities. Readers of the *Desk Reference* will discover, among other important facts and statistics, the types of cases most often litigated, the likelihood that an arrest for a serious crime will lead to conviction, and the percentage of murderers sentenced to life in prison.

In general, information about courts is not readily accessible. With respect to federal courts, the Framers of the U.S. Constitution gave judges built-in job security to insulate them from political backlash so they would not shrink from making unpopular decisions. Federal courts, unlike the executive and legislative branches, are not accountable to the ballot box, and therefore judges and court officials feel less compelled to make information about their operations available to the public. It is no coincidence that the Supreme Court is one of the last American institutions to be shielded from the glare of television cameras. Justices have lifetime tenure, assuming good behavior, and cannot be fired by the public. If they do not want television in their courtroom, it will not be allowed. Efforts to obtain certain basic information about federal courts were unsuccessful. A case in point is the nation's newest federal court, the Alien Terrorist Removal Court, created by Congress in 1996. Will it actually convene at some point, or will it quietly fade away? Only time will tell—the Administrative Office of the U.S. Courts either could not or would not.

The challenge of writing about the state courts is that there are fifty independent state court systems, each with different laws and different methods of selecting judges, processing cases, and reporting statistics. Only in recent years has any effort been made to centralize data on the operation of individual state court systems. Therefore information is sometimes dated and often scattered and incomplete. For example, the only courts with which most Americans have contact are small claims and traffic courts. One would expect these courts to receive a proportionate share of a state's attention and resources. But the reverse is true. Woefully little reliable information is available on these and other state courts of limited jurisdiction. Although the *Desk Reference* necessarily reflects such gaps in the source data, it nevertheless succeeds in bringing together the latest information and most up-to-date statistics available.

Readers can use the *Desk Reference* in two ways. This book is designed to be a convenient reference tool and to provide quick access to specific facts about the courts and court-related issues. A detailed index makes the book's contents instantly accessible. Readers also may proceed sequentially through the questions, from Chapter 1 through Chapter 6, to gain a broad understanding of the courts. The book's main subject areas include historic milestones, the U.S. Constitution, and the Supreme Court; U.S. courts of appeals and district courts; state constitutions; state supreme courts, appellate courts, and trial courts; court-related civil and criminal justice issues; and, finally, courts on the bottom rung of the court system, including magistrate and justice of the peace courts.

Many answers are cross-referenced to link readers to additional relevant information. Supplemental research aids are included in the Reference Materials section, which contains the text of the U.S. Constitution and Judiciary Act of 1789, a list of sources of Supreme Court decisions, a primer on how to read a Court citation, a glossary of legal terms, and a bibliography.

Many thanks to those who assisted in the completion of this book, including my editor at CQ Press, Patricia Gallagher, and her predecessor, Shana Wagger, who suggested the project. Special thanks to Christopher Karlsten, whose thoughtful comments and deft copy editing improved this work immeasurably. John R. McKivigan brought a helpful historian's eye to the project. Some of the better questions were suggested by Martha Barnes, Dennis McCurdy, Tom Miles, Susan Okula, Susan Shaw Sailor, Victoria Sandin, and Richard Veilleux. Finally, I would like to thank the research and information officers at the National Center for State Courts and at the Justice Department's Bureau of Justice Statistics, who were unfailingly knowledgeable and helpful.

—Patricia G. Barnes

INTRODUCTION TO THE AMERICAN COURT SYSTEM

Q 1. What is the American court system?

A A map of the American court system might look like the California freeway system—incomprehensible at first glance, a series of interlacing and seemingly haphazard roadways. Despite its apparent complexity, it is the same basic system of federalism that was envisioned by the Framers of the U.S. Constitution in 1787. Though far from perfect, it has made the United States a much-admired source of freedom and hope throughout the world.

Compared with the state court system, the federal system is a sleek interstate highway, a national thoroughfare with well-marked access and exit ramps. The mission of federal courts has always been far narrower than that of state courts. Federal court jurisdiction is circumscribed by the Constitution and Congress. Federal courts were designed to resolve disputes that would be difficult to resolve in state courts, such as feuding between two states or between citizens of different states. Federal courts also interpret the laws enacted to carry out national policies—those guaranteeing unrestricted interstate commerce, for example—and provide uniform federal control over important national activities. Moreover, federal courts interpret and enforce the Constitution, federal laws, and treaties with foreign governments.

The federal court system is essentially a pyramid. At the apex is the U.S. Supreme Court, the only court required by the Constitution. It is the highest court in the nation, the final arbiter of the meaning of the Constitution. Twelve regional U.S. courts of appeals are in the middle. They hear appeals from lower federal courts and administrative agencies. Ninety-four U.S. district courts are on the bottom. They are general trial-level courts for cases involving federal statutes or questions of federal law. Congress has established assorted other courts to carry out specific mandates, such as U.S. Tax Court and the U.S. Court of Federal Claims.

State court systems carry most of the traffic of litigation in the nation. State courts are the country's primary forums for resolving civil disputes and the chief tribunals for interpreting the criminal law. Each of the fifty states independently developed its court system to meet the unique needs of its population. It is not surprising that Louisiana's court system is markedly different from that of Massachusetts. The best state court systems are a wellspring of innovation and experimentation. The worst are fragmented and inefficient, with many different levels of courts, some with overlapping venues, statutory authority, and geographical jurisdictions.

There is no generic state court system in the United States. Despite their differences, however, there are many similarities among state court systems and between the federal and state systems. Every state, for instance, has the equivalent of a court of last resort, which is called, variously, a supreme court, court of appeals, court of criminal appeals, supreme court of appeals, or supreme judicial court. Most states have intermediate appellate courts, which decide routine appeals from lower state courts. All states have trial courts of general jurisdiction in which the facts of a criminal or civil case are presented to a judge or a jury. These courts are called circuit, district, or superior courts and are often grouped into geographical units. Most states also have special purpose courts, such as family or juvenile courts, and courts of limited jurisdiction, including municipal or justice of the peace courts. Since the 1980s many states have unified their court systems, consolidating courts and hiring state court administrators to achieve greater efficiency.

The federal and state legal systems intersect at various points. They share jurisdiction in many areas of both civil and criminal law. In recent years the state/federal divide has grown less sharp as Congress has created federal penalties for crimes that were once entirely within the realm of state courts. Today, federal courts have jurisdiction not only over serious multistate criminal activity such as drug trafficking but also over innocuous offenses such as bringing false teeth into a state without the approval of a local dentist.

Because of the vastness of the territory, it is possible here to offer only a glimpse of the American court system's great expanse. Indeed, some may find that the following explanations raise more questions than they answer. It is hoped that this volume will, at least, direct the reader to further study. As the marshal of the Supreme Court says at the beginning of Court proceedings, "Oyez, Oyez, Oyez" (French: "Hear ye, Hear ye, Hear ye." *See 196 What does the marshal of the Court do?*).

THE LAW

IN GENERAL

Q 2. What is the law?

A From the Old English *lagu*, of Scandinavian origin, the law is a rule or a system of rules of human behavior. There are many different kinds of laws, including those enacted by the legislature, those discerned through the interpretation of legal precedent by the judiciary, and those promulgated by administrative bodies. These laws collectively represent an expression of the will of the supreme power of the state and must be followed by citizens. Failure to do so could result in sanctions or legal consequences. There also are unwritten moral laws that arise from custom and usage, including ethical and religious doctrines. These laws generally are not enforceable by the state in a court of law. Jurist Oliver Wendell Holmes, Jr., traced the "secret root from which the law draws all the juices of life" to considerations of what is expedient for the community.

Q 3. Why is the American legal system adversarial rather than inquisitorial, as in Europe?

A Their experience with the British monarchy and colonial rule left the Framers of the U.S. Constitution with a deep distrust of government, lawyers, and the courts. They established three branches of government and put in place a system of checks and balances to prevent any one branch from becoming too powerful. Rather than establishing an all-powerful judiciary, they preferred to discover the true nature of the law through the clash of opponents in a courtroom. In the *adversarial system*, the judge is an independent magistrate and the criminal defendant is presumed innocent until found guilty by a jury beyond a reasonable doubt. In the *inquisitorial* system, which is used by many other countries to determine guilt, the judge serves as a prosecutor who conducts an inquiry into the truth of the charges that the state or a plaintiff has lodged against a defendant.

Q 4. What is *stare decisis*?

A *Stare decisis* is a Latin phrase meaning "let the decision stand." The complete phrase is *stare decisis et quieta non movere,* or "let the decision stand and do not disturb the calm." It refers to the American process of legal reasoning that requires judges to adhere to the rule of law established in prior decisions in similar, relevant cases. Important judicial opinions are published so that they may serve as precedents—that is, guides to judges who are considering similar cases. This process is designed to yield consistent and predictable results.

Q 5. How binding is precedent on courts?

A Not all precedents are treated the same and, in some cases, precedent is explicitly rejected in favor of politically popular change. The U.S. Supreme Court views *stare decisis* as a "principle of policy and not a mechanical formula of adherence to the latest decision, however recent and questionable, when such adherence involves collision with a prior doctrine more embracing in its scope, intrinsically sounder, and verified by expression."

Q 6. What is the difference between the letter and the spirit of the law?

A The letter of the law is the literal translation of the law as written. The spirit of the law is what the lawmakers intended to accomplish by the law's passage. Should a law be interpreted strictly as written, or should a judge attempt to discern and interpret the spirit of the law? This issue is at the heart of an important national debate. Some scholars say that judges who deviate from the text and commonly accepted meaning of the U.S. Constitution are improperly rewriting the document, while others insist that the Constitution can survive only if it is considered a "living" document that may be interpreted in light of modern-day developments.

Q **7. What is natural law?**

A Natural law refers to the fundamental laws of God and nature. Some theorists say that natural law is the basis for all man-made laws and that government exists to protect the natural rights of the people. This philosophy was developed in the writings of the English philosophers Thomas Hobbes (1588–1679) and John Locke (1632–1704). Locke asserted that all people are inherently equal and free to pursue "life, liberty, health and property." He argued that law and government are limited by the individual rights that morality requires human beings to extend to each other. In the state of nature, he writes, one man may have power over another to preserve the peace but no man can have absolute or arbitrary power over another. Government should be the servant of the people and not their master. The theory of natural law profoundly influenced the development of government and law in Western civilization and that of many major legal documents, including the U.S. Declaration of Independence (1776) and the U.S. Constitution (1787).

Q **8. What is common law?**

A The common law comprises the body of judicial opinions rendered by judges over the centuries. These decisions are handed down by one generation of attorneys and judges to the next. Judges interpret and adapt prior judicial decisions in light of the unique circumstances of constantly evolving legal situations. New judicial decisions become part of the body of precedent available to decide similar cases in the future. The American legal system's reliance upon judicial precedent ensures that the law is consistent and predictable. Common law is sometimes referred to as the "unwritten law" because much of it is not codified. A large part of American common law is derived from the statutes of ancient England, where the common law evolved from church law in the twelfth century to encompass a wide variety of customs, precedents, and legal commentaries.

Q **9. Is there a federal common law?**

A Technically, no. The common law is state law. The U.S. Supreme Court ruled that there is no federal common law in the landmark case *Erie Railroad Co. v. Tompkins* (1938). The Court held that when no specific federal law applies, federal courts hearing cases involving citizens of different states must apply the law of the applicable state (the state where the dispute occurred), including its written laws and the decisions of its courts. This decision was intended to limit the spread of federal jurisdiction and to eliminate disputes between federal and state courts regarding the interpretation of state laws. Earlier, in *United States v. Hudson and Goodwin* (1812), the Court held that federal courts' criminal jurisdiction is limited to that created by federal laws declaring certain offenses to be federal crimes.

Q 10. What is statutory law?

A Statutes are written enactments of state and federal legislatures. They have the force of law but are subject to review by the courts. This body of law is known as statutory law. A law passed by Congress is called an act; a law passed by a state legislature, a statute; and a law passed by a local legislative body, an ordinance.

Q 11. What is civil law?

A Civil law denotes the rules governing private rights and remedies, as opposed to criminal law. Civil law includes the law of contracts, or the rules governing legal obligations that arise between individuals, and the law of "torts," or the claims that ensue between private parties when one party alleges that the other has been negligent or has caused him or her to suffer damages by failing to carry out a duty. Civil law also encompasses a range of laws governing the actions of individuals and businesses with respect to public affairs, such as consumer and environmental protection laws.

Q 12. What is criminal law?

A The criminal law is the body of rules concerning crimes in which the state or the United States is the aggrieved party. A crime is an act committed in violation of what the government defines as an individual's duty to the community. Violations of criminal law carry penalties ranging from fines to disqualification from holding public office to capital punishment. Criminal acts may also give rise to civil lawsuits. In the case of an assault, for example, the state may seek to criminally prosecute and jail the perpetrator, while the victim may sue the perpetrator for monetary damages in civil court.

Q 13. What is equity?

A Equity provides a remedy when there is no law covering a situation, when the law is inadequate to remedy the wrong, or when a literal interpretation of the law would result in egregious unfairness. Aristotle once said that "equity is justice that goes beyond the written law." Equitable principles evolved as an alternative to the common law in England, where courts could impose only money damages. Equity jurisdiction covered matters that required some extraordinary remedy, such as an injunction or a court order commanding a person to do a specific act or forbear from doing something. The equity judge or chancellor was said to be the "keeper of the king's conscience." Law and equity have merged in the federal court system and in most state court systems. Only a few states still maintain separate courts for law and equity. The Delaware Court of Chancery is one such court. It has endured as a separate legal institution since 1792 and has been instrumental in the development of the nation's largest body of corporation law.

Q 14. What is administrative law?

A An administrative agency is a government body authorized to implement a particular legislative act. Article 1, Section 1, of the U.S. Constitution vests all federal legislative power in Congress, which exercises this authority by creating administrative agencies. These agencies, in turn, carry out the legislative will of Congress. Thus the Internal Revenue Service collects federal taxes, the Federal Communications Commission regulates the public airwaves, and the Securities and Exchange Commission regulates the sale of securities. Administrative law is the body of law created by public regulatory agencies to implement their powers and mission.

Q 15. Who oversees the actions of federal administrative agencies?

A All three branches of government oversee the actions of these agencies.

The appointments clause of the U.S. Constitution (Article 2, Section 2) empowers the president to appoint officers of the United States, subject to confirmation by the Senate. Presidents generally appoint officers who share their views. If displeased, the president may issue an executive order directing agency officials to act or refrain from acting, or may seek congressional approval to reorganize the agency. The executive branch also reviews agency budgets through the Office of Management and Budget.

Congress oversees regulatory agencies through the annual appropriations process, by which it determines how much money they will receive. An overreaching agency may receive a budget cut or face overhaul or even extinction.

Judges routinely review agency decisions to ensure that they comply with the law and that the agency did not violate any individual rights under the Constitution, including the right to due process of law.

IMMUNITIES

Q 16. What is an immunity?

A Some people are, in a sense, above the law. They're supposed to obey society's laws like everyone else, but if they fail to, there are no legal consequences. An immunity is the negation of liability and the freedom from suit or legal authority. It is conferred upon an individual because of the person's status or position, not for any moral reason. It is justified by the function that it serves and protects. For example, judges have absolute immunity from civil liability arising out of the discharge of the functions of their office, even when these actions are taken in bad faith. However, immunity is not granted for acts over which the court has no jurisdiction. The U.S. Supreme Court reasons that judicial immunity is justified because allowing unsatisfied litigants to sue a judge would lead to the intimidation of judges and undermine the legal system. A "quasi-judicial" immunity also extends to nonjudicial officers when they are performing tasks that are intimately related to the judicial process, such as a court clerk who prepares an arrest warrant.

Many other public officials are protected by immunities, including foreign diplomats and legislators.

The U.S. Constitution gives legislators a privilege "from Arrest during their Attendance" at sessions of Congress. While in session they may not be arrested for any crime except treason, felony, and a breach of peace. They also are privileged "for any Speech or Debate in either House" (Article 1, Section 6).

Q 17. What is sovereign immunity?

A The doctrine of sovereign immunity is derived from the Eleventh Amendment (1795), which states, "The Judicial power of the United States shall not be construed to extend to any suit in law or equity, commenced or prosecuted against one of the United States by Citizens of another State, or by Citizens or Subjects of any Foreign State."

Historically, the U.S. government and its subdivisions were immune from being sued in court without their consent. However, the doctrine of "sovereign immunity" has greatly eroded.

In 1855 Congress established the U.S. Court of Claims (the predecessor of the U.S. Court of Federal Claims) to hear cases against the United States involving certain contract disputes and claims against the government. In 1946 Congress passed the Federal Tort Claims Act, which authorizes federal courts to hold the United States liable for certain claims of negligence or damages committed by its agencies, officers, and employers.

Congress today allows suits by individuals who claim to have been threatened or injured by government officials acting in excess of their legal authority or under an allegedly unconstitutional law.

Q **18. What is executive privilege?**

A The U.S. president is exempt from disclosure requirements applicable to ordinary citizens when such an exemption is necessary to the discharge of highly important executive responsibilities. Executive privilege is not an unqualified right. In 1974 Republican president Richard Nixon, who was then under investigation for ordering the break-in of Democratic national headquarters at the Watergate complex in Washington, D.C., asserted executive privilege when a special prosecutor subpoenaed him to turn over secret tape recordings of conversations with his aides in his White House office. In *U.S. v. Nixon* (1974) the Supreme Court recognized a constitutional basis for executive privilege in the doctrine of separation of powers. However, the Court said that the need for confidentiality of high-level communications cannot, without additional justification, sustain an absolute unqualified presidential privilege of immunity from the judicial process. Nixon was forced to turn over the tapes. He later resigned to avoid impeachment proceedings.

MILESTONES

Q **19. What is the foundation of English constitutional liberty?**

A King John of England (1199–1216) put his seal on the Magna Carta on June 15, 1215, in a field at Runnymede to ward off a confrontation with rebellious barons who had threatened war if the king did not accede to their demands. The Magna Carta was intended to protect the rights of the nobility from royal abuses of power, but it did far more than that. The Magna Carta was a harbinger of modern constitutionalism. It was the first important document defining the rights of English citizens. Deriving its name from a Latin phrase meaning "great charter," the Magna Carta required that legal proceedings be conducted according to "the law of the land" and prohibited the sale, denial, or delay of justice. Freemen were granted the right to a trial by a jury of their peers, and the king was prohibited from levying taxes without the consent of the "Great Council of the Realm."

Q 20. What rule of law governed the American colonies?

A More than 150 years lapsed between the Puritans' founding of the Massachusetts Bay Colony and the signing of the Declaration of Independence. During that time the thirteen colonies developed their own independent legal systems grounded in English common law but without a rigid class structure based upon feudalism and inherited social distinctions. Their laws reflected the challenges of living in a new frontier with unlimited opportunity and in a climate and geography vastly different from those of their homeland. Their laws also reflected the sensibilities of the Puritans, strict Protestants who emphasized the duty of each individual church member to be virtuous and to work for the common welfare of the church and the community.

In the mid-eighteenth century one farmer wrote about life in what today is the state of Vermont. "I am living in God's noble and free soil, neither am I slave to others," he wrote. "I have now been on American soil for two and a half years and I have not been compelled to pay for the privilege of living. Neither is my cap worn out from lifting it in the presence of gentlemen."

Of course, not everyone enjoyed the rights of which this farmer wrote—the rights of men of property. Colonial laws generally accorded women the legal status of children, who had few rights because of their age, and black slaves, who comprised one fifth of the population of the colonies in 1760, were treated as property and denied the basic rights to life, liberty, and property.

Q 21. What are the Articles of Confederation?

A The Articles of Confederation, ratified in 1781, are the first written constitution of the United States, the forerunner of the U.S. Constitution of 1787. The articles were drafted by a committee led by John Dickinson of Pennsylvania that was appointed by the Continental Congress. They embodied Congress's wish for a central government strong enough to defeat Great Britain but not so strong as to threaten the rights of citizens and the states.

The articles required each state to provide full faith and credit to the laws of the others, and the free inhabitants of each state were granted the "privileges and immunities of free citizens" of the other states. The articles include an extradition provision for "any Person guilty of, or charged with treason, felony, or other high misdemeanor in any state." Congress also was given jurisdiction to settle disputes between the states.

See 24 What is the significance of the Ordinance of 1787?

Q **22. What were the major weaknesses of the Articles of Confederation?**

A Problems arose under the Articles of Confederation that threatened the health of the new nation. The articles left Congress powerless to intercede when powerful majorities in state legislatures passed laws that taxed their citizens more than the British had, interfered in the private lives of citizens, and violated the property rights of creditors and landowners. Furthermore, Congress could not prevent states from taxing goods from other states, a practice that hindered free trade. Finally, Congress had no power to collect taxes to pay for the American Revolution.

Q **23. What was Shays's Rebellion?**

A Shays's Rebellion was a series of protests during 1786 and 1787 by debt-ridden farmers who objected to government enforcement of tax collections and to judgments requiring payment of debts. Mobs in Massachusetts forcibly stopped the courts from sitting, thereby preventing them from ordering foreclosures on farms. They sought to prolong the protest until politicians willing to provide debtors with legislative relief could be elected. The rebellion was named after Daniel Shays of Massachusetts, a former captain in the Continental army. Massachusetts asked the federal government to quell the uprising, but the Congress was powerless to act under the terms of the Articles of Confederation. The rebellion was finally put down by the Massachusetts militia. Proponents of a strong constitution cited the rebellion as proof of the need to replace the articles with a stronger national constitution.

Q **24. What is the significance of the Ordinance of 1787?**

A The Ordinance of 1787, otherwise known as the Northwest Ordinance, was the most important law passed by Congress under the Articles of Confederation. It gave people in the Northwest the right to establish their own governments and to eventually become states. In effect it established a national legal system by extending basic law to the frontier, which later became Ohio, Indiana, Illinois, Michigan, and Wisconsin. Up to that point, frontier law was administered haphazardly by rough and sometimes corrupt men, often land speculators with little or no legal training. Under the Ordinance of 1787, a territory that had a population of "five thousand free maile inhabitants of full age" could send a representative to the territorial general assembly. The ordinance provided for statehood when sixty thousand freemen inhabitants lived in the territory.

See 21 What are the Articles of Confederation? 22 What were the major weaknesses of the Articles of Confederation?

25. What are *The Federalist Papers*?

A *The Federalist Papers* are a series of eighty-five letters written by Alexander Hamilton, James Madison, and John Jay to three New York newspapers from 1787 to 1788. Urging the adoption of a strong U.S. Constitution, the authors dismissed fears that a tyrannical central government would encroach on states' rights and individual liberties. The essays were published in a book called *The Federalist* in 1788 and have been widely studied by scholars seeking insight into the principles upon which the Constitution and the government of the United States were founded.

See 34 Who is known as the "Father of the Constitution"? 49 What individual rights did James Madison think were most important?

Q 26. What was the Judiciary Act of 1789?

A The Judiciary Act of 1789, the first law passed by the new Congress of the United States of America, established the basic structure of the federal court system, which is still in existence today. Through the act, Congress implemented the mandate of the U.S. Constitution that "the judicial Power of the United States, shall be vested in one supreme Court, and in such inferior Courts as the Congress may from time to time ordain and establish." The act created the Supreme Court, setting its size at six justices, including a chief justice, and gave the Court the power to order federal officials to carry out their legal responsibilities.

The act also created two lower-level trial courts—district courts and circuit courts—to exist alongside state courts. Circuit courts had limited appellate jurisdiction. District courts were located in each of the eleven states that ratified the Constitution and in Maine and Kentucky, which were then a district of Massachusetts and a county of Virginia, respectively. The jurisdiction of the district courts was limited mainly to admiralty cases, diversity cases (those involving citizens of different states), and cases in which the United States was a plaintiff. The districts were organized into three circuits: eastern, middle, and southern. Congress chose not to create any separate judgeships for the circuit courts, instead assigning two Supreme Court justices to sit with a federal district judge in each circuit.

The Judiciary Act also authorized the courts to appoint clerks and gave the president the power to appoint marshals, U.S. attorneys, and an attorney general.

See 41 What type of court system does the U.S. Constitution envision?

27. What is considered the first code of criminal procedure in the United States?

The Bill of Rights, or the first ten amendments to the Constitution, are considered by many to be the first real code of criminal procedure in the United States. The Fourth, Fifth, Sixth, and Eighth Amendments guarantee certain fundamental rights to criminal defendants, including the right to a speedy and public trial by an impartial jury and freedom from self-incrimination, double jeopardy, and excessive bail. The Bill of Rights were ratified on December 15, 1791.

Even before the adoption of the Bill of Rights, during the colonial period, many American colonies adopted documents to safeguard their freedoms. One of the first was the Massachusetts Body of Liberties of 1641, which included the right to trial by jury and prohibitions against self-incrimination and cruel and unusual punishment.

See 46 Why didn't the U.S. Constitution originally have a Bill of Rights? 47 Why was a Bill of Rights necessary? 48 What is the Bill of Rights? 50 Does the Bill of Rights apply to the states?

Q **28. Who were the "Midnight Judges"?**

A The Federalists lost control of Congress and the presidency when Republican president Thomas Jefferson was elected in 1800. Outgoing Federalist president John Adams was determined not to lose the judiciary, too. He managed to get the outgoing Congress to pass a law that let the president appoint as many justices of the peace as he deemed necessary for the District of Columbia. Adams named forty-two of these "Midnight Judges," including William Marbury, an aide to the secretary of the navy, Benjamin Stoddert. Most of the judges received their commissions, but at midnight on the day the administration changed hands, Jefferson instructed his acting secretary of state to cease delivery of the remaining commissions. Marbury and three other Adams appointees brought suit in the Supreme Court to force Jefferson's administration to deliver their commissions, prompting the landmark case of *Marbury v. Madison* (1803), in which the Court for the first time declared an act of Congress to be unconstitutional. The Court said that even though Marbury was entitled to his commission, it did not have the power to order Jefferson to deliver the commission. The Court also invalidated a section of the Judiciary Act of 1789 in which Congress expanded the Court's original jurisdiction. Marbury went on to become president of a bank in the Georgetown section of Washington, D.C., in 1814.

See 102 What is the significance of Marbury v. Madison?

Q **29. What was the Circuit Court of Appeals Act of 1891?**

A President Abraham Lincoln warned in his first message to Congress on the state of the Union in 1861 that "the country has outgrown our present judicial system." He complained that the system of circuit courts could not accommodate the growth of the country, and an explosion of hastily drawn federal statutes made it difficult to ascertain the state of the law. Numerous attempts to reform the system had little effect. Meanwhile, Congress expanded the Supreme Court's jurisdiction, resulting in a heavy backlog. In the Circuit Court of Appeals Act of 1891, Congress shifted the appellate caseload burden from the Supreme Court to a newly created court of appeals, the forerunner of the modern U.S. courts of appeals. Until then, Supreme Court justices were assigned to circuits and forced to travel regularly or "ride circuit" to hear appeals, which often meant long, arduous journeys. The new law created a circuit court of appeals, staffed by two circuit judges and a district judge, in each of the country's nine circuits. The intermediate appellate courts' jurisdiction included criminal, diversity (involving citizens of different states), admiralty, and revenue and patent cases. The courts' decisions could be appealed to the Supreme Court if the Court itself granted a petition for review or if the courts certified to the high court a question or proposition of law about which they desired the Court's instruction.

Q **30. What was the "golden age" of American law?**

A The period from 1787 to 1861 is known as the "golden age" of American law because English law was effectively Americanized by the federal and state governments. The establishment of a series of national treatises, reporting legal decisions by state supreme courts and the U.S. Supreme Court, helped create a national legal system and gave Americans access to judicial decisions, codes, and statutes.

III

THE U.S. CONSTITUTION

IN GENERAL

Q 31. What is a constitution?

A A constitution is the expression of the fundamental laws of the state, containing the basic principles of government and regulating the distribution of sovereign power. Taking its name from the Latin word *constitutio* (an arrangement or establishment), the constitution overrides any other legal consideration.

An English monarch once quipped, "The law is whatever I say it is." That was the case until King John of England signed the Magna Carta to quell an uprising by rebellious nobles in 1215, making his nation a constitutional monarchy. The Magna Carta acknowledged that "freemen" had certain inherent rights and privileges and that the power of English kings and queens was limited by the law. The Magna Carta is still part of the constitution of the United Kingdom (most of which is unwritten), along with several important statutes passed by Parliament and assented to by monarchs.

All written constitutions owe a debt to concepts of constitutional democracy forged in ancient Greece and Rome. In *The Politics* Aristotle defined a constitution as "the organization of offices in a state" which determines "what is to be the governing body and what is the end of each community." In the United States the Constitution is the supreme law of the land, the charter of the national system, and the source of its limits and power. Each state also has its own constitution, which is superseded only by the U.S. Constitution.

Q 32. What American colony is believed to have adopted the world's first written constitution?

A Planters of the Connecticut Colony towns of Windsor, Hartford, and Wethersfield are credited with adopting the first written constitution on January 14, 1639. This constitution, the Fundamental Orders of 1639, called for an independent government not beholden to England and marked the beginning of Connecticut as a commonwealth.

The Fundamental Orders provided for two general assemblies each year and for the annual election of a governor and six assistants, who should "have power to administer justice according to the law here established, and for want thereof according to the rule of the word of God."

The orders were combined with the colony's royal charter of 1662 to form the state's constitution when it entered the Union in 1788. In recognition of the historic milestone, Connecticut's legislature in 1959 designated the state as the "Constitution State."

Eighteen years before the signing of the Fundamental Orders, a group of English Puritans adopted the Mayflower Compact prior to disembarking from their ship in Massachusetts Bay. On November 11, 1620, these pilgrims agreed to adopt just and equal "Laws, Ordinances, Acts, Constitutions, and Officers, from time to time, as shall be thought most meet and convenient for the general Good of the Colony; unto which we promise all due Submission and Obedience. . . . " If not a constitution itself, the Mayflower Compact has been called the best authenticated social compact for the establishment of a new nation in world history.

Q **33. What is the preamble to the Constitution?**

A The preamble is the fifty-two-word preface to the U.S. Constitution: "We the People of the United States, in Order to form a more perfect Union, establish Justice, insure domestic Tranquility, provide for the common defence, promote the general Welfare, and secure the Blessings of Liberty to ourselves and our Posterity, do ordain and establish this Constitution for the United States of America." The word *preamble* is derived from the Latin words *pre* (before) and *ambulo* (to walk).

Q **34. Who is known as the "Father of the Constitution"?**

A James Madison is the principal architect of the political system defined by the U.S. Constitution. A delegate to the Constitutional Convention in Philadelphia in 1787, he introduced the concept of a strong government based upon the consent of the people with internal checks and balances. Earlier, Madison championed freedom of religion, or "liberty of conscience for all," at the Virginia convention of 1776. Madison also was instrumental in the drafting and passage of the Bill of Rights in 1791.

Madison was born on his family's plantation in Orange County, Virginia, on March 16, 1751. During an extraordinary career in public life, Madison served as secretary of state (1801–1809) under Thomas Jefferson and then as the fourth president of the United States (1809–1817). He died on June 28, 1836, at his home in Montpelier, Virginia.

See 25 What are The Federalist Papers? *36 What is the "Virginia Plan"?*

Q 35. Who are the Framers of the Constitution?

A The Framers of the Constitution are the fifty-five delegates from twelve of the thirteen states (Rhode Island did not send delegates) that took part in the Philadelphia constitutional convention in the summer of 1787. Congress invited the states to send delegates to the convention to improve the Articles of Confederation. The delegates instead drafted an entirely new constitution. The Framers include national political figures, such as George Washington of Virginia and Benjamin Franklin of Pennsylvania, and senior American statesmen, such as John Dickinson of Delaware, William Livingston of New Jersey, John Rutledge of South Carolina, and Roger Sherman of Connecticut. Just thirty-nine of the fifty-five convention delegates signed the Constitution. Some refused because the document lacked a bill of rights. It took ten months for the required nine states to ratify the Constitution.

Q 36. What is the "Virginia Plan"?

A The U.S. Constitution is based on a set of resolutions known as the Virginia Plan which was largely the work of James Madison, later a delegate from Virginia to the Constitutional Convention of 1787. The plan called for a supreme national government with separate legislative, executive, and judicial branches. A system of checks and balances prevents one branch from dominating the other and from becoming so powerful that it can ignore the limits placed on government by the Constitution. The president is the commander in chief of the armed forces, for example, but only Congress has the power to declare war.

Q 37. What is federalism?

A Under the concept of federalism, the people delegate certain specific powers to the national government but retain all other powers for the states. The Founders divided the power of the American people between the federal and state governments, believing that this division would reduce the chance of a tyrannical government's usurping the rights of individual citizens.

Q 38. What does separation of powers mean?

A Under the U.S. Constitution, the power of the federal government is distributed among three separate and coequal branches. All legislative powers in the United States are vested in the Congress (Article I, Section 1); all executive powers, in the president and vice president (Article II, Section 1); and all judicial powers, in "one supreme Court, and in such inferior Courts as the Congress may from time to time ordain and establish" (Article III, Section 1). A series of checks and balances gives each branch protection against the other and prevents any single branch of government from dominating the entire government. Separation of powers is designed to prevent tyranny and to protect individual liberties.

Q 39. Which was the first state to ratify the U.S. Constitution?

A The first state was Delaware, which approved the document by a unanimous vote of 30–0 on December 7, 1787.

Q 40. When was the U.S. Constitution finally adopted?

A The Constitution was declared adopted about ten months after the Framers approved it at the Constitutional Convention, held at the State House in Philadelphia on September 17, 1787. New Hampshire was the ninth state to ratify the Constitution and provided the final vote necessary for adoption. New Hampshire approved the Constitution on June 21, 1788, by a vote of 57–47.

Q 41. What type of court system does the U.S. Constitution envision?

A Only six paragraphs of the Constitution refer to the judiciary. Article III, Section 1, states that the "judicial Power of the United States, shall be vested in one supreme Court" and in whatever inferior courts Congress "from time to time" sees fit to establish. Article III, Section 2, extends the federal court system's jurisdiction to cases affecting ambassadors and consuls, suits involving admiralty and maritime jurisdictions, controversies to which the United States is a party, disputes between two or more states, and cases involving citizens of different states.

See 26 What was the Judiciary Act of 1789?

Q 42. Which state rejected the U.S. Constitution and faced treatment as a foreign government?

A Rhode Island rejected the Constitution in March 1788 by popular referendum. It called a ratifying convention after the Constitution was adopted by the other twelve original states and finally approved the document on May 29, 1790. Even then, Rhode Island's ratification vote was 34–32, the narrowest margin of any state.

Q 43. Does the U.S. Constitution say "all men are created equal"?

A No, that phrase is in the Declaration of Independence, written by Thomas Jefferson in 1776 to explain the reasons for America's break from England and to outline the fundamental principles of the new nation. The Declaration of Independence asserts that "all men are created equal, that they are endowed by their Creator with certain unalienable Rights" and "that to secure these rights, Governments are instituted among Men, deriving their just powers from the consent of the governed."

What did Jefferson mean by equality? People of his era often practiced overt discrimination against blacks, women, and the poor. In fact, Jefferson himself was a slaveholder. When he wrote that "all men are created equal," he was referring to white males who had suffered abuses under the king of England. He was attempting to persuade colonists that "it is their duty to throw off such government." The original draft of the declaration included a charge that the king had waged a cruel war against human nature by assaulting a distant people and "captivating and carrying them into slavery in another hemisphere." These words were removed because they offended delegates in slaveholding states, particularly South Carolina, which refused to acknowledge that slaveholding was a violation of human rights. The idea of equality did eventually make its way into the Constitution, through the adoption in 1868 of the Fourteenth Amendment, which provides all people with equal protection under the laws.

Q 44. Did the U.S. Constitution address the issue of slavery?

A Article IV, Section 2, of the Constitution contains a fugitive slave clause which requires the return of slaves who escape into neighboring states. The clause states: "No Person held to Service or Labour in one State, under the Laws thereof, escaping into another, shall, in Consequence of any Law or Regulation therein, be discharged from such Service or Labour, but shall be delivered up on Claim of the Party to whom such Service or Labour may due." This clause was superseded in 1865 by the

Thirteenth Amendment outlawing slavery. The Framers of the Constitution acceded to arguments that the federal government had no power over slavery in states where it existed and that slavery was basically an issue of states' rights.

INDIVIDUAL RIGHTS AND FEDERAL POWERS

Q 45. What colony's declaration of rights became the model for the Bill of Rights to the U.S. Constitution?

A Virginia was the first state to adopt a declaration of rights. Delegates to the Virginia convention voted on June 12, 1776, to support American independence from Great Britain and drafted the influential Virginia Declaration of Rights, which recognized that all men have certain inherent rights. The Virginia Declaration of Rights became the model for the Bill of Rights to the U.S. Constitution.

According to the declaration, "all men are by nature equally free and independent, and have certain inherent rights, of which, when they enter into a state of society, they cannot, by any compact, deprive or divest their posterity; namely the enjoyment of life and liberty, with the means of acquiring and possessing property, and pursuing and obtaining happiness and safety."

The principal architect of the Virginia Declaration of Rights was George Mason (1725–1792), an influential plantation owner and political leader who helped draft the Constitution.

Q 46. Why didn't the U.S. Constitution originally have a Bill of Rights?

A As a delegate to the Constitutional Convention in Philadelphia in 1787, George Mason, the principal architect of the Virginia Declaration of Rights, said he "wished the plan had been prefaced by a bill of rights." However, convention delegates, weary and uncomfortable in the Philadelphia heat, refused to approve a motion to appoint a committee to draft a bill of rights. Many felt a bill of rights was unnecessary because the U.S. Constitution specifically enumerated the federal government's powers, thereby limiting their impact on individual rights. Furthermore, none of these powers affected individual rights not addressed in the document. Alexander Hamilton later argued that a written bill of rights could actually be dangerous because it would give power-hungry politicians a "colorable pretext" to usurp power. Proponents of the Constitution were forced to agree to amend it in exchange for ratification in closely divided states. In 1791 a sufficient number of states ratified the amendments to make them part of the Constitution. They became known as the Bill of Rights.

See 27 What is considered the first code of criminal procedure in the United States? 48 What is the Bill of Rights? 50 Does the Bill of Rights apply to the states?

Q 47. Why was a Bill of Rights necessary?

A As Robert Whitehill told delegates at the Constitutional Convention of 1787 in Philadelphia, "There is no Security for People's Houses or Papers by the Constitution—All depends on the good Will of Congress and the Judges."

Q 48. What is the Bill of Rights?

A The Bill of Rights, ratified December 15, 1791, comprises the first ten amendments to the U.S. Constitution. It articulates the fundamental rights of an individual to be free from government interference, including the rights of freedom of speech and religion. The Bill of Rights also guarantees citizens certain procedural rights in civil and criminal proceedings, such as the right to be free from unreasonable searches and seizures and the right to receive a trial by jury in cases involving serious crimes. *(For the complete text of the Bill of Rights, see the U.S. Constitution in the Appendix.)*

See 46 Why didn't the U.S. Constitution originally have a Bill of Rights? 50 Does the Bill of Rights apply to the states?

Q 49. What individual rights did James Madison think were most important?

A James Madison, a Virginia delegate to the Constitutional Convention in Philadelphia in 1787, proposed forty-two rights for inclusion in the Bill of Rights, of which twenty-seven were adopted. Of all of the rights he proposed, Madison said that *"the most valuable in the whole list"* were "the equal rights of conscience or freedom of the press, or the trial by jury in criminal cases." In the final analysis, however, Madison thought written guarantees of rights were little more than "parchment barriers." He advocated the passage of the Bill of Rights to appease opponents of the U.S. Constitution and to secure its ratification.

See 34 Who is known as the "Father of the Constitution"?

Q **50. Does the Bill of Rights apply to the states?**

A Originally the Bill of Rights applied only to the federal government and not to the states. U.S. chief justice John Marshall reasoned in *Barron v. The Mayor and City Council of Baltimore* (1883) that if "the framers of [the Bill of Rights] Amendments intended them to be limitations on the powers of the state governments, they would have ... expressed that intention ... in plain and intelligible language." At that time the primary sources of protection of individual rights were state constitutions and state bills of rights.

However, starting in the 1890s, the U.S. Supreme Court began to extend major provisions of the Bill of Rights to the states, a process known as "incorporation." In the mid-1920s the Court interpreted the due process clause of the Fourteenth Amendment as prohibiting states from depriving "any person of ... liberty ..." without due process of law. The Court has interpreted the word *liberty* to include almost all of the rights in the first eight amendments of the Bill of Rights. In *Gitlow v. New York* (1925), for example, the Court ruled that the rights of freedom of speech and press are fundamental to liberty and must be observed by the states.

Not all of the rights in the Bill of Rights have been applied to the states. Among those that have not been incorporated are the right to indictment by a grand jury, the right to a jury trial in civil cases, and the prohibition against excessive bail.

Q **51. How is the U.S. Constitution amended?**

A Two methods for proposing an amendment to the Constitution are set forth in Article V, but only one has been used. Under that method, when two-thirds of the members of both the Senate and the House of Representatives deem it necessary, Congress may submit amendments to the states for ratification. Under the second method, Congress may convene a constitutional convention to propose amendments if asked to do so by the legislatures of two-thirds of the states. Either way, an amendment must be ratified by three-fourths of the states, either by the state legislatures or in state conventions, whichever method is proposed by Congress. The U.S. Supreme Court ruled in *Dillon v. Gloss* (1921) that Congress may set a reasonable deadline for ratification. In *Coleman v. Miller* (1939) the Court said that what constitutes a reasonable time limit is a political question that must be decided by Congress.

Q **52. How many amendments to the Constitution have been proposed and adopted?**

A Thirty-three amendments have been submitted to the states. Twenty-seven were ratified by Congress. The Twenty-seventh Amendment, adopted in 1992, limits the ability of members of Congress to raise their pay. It requires that an election take place before a congressional pay raise can take effect. *(For the complete text of the amendments, see the Constitution in the Appendix.)*

Q **53. What does "due process of law" mean?**

A The term "due process of law" refers to constitutional guarantees in the First and Fourteenth Amendments that laws will not be arbitrary and that no one will be deprived of life, liberty, or property without first receiving proper notice and the opportunity to be heard. These guarantees help to ensure that the legal system is fair. The concept of due process of law is woven throughout English constitutional history and can be found in the Magna Carta (1215), which required King John to act in accordance with the law of the land.

The due process clause of the Fifth Amendment, ratified in 1791, states that no person shall be "deprived of life, liberty, or property, without due process of law." This provision is considered by many to be the most important part of the U.S. Constitution. It applies only to the federal government.

The due process clause of the Fourteenth Amendment, ratified in 1868, applies to the states. It declares that no state shall "deprive any person of life, liberty, or property, without due process of law." Through the Fourteenth Amendment, the U.S. Supreme Court has held that most of the individual protections of the Bill of Rights apply to the states as well as to the federal government.

See 50 Does the Bill of Rights apply to the states?

Q **54. What is the difference between substantive and procedural due process?**

A Due process of law is an expansive concept that includes substantive and procedural due process. Due process traditionally referred to *procedural due process,* which requires that the government follow the proper procedures before it deprives anyone of life, liberty, or property. Due process is particularly critical in criminal cases and has been called the "heart of the law." The U.S. Supreme Court has ruled that the due process clause of the Fourteenth Amendment requires states to abide by the Sixth Amendment rights of persons to receive a speedy trial and to confront and cross-examine witnesses. In a civil context, the Court has ruled that consumers must be notified before their property is repossessed for nonpayment of debts, or before their wages are garnished.

Substantive due process protects individuals from government actions that infringe upon fundamental rights which are vested in the individual and may not be arbitrarily or unreasonably interfered with. The Supreme Court has relied on substantive due process to ensure personal and familial privacy. In *Griswold v. Connecticut* (1965) the Court said that specific guarantees in the Bill of Rights have "penumbras, formed by emanations from those guarantees that help give them life and substance." The right of association, for example, is located within the penumbra of the First Amendment. Without it, other First Amendment freedoms, including free speech and religion, would be weakened. The Court in *Roe v. Wade* (1973) used the concept of substantive due process to protect a woman's right to terminate an unwanted pregnancy under certain circumstances.

At one time, the Court provoked outrage when it used substantive due process to protect private economic interests. In *Lochner v. New York* (1905) the Court upheld a private employer's right to contract with an employee to require him to work in excess of the sixty hours per week allowed by state law. Since the late 1950s the Court has tended to defer to legislatures in matters involving economic and property rights.

Q 55. What is the supremacy clause?

A The supremacy clause appears in Article VI of the U.S. Constitution, which declares that the Constitution, all laws made "in Pursuance thereof," and treaties executed under the authority of the United States shall be the "supreme Law of the Land."

Q 56. What form of taxation is the federal government prohibited from imposing?

A The U.S. Constitution contains only one prohibition on the federal taxing power. Article I, Section 9, states, "No Tax or Duty shall be laid on Articles exported from any State."

Q 57. Where does the U.S. government derive its right to regulate commerce?

A Article I, Section 8, of the U.S. Constitution allocates to Congress the power to "regulate Commerce . . . among the several States." The Supreme Court interpreted this power in a landmark case, Gibbons v. Ogden (1824), saying that it gives Congress "complete" authority to regulate commerce between the states. Aaron Ogden held a license from New York state granting him a monopoly to operate a steam-driven ferry between New Jersey and New York. Thomas Gibbons obtained a federal permit to operate his two boats in New York. When Gibbons defied Ogden's monopoly, Ogden sued and, not surprisingly, New York courts sided with him. The Supreme Court invalidated the New York law granting Ogden a monopoly, holding that it interfered with Congress's power to regulate commerce.

Q 58. What is the equal protection clause?

A The Fourteenth Amendment says that no state shall "deny to any person within its jurisdiction the equal protection of the laws." This clause has been interpreted by the U.S. Supreme Court as preventing states from enforcing laws that discriminate on the basis of race, creed, or ethnic origin. The Court uses different standards when deciding whether the actions of state governments conform to equal protection guarantees. The standard it applies depends on how the victim is classified and takes into account the government's justification for acting, including whether it had a reasonable basis to act or a compelling necessity.

Q 59. Where is the right of privacy in the U.S. Constitution?

A The right of privacy is not explicitly stated in the Constitution, but neither are many rights that are central to the American way of life, including the freedom of association. In *Griswold v. Connecticut* (1965), the pivotal case in establishing the right to privacy, the U.S. Supreme Court reversed the conviction of two officers of Planned Parenthood League for providing contraceptive information to married couples in violation of an 1879 Connecticut law. The majority opinion held that the First, Third, Fourth, and Fifth Amendments of the Constitution provide degrees of privacy. A concurring opinion traced the right of privacy to the Ninth Amendment, which states, "The enumeration in the Constitution, of certain rights, shall not be construed to deny or disparage others retained by the people."

The Court also has ruled that the right to privacy forbids states from passing laws that forbid interracial marriage, the use of contraceptives, and abortion. Debate over the existence of a right to privacy is a relatively recent phenomenon, but as far back as 1886 Supreme Court justice Joseph P. Bradley declared that "constitutional provisions for the security of person and property should be liberally construed. A close and literal construction deprives them of half their efficacy and leads to gradual depreciation of the right."

60. Who is the "Expounder of the Constitution"?

A Daniel Webster (1782–1852)—statesman, lawyer, and orator—argued 168 cases before the U.S. Supreme Court, more than any other private attorney. Twenty-four of these cases involved important constitutional issues that related to the structure and workings of the American government. He won 13 of them. In *Dartmouth College v. Woodward* (1819), for example, the Court agreed with Webster that New Hampshire had violated the Constitution by revising the charter of Dartmouth College. Webster, a Dartmouth graduate, told the Court: "It is, sir, as I have said, a small college, but there are those who love it." Webster also argued the case of *Gibbons v. Ogden* (1824), in which the Court defined the federal power to regulate interstate commerce, and that of *McCulloch v. Maryland* (1819), in which the Court ruled that the Constitution gives Congress the power to enact laws that are "necessary and proper" to carry out its constitutional responsibilities.

Also known as the "Defender of the Constitution," Webster was a champion of a strong federal government over state governments. Webster served in the U.S. Senate from 1827 to 1841 and from 1843 to 1850. In an argument with Senator Robert Y. Hayne, fervent states' rights advocate from South Carolina, the great orator thundered, "Liberty *and* Union, now and forever, one and inseparable!"

Q **61. What is a writ of habeas corpus?**

A *Habeas corpus* is a Latin term meaning "you shall have the body." A writ of habeas corpus is used by courts to inquire into the reasons for an individual's detention or imprisonment by the government.

Q **62. Can any right guaranteed in the U.S. Constitution be suspended?**

A The Constitution allows Congress to suspend one individual right under certain circumstances. Article I, Section 9, allows Congress to suspend "[t]he Privilege of the Writ of Habeas Corpus . . . when in Cases of Rebellion or Invasion the public Safety may require it."

Habeas corpus has been suspended at least three times in U.S. history. During the Civil War President Abraham Lincoln unilaterally authorized military commanders to suspend the writ of habeas corpus. Supreme Court Chief Justice Roger B. Taney, acting in his capacity as a circuit judge, complained that Lincoln's actions were unconstitutional. Lincoln ignored an order from Taney and refused to release a civilian who was jailed for anti-Union activities. Habeas corpus was also suspended in 1871 in South Carolina to combat the Ku Klux Klan and in Hawaii during World War II.

Other constitutional rights have been "suspended" by the government, especially during wartime. In World War I, for example, Congress passed espionage and sedition laws that made it virtually impossible for those who opposed the war to express their views. The Espionage Act of 1917 also was used to justify the internment of Japanese citizens by the military during World War II.

Q 63. What is the only crime defined in the U.S. Constitution?

A Treason. According to Article III, Section 3, "Treason against the United States, shall consist only in levying War against them [the United States], or in adhering to their Enemies, giving them Aid and Comfort." To be convicted of treason, a person must be accused by two witnesses to "the same overt act," or must confess to the crime.

See 27 What is considered the first code of criminal procedure in the United States?

Q 64. What noted jurist questioned the ability of a constitution, law, and courts to protect liberty?

A In an address to a graduating class in 1941, Judge Learned Hand remarked, "I often wonder whether we do not rest our hopes too much upon constitutions, upon laws and courts. These are false hopes; believe me, these are false hopes. Liberty lies in the hearts of men; when it dies there, no constitution, no law, no court can save it; no constitution, no law, no court can even do much to help it. While it lies there it needs no constitution, no law, no court to save it." Hand served as senior circuit judge (in effect, chief judge) of the U.S. Court of Appeals for the Second Circuit from 1939 to 1953.

IV
THE FEDERAL COURT SYSTEM

IN GENERAL

Q **65. What is the federal court system?**

A The federal court system (see Figure 4-1) consists of courts that decide cases under a grant of authority from the U.S. Constitution. Federal courts complement state courts by serving as a judicial forum for cases that would not be appropriate in state courts, including suits between states. Federal courts also interpret national public policies, such as those directing the war on drugs or promoting free trade among the states.

The Supreme Court of the United States is the only court mandated by the Constitution. It is at the top of the federal court pyramid, followed by intermediate appellate courts and trial courts (see Figure 4-2).

The intermediate appellate courts are organized into thirteen judicial circuits, and the circuits are further divided into ninety-four judicial districts.

There are twelve regional circuits, each of which includes a U.S. court of appeals. This intermediate or mid-level appellate court decides most of the routine appeals from a circuit's federal district courts. There are two other mid-level appellate courts that have nationwide jurisdiction over specific types of federal appeals: the U.S. Court of Appeals for the Federal Circuit and the U.S. Court of Appeals for the Armed Forces.

Each of the ninety-four federal judicial districts contains at least two courts: a U.S. district court, a trial court in which federal civil and criminal trials are held; and a bankruptcy court, a separate unit of the district court that decides petitions from individuals and businesses seeking relief from overwhelming debt.

Finally, Congress has created several courts to fulfill specific legislative mandates. These include three territorial courts that function as district courts in Guam, the

Figure 4-1   The Federal Court System

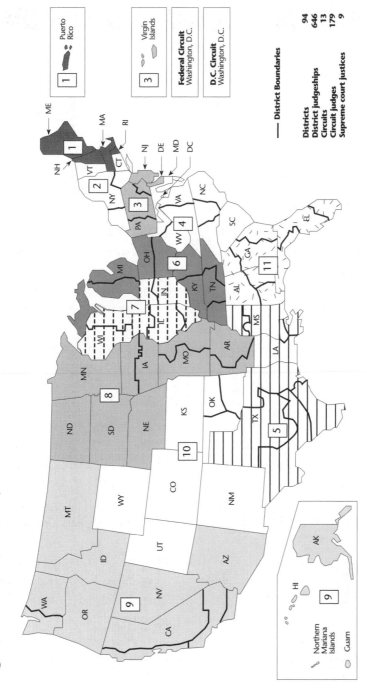

Districts	94
District judgeships	646
Circuits	13
Circuit Judges	179
Supreme court justices	9

Note: Number and composition of circuits set forth by 28 U.S.C. § 4. The large numerals indicate the Courts of Appeals.

Source: Administrative Office of the United States Courts.

Figure 4-2   The American Court System

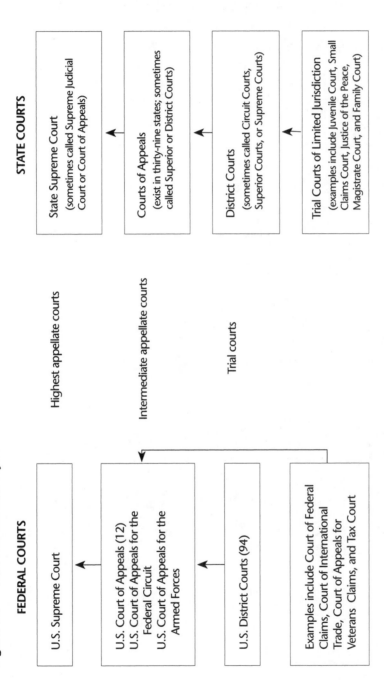

Source: Adapted from Lee Epstein and Thomas G. Walker, *Constitutional Law for a Changing America: Rights, Liberties, and Justice,* 2d ed. (Washington, D.C.: CQ Press, 1995), 865.

U.S. Virgin Islands, and the Northern Mariana Islands, and four courts that have nationwide jurisdiction over limited subject matter: the U.S. Tax Court, the U.S. Court of Federal Claims, the U.S. Court of Appeals for Veterans Claims, and the U.S. Court of International Trade.

Typically, federal cases begin in U.S. district court and work their way up through the system to the Supreme Court. Cases also originate in state courts, from which they are transferred to the federal courts, and in federal regulatory agencies.

Q 66. What is the source of the federal court system's power over citizens?

A The authority for the federal court system derives from Article III, Section 1, of the U.S. Constitution, which provides that the "judicial Power of the United States, shall be vested in one supreme Court, and in such inferior Courts as the Congress may from time to time ordain and establish." Congress used this power to create so-called *constitutional courts,* including the Supreme Court of the United States, U.S. courts of appeals, U.S. district courts, and the U.S. Court of International Trade. Judges in these courts are guaranteed life tenure during "good Behaviour," and their salaries cannot be reduced.

Article 1, Section 8, gives Congress the authority to "make all Laws which shall be necessary and proper for carrying into Execution" the authority granted to Congress in the Constitution. Congress has used this power to create *legislative courts* that carry out its specific legislative mandates. These courts may have nonjudicial, administrative, or quasi-legislative functions in addition to their purely judicial duties. Judges in these courts do not have the same job protections as constitutional court judges and may issue advisory opinions. Legislative courts include the three U.S. territorial courts, the U.S. Court of Appeals for the Armed Forces, the U.S. Court of Appeals for Veterans Claims, the U.S. Court of Federal Claims, and the U.S. Tax Court.

Q 67. What is the jurisdiction of federal courts?

A Jurisdiction describes the power of a court to rule on a case. Unlike the jurisdiction of state courts, that of federal courts is circumscribed by the U.S. Constitution and the laws of Congress.

Under Article III, Section 2, of the Constitution, the judicial power of the United States extends to "cases and controversies" that generally fall into one of two main categories.

The first category pertains to the subject matter of the dispute. Federal courts can hear cases arising under the Constitution and under federal laws and treaties of the

United States, as well as cases in maritime and admiralty jurisdiction. Federal courts also have jurisdiction over bankruptcy cases and trademark and copyright violations.

The second category pertains to the nature of the parties. Federal courts can hear cases involving citizens of different states ("diversity jurisdiction"); disputes between a state and citizens of another state, between two states, or between a state and the nation; and cases involving foreign countries or foreign citizens.

Federal and state courts have "concurrent," or shared, jurisdiction in many areas. For example, a suit that involves citizens of different states can be filed in either federal or state court, though it can only be heard in federal court if the amount in the controversy exceeds $75,000.

See 345 What is diversity jurisdiction?

Q **68. How is the federal court system governed?**

A The chief justice of the United States is the acknowledged leader of the federal court system. The chief justice presides over the Supreme Court of the United States and holds key leadership roles in the agencies that administer the federal court system, including the Judicial Conference of the United States, the Administrative Office of the U.S. Courts, and the Federal Judicial Center.

The chief justice works under the watchful eye of Congress and the executive branch. Congress holds the federal purse strings, approves judicial appointments, and passes laws that expand or limit the judiciary's freedom to act. The president approves such legislation, appoints the chief justice, and, subject to the Senate's approval, fills vacancies on the federal judiciary. Executive branch agencies also influence court operations, particularly the General Accounting Office, which plays a major role in decisions about the judiciary's space and facilities.

On a daily basis, federal district and appellate courts manage themselves, subject to statutory requirements and to the policies set by regional and national judicial agencies.

Each of the thirteen circuits into which the federal court system is organized has a Circuit Judicial Council, which manages the caseload and administers the federal courts within that circuit. This council consists of the chief judge of the circuit and an equal number of judges from both the court of appeals and the district courts in that circuit. Circuits also appoint a circuit executive to assist with the management of the circuit.

Each of the ninety-four federal districts within the thirteen federal circuits has a chief judge, who is the leader within the district.

See 133 How often has the Court "overruled" Congress? 135 How many Court decisions were reversed by amendments to the U.S. Constitution?

Q 69. What is the Judicial Conference of the United States?

A The Judicial Conference of the United States is, by statute, the chief policymaking body for the administration of the federal courts (28 U.S.C., Section 331). Known originally as the Conference of Senior Circuit Judges, the conference was established by Congress in 1922 to help presiding judges of the courts of appeals to improve the performance of district courts. It also establishes national standards for the federal judiciary. The conference's name was changed in 1948 and its duties expanded.

The conference is chaired by the chief justice of the United States, who is required to submit to Congress an annual report of the proceedings of the conference. Conference members include the chief judge of each federal court of appeals, the chief judge of the U.S. Court of International Trade, and a district judge from each of the thirteen judicial circuits. The chief justice is required to convene the conference at least once a year but, since 1949, has held two meetings a year, one in the spring and one in the fall. An executive committee acts on behalf of the full conference between sessions.

The conference develops the federal judiciary's budget for presentation to Congress and recommends and comments upon federal legislation that affects the judiciary. It biennially surveys federal appellate and district courts to evaluate judges' needs based on caseload demands and other relevant factors. It makes recommendations to Congress, which has the authority to establish or eliminate Article III judgeships and to define the jurisdiction and workload of the federal courts. The conference also promulgates a code of conduct that applies to all federal judges, though this code is not binding on Supreme Court justices.

Much of the work of the conference is carried out by twenty-five standing and special committees, on which an estimated 240 federal judges serve. Some committees include officials from the U.S. Justice Department, state supreme court justices, law professors, and practicing lawyers. The chief justice appoints committee members.

Another responsibility of the conference is supervising the Administrative Office of the U.S. Courts.

Q 70. What is the Administrative Office of the U.S. Courts?

A The Administrative Office of the U.S. Courts (AO) was created by Congress in 1939 to manage the federal court system. The AO maintains workload statistics and disburses funds appropriated to maintain the U.S. judicial system. In addition, it provides administrative support to federal court staff, the Judicial Conference of the United States, and the conference's committees. The AO is supervised by the Judicial Conference. The chief justice of the United States appoints the director and deputy director of the AO after consulting with the Judicial Conference. The budget of the AO in a recent year totaled $54,500,000. The AO can be reached at:

Administrative Office of the United States Courts
Thurgood Marshall Federal Judiciary Building
One Columbus Circle, N.E.
Washington, D.C. 20544
(202) 273-2150
http://www.uscourts.gov/

Q 71. What is the Federal Judicial Center?

A The Federal Judicial Center is an independent agency that was created by Congress in 1967 "to further the development and adoption of improved judicial administration" in the courts of the United States. The center conducts policy research, oversees continuing educational programs, and makes recommendations to the Judicial Conference of the United States to improve the federal judiciary. The chief justice of the United States chairs the center's nine-member board of directors, which also includes seven judges elected by the Judicial Conference and the director of the Administrative Office of the U.S. Courts. The center has 138 permanent staff positions, and its budget in a recent year was $17,716,000. It can be reached at:

Federal Judicial Center
Thurgood Marshall Federal Judiciary Building
One Columbus Circle, N.E.
Washington, D.C. 20002-8003
(202) 273-4160
http://www.fjc.gov/

Q 72. How much does the United States spend annually on the federal judiciary?

A In 1998 Congress allocated $3.719 billion to the federal judiciary. Annual spending for other recent years is as follows:

Year	Annual U.S. spending on federal judiciary (billions)	Year	Annual U.S. spending on federal judiciary (billions)
1997	$3.26	1979	$0.48
1996	3.06	1978	0.44
1995	2.90	1977	0.39
1994	2.67	1976	0.33
1993	2.62	1975	0.28
1992	2.30	1974	0.21
1991	1.99	1973	0.19
1990	1.64	1972	0.17
1989	1.49	1971	0.15
1988	1.34	1970	0.13
1987	1.18	1969	0.11
1986	1.07	1968	0.94
1985	0.97	1967	0.88
1984	0.87	1966	0.80
1983	0.78	1965	0.75
1982	0.71	1964	0.66
1981	0.64	1963	0.62
1980	0.57	1962	0.57

Source: Budget for Fiscal Year 1999, Historical Tables (Washington, D.C.: GPO, 1998).

Q 73. What percentage of the national budget does the federal judicial branch account for?

A Compared to the executive and legislative branches of government, the federal judicial branch is small. It represents less than two-tenths of one percent of the federal budget.

Q 74. What is the budget process for the federal judicial branch?

A The Administrative Office of the U.S. Courts develops budget estimates for the Supreme Court of the United States and for the lower courts. These budget estimates are submitted for consideration to the Judicial Conference of the United States and its committees. When the conference approves a budget request, it is transmitted to the executive branch's Office of Management and Budget, which may review and comment upon the judiciary's budget request but has no authority to change it. The Administrative Office then submits the proposed judicial budget to the House and Senate Appropriations Committees. When both houses of Congress have approved the judiciary's budget, it is sent to the executive committee of the Judicial Conference, which approves a spending plan for the federal courts. The Administrative Office implements the plan. However, each federal court controls its own budget and can shift resources among activities to meet its needs.

Q 75. How is the federal judicial budget allocated?

A In 1998 5 percent of the judiciary's budget went to the Supreme Court of the United States, U.S. Court of Appeals for the Federal Circuit, U.S. Court of International Trade, Administrative Office of the U.S. Courts, Federal Judicial Center, Judiciary Trust Fund, and U.S. Sentencing Commission. The remaining 95 percent was allocated to the U.S. courts of appeals, U.S. district courts, and other judicial services, including juror and commissioner fees, court security, public defender services, and salaries and expenses. The judicial branch has twenty-eight thousand employees.

Q 76. How are federal judges appointed?

A Under Article II, Section 2, of the U.S. Constitution, the president nominates and, "with the Advice and Consent of the Senate," appoints judges to the Supreme Court and the federal judiciary (U.S. courts of appeals and U.S. district courts). Potential nominees often are recommended to the president by members of the Senate who are of the president's political party. The Federal Bureau of Investigation conducts a background check on potential nominees. After the president selects a nominee, the Senate Judiciary Committee conducts confirmation hearings to determine the nominee's fitness for the position. If the committee's vote is favorable, the nomination is sent to the floor of the Senate, where it is approved or rejected by majority vote (a nominee is not considered appointed until he or she is confirmed by the entire Senate). In recent years, delays in the Senate confirmation process have proved to be a major obstacle to judicial appointments, resulting in more than one hundred vacancies on the federal bench in 1997.

Q **77. What is the American Bar Association's role in the appointment of federal judges?**

A The U.S. Constitution sets forth no specific requirements for becoming a federal judge. President Harry S. Truman agreed in 1952 to allow the American Bar Association's Standing Committee on the Federal Judiciary to evaluate potential nominees for federal courts. President Dwight D. Eisenhower's administration was the first to use this procedure. Today, the fifteen-member committee evaluates the qualifications of candidates to the Supreme Court, U.S. courts of appeals, U.S. district courts, and Court of International Trade. The committee reviews a candidate's experience, temperament, and character, and rates him or her as well qualified, qualified, or not qualified. The president does not have to seek or follow the ABA's recommendation. The ABA was not consulted, for example, when President Ronald Reagan appointed Sandra Day O'Connor to the Supreme Court.

From 1993–1996 the ABA rated exceptionally well-qualified 63.9 percent of President Bill Clinton's appointees to the federal bench. It found 34.3 percent to be qualified and 1.8 percent to be unqualified.

Q **78. What is the average time from judicial nomination to confirmation by the Senate?**

A In recent years the average time from a judicial nomination to confirmation was 78 days. However, in 1997, the time more than doubled, to 192 days. The slow pace is believed to reflect increased partisanship in the nomination process.

Q **79. How many federal judges are there?**

A In 1997 there were 835 authorized (congressionally approved) life-tenured federal judges and 365 senior or semiretired judges who perform some judicial service. The number of judges has roughly doubled every thirty years since the end of the Civil War. Federal judges and magistrates work in more than eight hundred locations in the United States and its territories.

There are 9 justices on the Supreme Court of the United States, 179 authorized judges on the U.S. courts of appeals, and 647 authorized judges on the U.S. district courts. As of September 1997 there were 24 vacancies on the federal courts of appeals and 69 on the district courts.

There are also 326 authorized federal bankruptcy judges, 432 full-time magistrate judges, and 75 part-time magistrate judges. These judicial officers serve fixed terms and are not protected under the U.S. Constitution from arbitrary dismissal or salary reductions while in office.

There are more than 25,000 nonjudges (for example, clerks and administrators) working in the federal judicial system.

Q 80. What U.S. president appointed the most women and minorities to the federal bench?

A President Bill Clinton set records in his first term (1993–1997) for appointing the most women and minorities to federal judgeships. Of Clinton's appointees, 69.8 percent were men and 72.2 percent were white.

Clinton's most recent predecessors made the following judicial appointments:

President	Federal judicial appointments
George Bush (1989–1992)	80.4 percent male 89.2 percent white
Ronald Reagan (1985–1988)	92.5 percent male 91.9 percent white
Ronald Reagan (1981–1984)	90.7 percent male 93.0 percent white
Jimmy Carter (1977–1980)	85.6 percent male 78.7 percent white
Gerald Ford (1974–1976)	98.1 percent male 88.5 percent white
Richard M. Nixon (1969–1974)	99.4 percent male 95.5 percent white
Lyndon B. Johnson (1963–1968)	98.4 percent male 93.4 percent white

According to Alliance for Justice, a Washington, D.C.–based group that monitors judicial appointments, Clinton by 1998 had doubled the number of women judges on the federal bench and had increased the number of African American and Hispanic judges by 56 percent and 39 percent, respectively.

Q 81. What is the demographic profile of the federal judiciary?

A According to the Alliance for Justice, a Washington, D.C.–based group that monitors the judicial branch, the active federal judiciary had the following demographic characteristics as of April 7, 1998:

- 80.2 percent male
- 19.8 percent female
- 83.9 percent white
- 10.3 percent African American
- 0.9 percent Asian American
- 0.3 percent Hispanic
- 0.1 percent Native American.

Forty-seven percent of the federal judges confirmed in 1997 had a net worth of more than $1 million, while 28 percent had a net worth of less than $500,000.

Q 82. Who was the first female federal judge?

A The first female federal judge was Genevieve Cline, who was appointed to the U.S. Customs Court by President Calvin Coolidge in 1938.

Q 83. Why do federal judges have lifetime tenure?

A The drafters of the U.S. Constitution believed that only an independent judiciary could render impartial decisions and be an effective check and balance against the legislative and executive branches of government. As a result, the Constitution makes it difficult to remove federal judges from office during "good Behaviour" and states that their salaries may not be diminished during their term in office. Without job security, federal judges would find it difficult, if not impossible, to protect unpopular individuals and causes or to attack political corruption. For example, during the civil rights struggle in the South, some courageous southern judges upheld desegregation laws in the face of tremendous opposition.

Q 84. Can federal judges be fired?

A No. The only way to remove a judge appointed under Article III of the U.S. Constitution is through the impeachment process. Article II, Section 4, states: "The President, Vice President and all civil Officers of the United States, shall be removed from Office on Impeachment for, and Conviction of, Treason, Bribery, or other high Crimes and Misdemeanors." Impeachment requires indictment by a simple majority vote of the House of Representatives. A vote of two-thirds of the senators who are present, following a trial, is required to remove a judge from office.

See 88 Is there any appeal from impeachment?

Q 85. How many federal judges were impeached?

A Seven federal court judges were removed from office through the impeachment process. All were found guilty of judicial misconduct or criminal behavior. They include the following U.S. district court judges:

- John Pickering of New Hampshire: engaged in drunken and profane behavior, 1804
- West H. Humphreys of Tennessee: supported secession, 1862
- Robert W. Archibald, an associate judge of the U.S. Commerce Court, was impeached for financial misconduct in 1913.
- Halsted L. Ritter of Utah: brought office into disrepute, 1936
- Harry E. Claiborne of Nevada: convicted of tax fraud, 1986
- Alcee L. Hastings of Florida: convicted of conspiracy to accept a bribe, 1989
- Walter L. Nixon, Jr., of Mississippi: lied under oath, 1989

Impeachment proceedings against two other judges failed. Supreme Court justice Samuel Chase, a radical Federalist who pushed his political views from the bench, was acquitted by the Senate after the House voted to impeach him in 1805. U.S. district court judge Charles Swayne of Florida was acquitted in 1905 in impeachment hearings.

Impeachment proceedings against George W. English, a U.S. district court judge from Illinois, were dismissed when he resigned in 1926.

Q 86. What is an impeachable offense?

A Perhaps the best definition of an impeachable offense came from President Gerald Ford. When he was a member of Congress in 1970, Ford spoke in favor of the impeachment of Supreme Court justice William O. Douglas on the grounds of alleged financial conflict of interest. "An impeachable offense is whatever a majority of the House of Representatives considers it to be at a given moment in history," said Ford.

Under Article II, Section 4, of the U.S. Constitution, all civil officers of the United States may be removed "from Office on Impeachment for, and Conviction of, Treason, Bribery, or other high Crimes and Misdemeanors." No definition of high crimes and misdemeanors is provided in the Constitution.

Q 87. Must an impeachable offense include criminal misconduct?

A There is no clear answer to this question. However, in *Federalist* No. 65, Alexander Hamilton wrote that an impeachment should "proceed from the misconduct of public men, or, in other words, from the abuse or violation of some public trust. They are of a nature which may with peculiar propriety be denominated political, as they relate chiefly to injuries done immediately to the society itself."

See 25 What are The Federalist Papers?

Q 88. Is there any appeal from impeachment?

A No. Article II, Section 2, of the U.S. Constitution gives the president the power to grant reprieves and pardons for offenses against the United States, except in cases of impeachment.

Q 89. Must federal judges retire?

A Judges of so-called constitutional courts who were appointed under Article III of the U.S. Constitution serve for life or during "good Behaviour." They include judges of the Supreme Court of the United States, U.S. court of appeals, U.S. Court of International Trade, and U.S. district court.

Not all federal judges are appointed for life. Judges of so-called legislative courts who were appointed under Article I of the Constitution are appointed to fixed terms. They include judges of the territorial district courts, U.S. Tax Court, Court of Appeals for Veterans Claims, Court of Federal Claims, and Court of Appeals for the U.S. Armed Forces, as well as magistrate judges and bankruptcy judges.

See 91 What is the chief difference between federal constitutional and legislative courts?

Q 90. What is the "Rule of 80"?

A Congress attempted in 1984 to make retirement an appealing option to federal judges who are aged and infirm by adopting the "Rule of 80." This rule allows a judge, beginning at age sixty-five, to retire at his or her current salary or to take senior status if the sum of the judge's age and years of service equals eighty. Thus a judge who is aged sixty-five may retire or choose senior status if he or she has fifteen years of active service in the federal judiciary. Similarly, a justice may retire or become a senior judge at the age of seventy if he or she has ten years of active service. Senior judges may keep their office if they continue to work, albeit with a reduced caseload. They typically handle about 15 percent of the federal courts' workload annually.

Q 91. What is the chief difference between federal constitutional and legislative courts?

A Legislative courts, created under Article I of the U.S. Constitution, are considered creatures of Congress. They are much more vulnerable to congressional control than so called constitutional courts, created under Article III. Legislative court judges lack the same constitutional protections as their constitutional court peers. They do not have lifetime tenure but are appointed by Congress to fixed terms, with no assurance of reappointment. They also lack the constitutional protection afforded to constitutional court judges against arbitrary dismissal or salary reductions.

THE SUPREME COURT OF THE UNITED STATES

IN GENERAL

Q 92. What is the Supreme Court of the United States?

A The Supreme Court is the highest court in the land. It has the ultimate power to determine whether Congress, the president, or a state has acted within the bounds of the U.S. Constitution. The Court consists of a chief justice and eight associate justices who are appointee for life by the president, subject to confirmation by the Senate. The Court's jurisdiction extends to disputes involving the Constitution, laws and treaties of the United States, foreign diplomats, citizens of different states, and cases in which the United States is a party.

As the ultimate authority on the U.S. Constitution, the Court effectively exercises veto power over acts of the executive and legislative branches of the federal government. If the Court declares a law or executive action to be unconstitutional, its decision may be reversed only through an amendment to the Constitution or by the Court itself. The Court's term begins each year at 10 A.M. on the first Monday in October and continues until the summer recess, which usually begins in late June or early July. The Court hears fewer than one hundred cases annually.

Q **93. How can the Court be reached?**

A The Court can be reached at the following address:

> Supreme Court of the United States
> U.S. Supreme Court Building
> One First Street, N.E.
> Washington, D.C. 20543
> (202) 479-3000

Q **94. Where has the Court been located since its inception?**

A The Court's first meeting was on February 1, 1790, at the Royal Exchange Building at the intersection of Broad and Water Streets in New York City, then the nation's temporary capital. The Court occupied the second floor; an open-air market was located on the first. Only three of the Court's six justices were present for its opening session, forcing Chief Justice John Jay to postpone it until the next day.

In 1791 the Court moved, along with the nation's capital, to Philadelphia. It shared a room with the mayor's court in the new city hall.

In 1800 the Court moved to Washington, D.C., where it heard arguments in several different places, including a tiny basement room in the Capitol Building that one observer described as "little better than a dungeon," a chilly library formerly occupied by the House of Representatives, and Long's Tavern on First Street, where the Library of Congress now stands. In 1810 the Court met in the first courtroom designed specifically for it, a basement room underneath the Senate chambers.

The British reportedly used Supreme Court documents to set fire to the Capitol during the War of 1812. From 1814 to 1816, while the Capitol was being restored, the Court held sessions in a home on Capitol Hill that was rented by its clerk, Elias Boudinot Caldwell. The house later became Bell Tavern. The Court returned to the Capitol in 1817, meeting in a section of the North Wing that had been not been destroyed by fire. The Court finally returned to its newly restored basement location beneath the Senate chambers in 1819. It remained there until 1860, when it moved to the old Senate chamber on the first floor of the Capitol.

In all, the Court convened in about a dozen different places until in 1935 it moved into the new U.S. Supreme Court Building, across the street from the U.S. Capitol Building at One First Street, N.E., in Washington, D.C. In laying the cornerstone for the building on October 13, 1932, Chief Justice Charles Evans Hughes said, "The Republic endures and this is the symbol of its faith."

Q 95. Which of the seven wonders of the ancient world is the U.S. Supreme Court Building patterned after?

A The Court's permanent home, designed by architect Cass Gilbert, is patterned after the Temple of Diana at Ephesus, one of the seven wonders of the ancient world.

Q 96. How many security X-ray machines does the Court have?

A The Court has four security X-ray machines which are used by police to inspect packages at the entrance of the building.

Q 97. What words are written over the main entrance of the U.S. Supreme Court Building?

A "Equal Justice Under Law" is carved over the great bronze doors of the Court's entrance.

Q 98. What figures stand on each side of the steps of the main entrance of the U.S. Supreme Court Building?

A Two marble sculptures by James Earle Fraser. On the left is a female figure representing the contemplation of justice. On the right is a male figure representing the executor of law. Carved in 1935, the figures have suffered significant deterioration due to air pollution and weather damage, which have eroded some of their features. The Court hopes to undertake a preservation effort in the year 2000.

Q 99. What does the star on the seal of the Supreme Court signify?

A The seal includes a single star beneath eagle claws. The star signifies the U.S. Constitution's creation of "one supreme Court." The seal is kept by the clerk of the Court and is stamped on official papers.

Q 100. What colors did the justices wear before they settled on basic black?

A Prior to the 1800s the justices wore black robes with a wide scarlet facing, gold piping, and twelve- or fourteen-inch scarlet cuffs.

See 153 Which justice adorns his black robe with fanciful gold stripes?

Q 101. What is judicial review?

A Judicial review describes the power of the Supreme Court of the United States to review and either uphold or declare unconstitutional acts of Congress and state statutes, to order state officers to perform acts that the Court concludes are required by the Constitution, and to order the president to discharge duties that the president claims are protected by the constitutional right of executive privilege. The latter power is seldom invoked by the Court. The Court ordered President Richard Nixon to turn over tape recordings secretly made in his office during the Watergate scandals of the early 1970s.

See 103 Was Marbury v. Madison *the first case to assert the power of judicial review? 157 Who is the "father of constitutional law"?*

Q 102. What is the significance of *Marbury v. Madison*?

A The Judiciary Act of 1789 established the framework for the modern-day court system. It gave the Supreme Court the power to review state laws, but it was unclear whether the Court could review acts of Congress. In the landmark case of *Marbury v. Madison* (1803), the Court announced that it may declare an act of Congress void if the act violates the Constitution. The Court invalidated a provision of the Judiciary Act that empowered the Court to issue a "writ of mandamus" (Latin, "we command"), a judicial order compelling a government action.

The case involved William Marbury, who received an appointment as a justice of the peace for the District of Columbia in the waning hours of the administration of Federalist president John Adams. Adams's successor, Republican Thomas Jefferson, refused to give Marbury his commission. Marbury asked the Court to issue a writ of mandamus compelling the delivery of the commission.

In a decision written by Chief Justice John Marshall, the Court unanimously agreed that Jefferson wrongfully withheld Marbury's commission but denied Marbury the relief he sought. Congress in the Judiciary Act had granted the Court the power to issue writs of mandamus "to persons holding office under the authority of the United States." The Court ruled that Congress impermissibly enlarged the Court's power beyond the provisions of Article III of the Constitution. Marshall reasoned that the Court's original jurisdiction as stated in the Constitution cannot be enlarged or diminished, except by constitutional amendment.

With this ruling the Court announced that it had the power to invalidate federal laws that violate the Constitution. It also avoided a showdown with Jefferson, who might have ignored a Court order to deliver Marbury's commission.

Jefferson feared that the *Marbury* decision would lead the judiciary to become the "despotic branch."

See 28 Who were the "Midnight Judges"?

Q **103. Was *Marbury v. Madison* the first case to assert the power of judicial review?**

A No. The principle of judicial review had been asserted and established in some states prior to 1803. The first case in which an American court explicitly articulated the principle of judicial review was the North Carolina case of *Bayard v. Singleton* (1787).

Q **104. What is the Court's jurisdiction?**

A Article III of the U.S. Constitution empowers the Court to decide "cases" and "controversies" in law and equity arising under the Constitution and the laws of the United States.

The Court has original jurisdiction—meaning it can hear a case from beginning to end—in cases arising out of disputes between states or between a state and the federal government. These cases represent a tiny fraction of the Court's workload, largely because few such cases are ever filed. In 1998 the Court disposed of a single case of original jurisdiction. In all other cases, the Court has appellate jurisdiction "with such Exceptions, and under such Regulations as the Congress shall make." Appellate jurisdiction has been conferred upon the Court by various statutes. The statutes effective at this time in conferring and controlling the jurisdiction of the Supreme Court are 28 U.S.C. 1251, 1253, 1254, and 1257–1259, as well as various special statutes. The Court may hear appeals from lower federal courts, including intermediate appellate and district courts, and state courts of last resort when the issue involves a substantial question of federal law.

Congress has also conferred upon the Court the authority to make rules of procedure to be followed by lower federal courts.

See 67 What is the jurisdiction of federal courts? 131 What is judicial restraint? 132 What is judicial activism?

Q 105. Can a litigant appeal any state court decision to the U.S. Supreme Court?

A No. Even if the case is a proper one for the Court's consideration, the Court still cannot review it unless it represents the final judgment or decrees of the highest court of the state in which a decision could be had. A litigant must appeal his or her case as far as possible through the state court system before the Supreme Court will consider the appeal.

Q 106. What kind of district court decision can be appealed directly to the U.S. Supreme Court?

A Only a few federal statutes remain in existence that require the Supreme Court to review an appeal. They involve the decisions of a three-judge district court panel. Such panels hear cases that involve apportionment and certain voting practices. The panel's decision does not have to be appealed first to a federal intermediate appellate court but can be appealed directly to the Supreme Court. These appeals are extremely rare.

Q 107. What is a writ of certiorari?

A Prior to 1891 virtually all of the U.S. Supreme Court's jurisdiction was mandatory. That is, Congress required the Court to hear most of the appeals filed with the Court. Today, the reverse is true. Congress has eliminated most of the Court's mandatory jurisdiction.

Virtually all of the Supreme Court's jurisdiction today is discretionary. The Court is not required by statute to hear a case. An appellant must ask the Court to review his or her case by filing a *writ of certiorari* (a Latin term roughly translated as "made more certain"). A writ of certiorari is a request for a written order commanding a lower court to prepare the record of a case and send it to the higher court (in this case, the Supreme Court) for its review. When the Court grants certiorari, it reserves the right to review the merits of a case before adding it to its docket.

108. How does the Court decide whether to grant certiorari?

In recent years most justices have used a "cert pool" composed of law clerks to screen petitions for writs of certiorari and to recommend cases for the Court's review.

According to the Rules of the Supreme Court of the United States, "Review on a writ of certiorari is not a matter of right, but of judicial discretion. A petition for a writ of certiorari will be granted only for compelling reasons." Important factors considered by the Court include whether there is a conflict between different federal courts of appeals or between the highest courts of two or more states, or if the issue raises an important unsettled question of federal law.

Among the rules adopted by the Court to guide the use of its discretionary jurisdiction is the so-called Rule of Four. The Court will not accept a case for review unless four justices feel that it merits the Court's consideration. The Supreme Court grants a petition for a writ of certiorari only about 1 percent of the time. Denial of "cert" does not reflect the merits of a case but only the Court's unwillingness to consider it.

109. How many new cases are filed with the Court each year?

A total of 6,781 cases were filed with the Court in 1997. Totals from other recent years were:

Year	Cases filed	Year	Cases filed
1996	6,634	1986	4,240
1995	6,597	1985	4,413
1994	6,996	1984	4,047
1993	6,897	1983	4,222
1992	6,303	1982	4,201
1991	5,866	1981	4,422
1990	5,502	1980	4,174
1989	4,918	1975	3,940
1988	4,776	1970	3,419
1987	4,493		

Source: Supreme Court of the United States, *Budget Estimates for Fiscal Year 1999, Congressional Submission* (Washington, D.C.: GPO, 1998).

Q 110. What types of cases are filed with the Court?

A The types of cases docketed by the Court in its 1996 term were: civil, 43.5 percent; criminal, 36.5 percent; petitions for a writ of habeas corpus, 18.7 percent; and other, 1.3 percent. Habeas corpus petitions typically are filed by prisoners who allege that they are being wrongfully detained and who have exhausted their claims in state courts.

See 61 What is a writ of habeas corpus? 62 Can any right guaranteed in the U.S. Constitution be suspended?

Q 111. What types of cases does the Court accept for argument?

A The Court is much more likely to accept a civil case for argument than a criminal case. The types of cases argued before the Court in 1996 were: civil, 77.8 percent; criminal, 14.4 percent; habeas corpus, 6.7 percent; and cases in which the Court has original jurisdiction, such as election disputes, 1.1 percent.

See 61 What is a writ of habeas corpus? 104 What is the Court's jurisdiction?

Q 112. How many cases on its docket does the Court actually decide?

A The Court decides only about 1 percent of the appeals filed with it. In 1997 the Court issued ninety-three signed opinions and one unsigned opinion. The Court summarily decided fifty cases on its docket, which means that it declined to consider the merits of these cases because they involved issues that had been raised in a case already decided by the Court. Fifty-four cases were carried over to the next term. The rest of the cases were either denied, dismissed, withdrawn, or not acted upon.

Q 113. Is the Court issuing fewer or more decisions these days?

A Far fewer. Petitions today are five times more likely to be denied review than they were twenty years ago. Some observers say the modern-day Court is deferring to the elected branches of government for decisions on hot-button issues and is attempting to improve the quality of the justice that it dispenses. Others say the Court is retrenching in the face of a backlash from the public. Justice Anthony Scalia was quoted as stating, "It's better if the people decide."

The Court issued the following number of (signed and unsigned) opinions per year:

Year	Opinions	Year	Opinions
1997	94	1990	125
1996	90	1989	146
1995	90	1988	168
1994	94	1987	160
1993	99	1986	174
1992	115	1985	171
1991	123		

Source: Supreme Court of the United States, *Budget Estimates for Fiscal Year 1999, Congressional Submission* (Washington, D.C.: GPO, 1998).

Q 114. What is the significance of the Court's refusal to review an appeal?

A The Court does not endorse a lower court ruling when it refuses to consider an appeal of the ruling. However, its decision effectively allows the lower court ruling to stand as the law of the jurisdiction that it came from, even if that law conflicts with the law in other jurisdictions. For example, the Court refused to hear an appeal of a decision by the U.S. Court of Appeals for the Fifth Circuit, which includes Texas, Louisiana, and Mississippi. The appeals court ruled that race could not be considered as a factor in admissions and financial aid at a state university. As a result, consideration of racial factors is taboo in the states of the Fifth Circuit but is permissible in other states, such as Pennsylvania.

Q 115. Is the Court more likely to hear an appeal by the federal government than by the average citizen?

A Yes. The Court grants certiorari as often as 70 percent of the time when the United States seeks to appeal a case in which it is the losing party, compared with no more than 8 percent of the time for other parties. Furthermore, the United States won 62 percent of its cases before the Court between 1801 and 1958.

See 107 What is a writ of certiorari? 108 How does the Court decide whether to grant certiorari?

116. Can you ask the Supreme Court of the United States for advice?

A No. Article III, Section 2, of the U.S. Constitution limits the Court's jurisdiction to definite "cases" and "controversies." This provision was clarified by the Court's first chief justice, John Jay, who refused to advise President George Washington about the constitutional implications of a proposed foreign policy decision. The Court will not consider abstract, hypothetical questions or rule on matters in which no party is properly before the Court.

Q **117. Can anyone with a claim make a federal case out of it?**

A Only a litigant who has "standing" may assert a claim in state or federal court. Standing requires a party to have a significant interest in the outcome of the matter. A party must allege a concrete and direct injury—not simply general harm—caused by the challenged action. For example, the Court has refused to hear claims asserted by taxpayers who are dissatisfied with the way in which their money is being spent by the federal government. A case must also fall within the Court's jurisdiction.

See 104 What is the Court's jurisdiction?

Q **118. What is a federal question?**

A Federal courts have jurisdiction to resolve "federal questions," or those that involve the interpretation and application of the U.S. Constitution, acts of Congress, and treaties. Authority for this jurisdiction is derived from Article III of the Constitution and federal statutes.

See 67 What is the jurisdiction of federal courts?

Q **119. What is the Ripeness Doctrine?**

A The Ripeness Doctrine bars the Supreme Court from deciding a case before an injury or threatened injury occurs. It is intended to avoid the resolution of injuries that may never occur. For example, public employees in *United Public Workers v. Mitchell* (1947) claimed their free speech rights had been violated by a government law prohibiting civil servants from working in political campaigns. The Court ruled that this scenario was not ripe for decision because the employees had merely desired to work on political campaigns. Since they had not actually done so, and therefore had not suffered any adverse consequences, their suit could not be decided by the Court.

See 117 Can anyone with a claim make a federal case out of it?

Q **120. What is a "political question"?**

A In deference to the separation of powers clause of the U.S. Constitution, the Supreme Court will not consider issues that it determines are properly within the purview of the legislative or executive branch of government. These matters are said to involve non-justiciable "political questions."

In *Baker v. Carr* (1962) the Court said political questions involve a "lack of judicially discoverable and manageable standards." The Court said it wished to avoid embarrassing "multifarious pronouncements" by various departments of government, and to show the proper respect for coordinate branches of government. A political question must have "a textually demonstrable constitutional commitment of the issue to a coordinate political department."

The Court has refused to consider the following political questions: whether the president can terminate a foreign treaty, whether lower courts have applied the law correctly in cases involving the war in Vietnam, and what constitutes a reasonable time period for states to ratify a proposed amendment to the U.S. Constitution.

See 38 What does separation of powers mean?

Q **121. Who decides which justice will write the opinion in a case?**

A When the Supreme Court is unanimous, which it is about a quarter to a third of the time, the chief justice decides who will write the opinion in the case. If there is a split of opinion and the chief justice is on the minority side, the senior associate justice on the prevailing side may assign a justice to write the opinion. Any justice who disagrees with the majority may write a dissent. The justices announce their written opinions from the bench.

Q **122. How does the Court arrive at a final decision?**

A The justice who is assigned to write the opinion drafts a proposed opinion, which is printed by the Court's basement printing office and circulated among the members of the Court. This process continues until one draft proves acceptable to a majority of the Court.

Q **123. What percentage of Court decisions involve dissent?**

A Dissents are filed in about two-thirds of all of the cases in which the Court issues written opinions. During its first decade the Court issued *seriatim* opinions, or separate opinions by each justice. Chief Justice John Marshall had a policy of encouraging unanimity among the justices. The first real dissent was issued by Justice William Johnson in the case of *Huidekoper's Lessee v. Douglass* (1805). Johnson later complained that his dissent provoked other justices to issue "lectures on the Indecency of Judges cutting at each other."

Q **124. What is the "conference handshake"?**

A Chief Justice Melville W. Fuller, who presided over the Court from 1888 to 1910, instituted a tradition whereby the justices shake hands when they assemble to go on the bench or into a private conference. This practice is intended to be a reminder that differences of opinion on the Court do not preclude harmony of purpose.

When the Court is in session, the justices assemble at a weekly conference, usually on Friday, to discuss the Court's business. The justices meet in a conference room adjacent to the chief justice's chambers, shake hands, and take their seats behind a large mahogany conference table. They discuss which cases the Court will accept for review and those they have recently heard in oral argument. Votes are recorded in a red leather docket book. Only the justices attend these conferences, and the proceedings are kept strictly confidential. Six justices are needed for a quorum.

Q **125. What traditional beverage is served at Court conferences?**

A The Court has a long-standing tradition of serving wine at its conferences when the weather is bad. Legend has it that the famous fourth chief justice, John Marshall, would sometimes say to his colleagues on sunny days, "Our jurisdiction extends over so large a territory that the doctrine of chances makes it certain that it must be raining somewhere."

Q **126. What forms do Court opinions take?**

A The Court issues the following types of opinions:

1. Written opinion, signed by the justice who wrote the opinion for the majority.
2. *Per curiam* (Latin, "by the court") opinion, which generally does not identify the author of the opinion.

3. Concurring opinion, in which a justice agrees with the outcome of the majority's opinion but may disagree on some aspect of the opinion or the majority's rationale.

4. Dissenting opinion, in which one or more justices express their opposition to the majority's opinion.

5. Summary opinion, in which the Court effectively dismisses the case because the legal issue in question was already decided in an earlier opinion of the Court.

Q **127. Where can decisions of the Court be found?**

A The official repository for the Court's decisions is the *United States Reports,* a bound, permanent edition of the Court's decisions that is published by the U.S. Government Printing Office and can be found in any law library. Decisions of the Court may also be found in *United States Supreme Court Reports, Lawyers' Edition,* published by Lawyers Cooperative Publishing, and in West Publishing Company's *Supreme Court Reporter.* The Court's decisions also are accessible via the Internet at several Web sites, including one operated by The Legal Information Institute under the auspices of Project Hermes, the Court's electronic dissemination project: *http://supct.law. cornell.edu/supct/.*

Q **128. What limits does the Court impose on the size of a written brief?**

A The Court has imposed a forty-page limit for a petition for a writ of certiorari, a jurisdictional statement, a petition for an extraordinary writ, a brief in opposition, or a motion to dismiss or affirm. The Court has imposed a fifteen-page limit for a reply to a brief opposing a motion to dismiss or affirm, a supplemental brief, or a petition for a rehearing.

Q **129. How do public interest groups attempt to influence the Court?**

A Both liberal and conservative interest groups work in many ways to influence the Court and its proceedings. Interest groups raise money for and file appeals on test cases to advance a position supported by the group. The NAACP Legal Defense Fund, for example, sponsored the landmark 1954 case that led to the desegregation of American schools (*Brown v. Board of Education of Topeka,* 1954). In another case the American Civil Liberties Union represented various interest groups, including members of the clergy, to challenge a law in 1988 that prevented the use of federal funds to promote abortion (*Brown v. Kendrick,* 1998). Interest groups also seek the permission of the Court to file briefs supporting the arguments of independent parties in a case, use coalition building and group litigation networks to build pressure for issues, and stage protests and demonstrations before the Court.

Q 130. What is an *amicus curiae* brief?

A *Amicus curiae* is a Latin term meaning "friend of the court." Interested individuals or groups may, with the permission of the Court or the parties, submit an amicus curiae brief in a case to ensure that their viewpoints are heard or to bolster the argument of one of the parties. More than four hundred groups, for example, participated in a controversial 1989 case on abortion, *Webster v. Reproductive Health Services.* The U.S. government was not a party in the landmark 1954 case *Brown v Board of Education* but filed a brief supporting desegregation. Overall, 84.4 percent of all full-opinion cases decided by the Supreme Court between 1986 and 1991 contained at least one amicus curiae brief.

Q 131. What is judicial restraint?

A The Supreme Court of the United States exercises judicial restraint overtly and through a variety of legal doctrines that limit its caseload. These include requirements that litigants have standing to sue and that a case be neither premature nor moot.

The philosophy of judicial restraint undergirded an unusual joint opinion by Justices Sandra Day O'Connor, Anthony M. Kennedy, and David Souter in the 1991 case of *Planned Parenthood of Southeastern Pennsylvania v. Casey.* Emphasizing the importance of precedent, the three justices declined to outlaw abortion rights because, they noted, their doing so would cause social upheaval. People who have lived for decades with the idea that abortion is available if contraception fails would react strongly against the decision, destabilizing the social order.

Q 132. What is judicial activism?

A Judicial activism occurs when judges allow their political views to influence their decisions on questions of law and effectively substitute their judgment for those of elected legislators and policy makers.

In the early twentieth century, the charge of judicial activism was often made by liberals who objected to conservative judges striking down social welfare programs. In a two-year period during the 1930s, the Court struck down a series of laws that Congress had passed as part of President Franklin Delano Roosevelt's New Deal program to combat the depression. After Roosevelt attempted unsuccessfully to "pack" the Court with justices favorable to his programs, the Court backed away from deciding issues involving economic rights, deferring to state legislatures.

Today, the charge of judicial activism is most often heard from conservatives who object to Court rulings upholding antidiscrimination measures that benefit minorities and women.

Q 133. How often has the Court "overruled" Congress?

A The Court has declared at least 135 acts of Congress to be unconstitutional. Congress may "reverse" a Court decision that restricts or invalidates a congressional action by enacting new legislation. Such a reversal occurred, for example, when Congress passed the Clayton Act of 1914, allowing an antitrust exemption for labor unions pursuing lawful objectives. More recently, Congress in 1998 passed the Civil Rights Restoration Act, requiring an entity receiving federal funds to abide by federal laws prohibiting discrimination in education.

Q 134. How many times has the Court overruled itself?

A The Court has overruled itself, or overturned earlier rulings, more than two hundred times since its founding. The Court's first major reversal occurred in 1871 when it upheld legislation passed by Congress allowing the use of paper money to pay debts. The reversal overturned a decision by the Court just fifteen months earlier.

Q 135. How many Court decisions were reversed by amendments to the U.S. Constitution?

A Four. In *Chisholm v. Georgia* (1793) the Court upheld the right of South Carolina citizens to sue the sovereign state of Georgia. This decision provoked Congress to draft the Eleventh Amendment, which barred the judiciary from hearing cases brought against a state by a citizen of another state. The drafting of the amendment marked the first substantial alteration in the original language of the Constitution of 1787. Other amendments and the decisions they overturned are:

- Thirteenth (1865) and Fourteenth (1868) Amendments: prohibited slavery and granted blacks equal rights; overturned the Court's decision in *Dred Scott v. Sandford* (1857).

- Sixteenth Amendment (1913): gave Congress the right to levy an income tax without apportionment among the states; overturned the Court's decision in *Pollock v. Farmers' Loan and Trust Co.* (1895).
- Twenty-sixth Amendment (1971): gave all citizens who are eighteen years of age or older the right to vote; overturned the Court's decision *Oregon v. Mitchell* (1970).

Q 136. What is often said to be the low point in the Court's history?

A If not the absolute lowest point in its history, the Court's decision in the 1857 case of *Dred Scott v. Sandford* is certainly a graphic example of the Court's fallibility. The Court ruled that blacks, slave or free, "are not included . . . under the word *citizens* in the Constitution." The Court also held that Congress could not prevent slavery in the western territories.

Scott was a black slave who was owned by an army surgeon and lived on military bases in Illinois and Minnesota, areas that were free under the Missouri Compromise of 1820, which prohibited slavery in the territories. After the surgeon died, a St. Louis court held that Scott had become free while living in nonslave jurisdictions. The case eventually wound up before the Court, which ruled against Scott.

The majority held that Scott, who was then owned by a New Yorker, could not sue in federal court as a citizen of a different state because he was not a citizen. The decision, written by Supreme Court Justice Roger B. Taney, said, "[T]he right of property in a slave is distinctly and expressly affirmed in the Constitution. The right to traffic in it, like an ordinary article of merchandise and property, was guaranteed to the citizens of the United States, in every State that might desire it . . . And the Government in express terms is pledged to protect it in all future time, if the slave escapes from his owner."

Scott was later sold to a prior owner and freed from slavery. He died in St. Louis on Sept. 17, 1858. Many believe the landmark decision that bore his name set the stage for the Civil War.

See 43 Does the U.S. Constitution say "all men are created equal"? 44 Did the U.S. Constitution address the issue of slavery?

Q 137. What is the Court's most controversial modern-day decision?

A The Court's decision in *Roe v. Wade* (1973) is certainly its most controversial in modern times. The Court's 7–2 decision limited the federal and state legislature's right to proscribe and regulate abortion, finding that women have a qualified right to abort a fetus that is based on the right to privacy guaranteed to all Americans in the U.S. Constitution. The Court said states could not ban abortion during the first three months of pregnancy, when the mother's health takes precedence over the fetus. The state can regulate abortion during the second trimester, and may even prescribe it during the last three months of pregnancy, when the fetus is capable of a meaningful life outside the mother's womb. The Court reaffirmed this basic premise in a fractious 5–4 vote in *Planned Parenthood of Southeastern Pennsylvania v. Casey* (1992). However, the Court instituted a new standard for testing whether state restrictions infringe upon the abortion right—whether the restriction poses an "undue burden" on the woman seeking an abortion.

Q **138. What is the most quoted footnote in any Supreme Court decision?**

A In an obscure footnote in *U.S. v. Carolene Products Co.* (1938), the Court signaled its intention to devote greater attention to how legislation affects the noneconomic rights of citizens, especially those rights necessary to the operation of the political system. When a law violates an economic right, the Court said, the law should be presumed to be valid. However, when a law violates a personal right guaranteed by the Bill of Rights of the U.S. Constitution, the Court should adopt a higher standard of review.

"Prejudice against discrete and insular minorities may be a special condition, relied upon to protect minorities, and which may call for a correspondingly more serious judicial inquiry," wrote Justice Harlan Fiske Stone in the footnote.

The Court subsequently adopted a standard reserving its highest level of scrutiny for cases alleging discrimination on the basis of race or national origin. This means a statute will be upheld only if it is found necessary to attain some compelling government interest.

The case in which the footnote appears involved a challenge to a federal law prohibiting the interstate shipment of certain "filled milk" products deemed injurious to the public's health. The Court held the act was a valid exercise of Congress's power to regulate interstate commerce.

Q **139. The Court has held a special term only four times in its history. Why?**

A The Court held special sessions to decide the urgent cases that arose after it had adjourned its regular term. When possible, the Court has extended its regular term to hear urgent matters. However, it was forced to hold special terms four times in its history for cases that occurred during the its summer recess. Those cases were:

Ex Parte Quirin (1942). Nine Nazi saboteurs arrested in the United States challenged President Franklin D. Roosevelt's decision to have them tried by a presidentially established military commission instead of by civilian courts. The Court convened a special term on July 29–30, 1942, and unanimously upheld the saboteurs' conviction, finding that Roosevelt's actions were within the powers delegated to him by Congress.

Rosenberg v. United States (1953). In a special term on June 18, 1953, the Court, by a 6–3 vote, lifted a stay of execution granted by Justice William O. Douglas in the case of Julius and Ethel Rosenberg, a husband and wife who were convicted of violating the Espionage Act of 1917 by providing secrets about the atomic bomb to the Soviet Union at the height of the cold war. The Court ruled the adoption of the Atomic Energy Act of 1946 did not repeal penalty provisions of the Espionage Act. The Rosenbergs were executed a few hours later.

Cooper v. Aaron (1958). In a special session on August 28, 1958, the Court refused a request by Little Rock, Arkansas, school officials to delay school desegregation. Arkansas governor Orval Faubus had called out the national guard to prevent black students from entering a local high school, and federal troops were summoned to protect the students. In this volatile climate a federal judge suspended the district's desegregation plan for two-and-a-half years, a decision that was reversed by the U.S. court of appeals. The Court, in a decision signed personally by each justice, unanimously ruled that "law and order are not here to be preserved by depriving the Negro children of their constitutional rights."

O'Brien v. Brown (1972). The Court called a special session on July 6, 1972, to consider challenges to the unseating of Illinois and California delegates to the Democratic National Convention. The Court concluded that it lacked sufficient time to rule upon important constitutional issues raised in the case given the convention was due to start in four days. It took no action on those matters.

Q 140. How much does it cost to appeal a case to the Supreme Court of the United States?

A Most of the cases on the Court's docket are filed by indigent parties who are not required to pay the Court's usual $300 filing fee. Of the 6,779 cases filed with the

Court in 1997, 4,694 were filed *in forma pauperis* ("in the manner of a pauper"). Attorneys' fees aside, a major cost of filing a brief with the Court is the high number of copies required, usually forty. A party proceeding *in forma pauperis* need file only the original brief and ten copies. If the indigent party is a prison inmate who is not represented by counsel, the Court requires only the original appeal, without any additional copies. Typically, the Court grants review to very few of the cases filed by indigent parties. The Court agreed to review only 21 of the cases on its *in forma pauperis* docket in 1997.

Q 141. Which branch of government does the public have the most confidence in?

A In a 1998 poll by Louis Harris and Associates, Inc., 37 percent of those polled expressed "a great deal of confidence" in the Supreme Court of the United States, compared with 12 percent for Congress and 20 percent for the White House. In fact, the Court was second only to the military as the most respected institution in the country. Thirty-eight percent of those polled said they have great confidence in the military.

Q 142. What are the ten greatest Court decisions?

A No such list is definitive, but here are ten cases considered "great" for their profound impact on American history:

Marbury v. Madison (1803). Chief Justice John Marshall established the Court as the primary interpreter of the U.S. Constitution, capable of invalidating acts of Congress.

McCulloch v. Maryland (1819). This decision established the priority of federal law over state law. The Court held that Congress can enact all laws that are "necessary and proper" to execute its responsibilities under the Constitution. "We must never forget that it is a constitution we are expounding . . . intended to endure for ages to come, and, consequently, to be adapted to the various crises of human affairs," wrote Chief Justice John Marshall. The Court ruled that Maryland could not tax federal bank notes.

Gibbons v. Ogden, 9 Wheat 1 (1824). The Court ruled that Congress can regulate all commerce affecting more than one state. Chief Justice John

Marshall nullified a New York law granting a monopoly on the use of its waters.

National Labor Relations Board v. Jones & Laughlin Steel Corp. (1937). The Court sustained the constitutionality of the National Labor Relations Act of 1935, which gave workers the right to organize collectively in unions.

Brown v. Board of Education of Topeka (1954). Separate schools for blacks and whites are inherently unequal, said the justices, and violate the equal protection guarantee of the Fourteenth Amendment.

Gideon v. Wainwright (1963). The Court decided that all persons accused of a serious crime are entitled to a lawyer.

Baker v. Carr (1992). This ruling gave federal courts the power to resolve equal protection challenges to legislative apportionment schemes.

New York Times Co. v. Sullivan (1964). The Court said that public officials must prove actual malice to prevail in libel suits against the press.

Roe v. Wade (1973). The ruling found that the right to privacy protects a woman's decision to abort a fetus.

Charles River Bridge v. Warren Bridge, (1837). The Court ruled that the community's interest in economic development trumped a private company's right to property under the U.S. Constitution.

Q 143. How does a case get to the Supreme Court of the United States?

A Cases reach the Court in one of three ways (see Figure 4-3):

(1) An appeal as a matter of right: A case comes before the Court when a special three-judge district court has granted or refused to issue a final court order in a proceeding that the district court was required to hear.

(2) A writ of certiorari or a matter of court discretion: The Court may grant "cert" when the validity of a treaty or federal statute is questioned, when there is a serious constitutional question about a state law, when a case is appealed from a lower federal appeals court, or when a decision involving a serious constitutional question is appealed from a state court of last resort.

Figure 4-3 How Cases Reach the Supreme Court

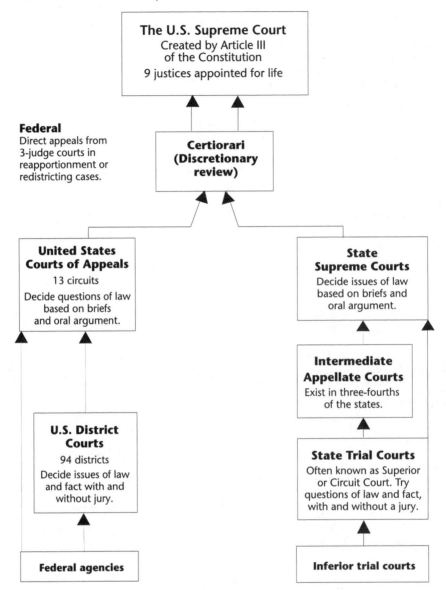

Source: Theodore J. Lowi and Benjamin Ginsberg, *American Government: Freedom and Power,*
5th ed. Copyright © 1998, 1996, 1995, 1994, 1993, 1992, 1990 by W. W. Norton &
Company, Inc. Reprinted by permission of W. W. Norton & Company, Inc.

(3) Certification: In this seldom-used process, a lower court, such as the U.S. court of appeals, seeks instructions from the high court to resolve a question of law in a civil or criminal case.

Q 144. Is there any appeal from a decision of the Supreme Court?

A No, but Congress can pass "remedial legislation" to reverse a Court decision, or can join with the states to seek passage of an amendment to the U.S. Constitution that effectively overrules the Court.

See 135 How many Court decisions were reversed by amendments to the U.S. Constitution?

PERSONNEL

Justices

Q 145. Who sits on the Supreme Court of the United States?

A The chief justice of the United States is William H. Rehnquist, who was appointed on September 26, 1986. The eight associate justices on the Court are John Paul Stevens, Sandra Day O'Connor, Antonin Scalia, Anthony M. Kennedy, David H. Souter, Clarence Thomas, Ruth Bader Ginsburg, and Stephen G. Breyer. There have been a total of 108 justices on the Court, the latest being Justice Breyer.

Q 146. Why are Supreme Court members called "justices" instead of "judges"?

A The U.S. Constitution refers to the "judges, both of the supreme and inferior courts. . . ." However, when Congress created the Court in the Judiciary Act of 1789, it said the Court should "consist of a chief justice and five associate justices. . . ." It is not clear why the title was changed from "judge" to "justice." Some observers attribute the switch to the fact that the Court was not held in as high esteem when it was formed as it is today. The enhanced title was intended to stress the unique role of the Court at the pinnacle of the federal judicial system.

Q 147. What qualifications are necessary to be a justice?

A There are no statutory or constitutional requirements for eligibility for a federal judgeship, though a law degree is considered essential today. As for judicial experience, 43 of the 106 men and 2 women who served on the Court between 1789 and 1996 had none.

Q **148. Has the Court always had nine justices?**

A No. The U.S. Constitution requires the formation of a Supreme Court but is silent on the number of judges who must staff the Court. The number of justices has changed six times since Congress passed the Judiciary Act of 1789, which created the Court and specified that it "shall consist of a chief justice and five associate justices, any four of whom shall be a quorum. . . . " The largest number of seats on the Court was ten during the Civil War, when President Abraham Lincoln sought to solidify support on the bench for the Union cause. In 1866 Congress reduced the size of the Court to seven. Congress fixed the number of seats on the Court at nine in 1869, and that number has not changed since that time.

Q **149. What was President Franklin D. Roosevelt's 1937 "Court Reform Plan"?**

A Politicians occasionally attempt to tinker with the size of the Court to win political advantage. Shortly after President Franklin D. Roosevelt won a landslide reelection victory in 1937, he presented a bill to Congress to "reorganize" the federal judiciary, ostensibly to decrease delays in the administration of justice. Roosevelt was irked that virtually all of his New Deal measures had been struck down by the Supreme Court of the United States. Among other things, he sought to expand the Court by up to six members. Opponents charged that Roosevelt was really attempting to subvert the U.S. Constitution and to erode the independence of the federal judiciary by packing the Court with sympathizers.

Roosevelt's plan failed, but it was not a complete loss. The Court subsequently upheld several major pieces of New Deal legislation, including the Social Security Act and the National Labor Relations Act.

Q **150. Who were the "Four Horsemen"?**

A They were the four justices who constituted the conservative wing of the Court and consistently opposed Franklin D. Roosevelt's New Deal program in the 1930s. Named after the Book of Revelation's Four Horsemen of the Apocalypse, they were Justices Willis Van Devanter, James McReynolds, George Sutherland, and Pierce Butler.

Q **151. What is the correct title for the presiding officer on the Court?**

A The correct title is chief justice of the United States.

Q **152. What are the duties of the chief justice?**

A The chief justice is the leader of the federal court system and presides over the Supreme Court of the United States. The chief justice serves in key leadership positions on the Judicial Conference of the United States, Administrative Office of the U.S. Courts, and Federal Judicial Center. There is little consensus on exactly what the job of chief justice entails. It is mostly what the officeholder makes of it. Some chief justices are hands-on executives while others are happy to delegate much of their authority to support staff.

See 69 What is the Judicial Conference of the United States? 70 What is the Administrative Office of the U.S. Courts? 71 What is the Federal Judicial Center?

Q **153. Which justice adorns his black robe with fanciful gold stripes?**

A Chief Justice William Rehnquist began wearing four gold stripes on each sleeve in 1995 after seeing a production of Gilbert and Sullivan's operetta "Iolanthe," in which the lord chancellor wore a similarly adorned frock. The "highly susceptible" chancellor in the operetta sings of his weakness for young ladies, including his wards. Rehnquist wore the striped robe when he presided over President Bill Clinton's impeachment trial in the U.S. Senate. It was noted with some irony that Clinton was enmeshed in an adulterous scandal with a young White House intern, Monica Lewinsky.

Q **154. Do associate justices answer to the chief justice?**

A No. As a Supreme Court member, the chief justice is just the "first among equals." The chief justice lacks formal authority to require other justices to do his or her bidding but does possess indirect authority to influence Court proceedings. The chief justice controls the discussion during judicial conferences, assigns Court opinion writing duties, oversees the Court's administration, and sets the tone for the Court.

Q **155. What U.S. president's true ambition was to serve as chief justice of the United States?**

A William Howard Taft, who served as president from 1909 to 1913, was appointed chief justice of the United States in 1921, eight years after losing a second bid for the presidency to Democrat Woodrow Wilson. In fact, Taft was a reluctant politician who called his first campaign "one of the most uncomfortable four months of my life." His true ambition was to serve on the Supreme Court of the United States. After losing to Wilson, Taft taught at Yale law school until President Warren Harding, a fellow Republican, appointed him to serve as chief justice. Drawing upon his experience as the nation's chief executive, Taft transformed the role of chief justice into that of a true leader of the federal judicial branch. He lobbied Congress for judicial reforms, pushed through legislation that drastically reduced the Court's docket, and secured the construction of the Supreme Court Building. Judge Learned Hand said Taft was "the first Chief Justice that ever recognized such things as district courts except when they were officially brought to their attention to reverse."

Q 156. Who has served as chief justice?

A The sixteen chief justices who have served on the Court since its first session in 1789 are:

Name	Years served	Appointed by	Home state
John Jay	1789–1795	Washington	New York
John Rutledge	1795 [a]	Washington	South Carolina
Oliver Ellsworth	1796–1800	Washington	Connecticut
John Marshall	1801–1835	Adams	Virginia
Roger B. Taney	1836–1864	Jackson	Maryland
Salmon P. Chase	1864–1873	Lincoln	Ohio
Mornson R. Waite	1874–1888	Grant	Ohio
Melville W. Fuller	1888–1910	Cleveland	Illinois
Edward D. White	1910–1921	Taft	Louisiana
William Howard Taft	1921–1930	Harding	Ohio
Charles Evans Hughes	1930–1941	Hoover	New York
Harlan Fiske Stone	1941–1946	Roosevelt	New York
Fred M. Vinson	1946–1953	Truman	Kentucky
Earl Warren	1953–1969 [b]	Eisenhower	California
Warren E. Burger	1969–1986	Nixon	Minnesota
William H. Rehnquist	1986–	Reagan	Arizona

[a] Rutledge accepted a recess appointment and presided over the Court during its August 1795 term, at which two cases were decided. In December 1795, however, the Senate refused, 14–10, to confirm him.

[b] Warren accepted a recess appointment as chief justice in September 1953 and was confirmed by the Senate in March 1954.

Q 157. Who is the "father of constitutional law"?

A Chief Justice John Marshall is credited with establishing the Court as the supreme authority on the meaning of the U.S. Constitution. Marshall was born in a log cabin in Virginia on September 24, 1755, the son of a member of the Virginia House of Burgesses. He served in the Revolutionary War as a member of the Third Virginia Regiment. He was admitted to the bar in 1780 after attending a course of law lectures at the College of William and Mary. Marshall established a successful practice representing debtors against their prewar British creditors. He served terms in Virginia's House of Delegates and in the U.S. House of Representatives, and acted as secretary of state under President John Adams. Marshall also authored a series of five books on the life of George Washington.

Marshall achieved a measure of fame in 1797 when he was sent to France as an American envoy to negotiate a treaty with the new revolutionary government. He refused to pay a bribe for foreign minister Charles-Maurice de Talleyrand, calling the shakedown an affront to the United States. Marshall's tersely worded message home was "Millions for defense, but not one cent for tribute!"

Although Marshall had no prior judicial experience, Adams appointed him to the position of chief justice on the Court in 1801 after Adams's first choice, John Jay, declined the post. During his thirty-four-year tenure, Marshall participated in more than one thousand decisions and wrote more than five hundred opinions. None was more important than his ruling in *Marbury v. Madison,* which established the principle of judicial review. The Liberty Bell was tolled on July 6, 1835, to mark Marshall's death at the age of seventy-nine.

See 28 Who were the "Midnight Judges"? 102 What is the significance of Marbury v. Madison? *103 Was* Marbury v. Madison *the first case to assert the power of judicial review? 159 Have all Supreme Court justices been lawyers?*

Q 158. What U.S. president wouldn't give Chief Justice John Marshall the time of day?

A President Thomas Jefferson said Marshall's powers of intellectual persuasion were so great that "you must never give him an affirmative answer or you will be forced to grant his conclusion. Why, if he were to ask me if it were daylight or not, I'd reply, 'Sir, I don't know, I can't tell.'"

Q **159. Have all Supreme Court justices been lawyers?**

A No. Arguably the greatest justice in the Court's history, Chief Justice John Marshall (1755–1835), was self-taught in the law, having taken only a few law courses at William and Mary College in the 1770s. Until recent times, many justices studied the law but lacked a law degree. Justice Stanley F. Reed, a native of Minerva, Kentucky, who served on the Court from 1938 to 1957, was the last justice who did not have a law degree, this despite the fact that he attended both the University of Virginia and Columbia University law schools and studied civil and international law at the Sorbonne in Paris. Since 1957 every justice on the Court has been a law school graduate.

Q **160. Which president appointed the most justices?**

A President George Washington appointed the largest number of justices. In addition to the six original justices on the Court, Washington appointed four more justices by the end of his second term. President Franklin D. Roosevelt is second to Washington, having appointed eight justices to the Court and elevated Justice Harlan Fiske Stone to chief justice.

Q **161. Which president appointed the fewest justices?**

A Four presidents tie for that distinction. William Henry Harrison, Zachary Taylor, Andrew Johnson, and Jimmy Carter each made no appointments to the Court. Carter is the only full-term president to make no appointments because no vacancies occurred during his term.

Q **162. What U.S. senator lost his chance to serve on the Supreme Court when he asked for a night to think it over?**

A In 1971 President Richard M. Nixon authorized Attorney General John Mitchell to ask the Republican senator Howard Baker if he was interested in serving on the U.S. Supreme Court. Baker allegedly responded, "I want overnight to think about it." Mitchell preferred William Rehnquist, a former head of the Justice Department's Office of Legal Counsel, and decided to back him instead. When Baker tried to accept the offer to serve on the Court, it was too late. Rehnquist, who was Nixon's second choice, went on to become the chief justice of the Court in 1986.

Q 163. What is the longest vacancy in the history of the court?

A The longest vacancy was two years, three months, and twenty-three days. This vacancy was created when Justice Henry Baldwin died on April 2, 1844. The Senate rejected President John Tyler's first three nominations to fill the vacancy, and it rejected the first nomination by Tyler's successor, James K. Polk. Meanwhile, both Tyler and Polk beseeched James Buchanan, a future U.S. president, to take the slot, to no avail. On August 4, 1846, the Senate finally confirmed Polk's nomination of Robert C. Grier, a district court judge from Pennsylvania.

Q 164. Does politics influence the appointment of justices?

A Does it rain in Indianapolis in the summertime? At least ninety percent of federal judicial nominees are of the same political party as the appointing president. And the ease of the candidate's confirmation by the Senate is influenced by whether the president's political party is in the majority or minority.

The political nature of the process is particularly apparent when a candidate is not a moderate in his or her views. President Ronald Reagan nominated conservative Robert H. Bork, a judge on the D.C. Circuit Court of Appeals, to the Court in 1987. Bork had espoused a literal interpretation of the U.S. Constitution consonant with the public understanding of the time in which it was written. Bork had also played a leading role in the infamous "Saturday Night Massacre." In 1973 President Richard M. Nixon had ordered Attorney General Elliot Richardson, and then Deputy Attorney General William Ruckelshaus, to fire Archibald Cox, the special prosecutor in the Watergate scandal. Both men resigned rather than carry out the order. The task fell to Bork, then U.S. solicitor general, who fired Cox. The Senate rejected Bork's nomination.

See 6 What is the difference between the letter and the spirit of the law?

Q 165. Has any justice ever died on the bench?

A No, but a few came close and at least fifty justices have died while in office. An appointment to the Court is for life or during "good Behaviour." Many aging justices refuse to resign because they enjoy the perks of office or fear the philosophical bent of the nominee who is likely to replace them.

In the 1970s several members of the Court were battling the ravages of age. Justice William O. Douglas suffered a paralytic stroke in 1975 but refused to resign when urged to do so by Chief Justice Warren Burger. Douglas's health deteriorated to such an extent that he is said to have demonstrated symptoms of paranoia and odd behavior, and could barely make his voice heard.

Douglas's fellow justices, Hugo Black and John Harlan, also were aged and infirm. In fact, Douglas had urged the eighty-five-year-old Black to retire, without success. Harlan, who suffered from cancer of the spine and was almost blind, once signed a hospital bed sheet thinking it was an emergency petition.

After suffering an incapacitating stroke, Black resigned on September 17, 1971, and died eight days later. Harlan resigned on September 23, 1971, and died about a month later. Douglas finally retired on November 12, 1975. He died in Washington, D.C., on January 19, 1980.

The oldest justice to serve was Oliver Wendell Holmes, who was ninety when he retired in 1932 at the suggestion of his colleagues, after twenty-nine years on the bench.

See 89 Must federal judges retire? 90 What is the "Rule of 80"?

Q 166. Who is the only justice to never engage in any political or judicial activities prior to his appointment?

A Justice George Shiras, Jr., who served on the Court from 1892 to 1903, is unique in that he never engaged in political or judicial activities before his appointment to the Court. A native of Pittsburgh, Shiras obtained an undergraduate degree from Yale University and then studied law at Yale without graduating. Shiras was admitted to the Allegheny County bar in 1855 and practiced law successfully in Pittsburgh until his nomination to the Court in 1892 by President Benjamin Harrison. Shiras's nomination was backed by his former Yale classmates and Pittsburgh's steel and coal interests, including robber baron Andrew Carnegie. Despite some initial opposition by Pennsylvania Republican senators, who were peeved that they had not been consulted by Harrison before Shiras's name was sent to the Senate, Shiras's nomination was unanimously confirmed.

Q 167. Which justice wrote the fewest decisions?

A Three justices wrote only one decision. Justice Alfred Moore wrote only one decision during his term on the Court from 1800 to 1804, when he resigned, citing ill health, and returned to his home state of North Carolina to help found the University of North Carolina. Moore served considerably longer than the two other justices who wrote only one opinion, John Rutledge and Thomas Johnson. Rutledge was confirmed as an associate justice in 1789 but never sat on the Court because of illness. He resigned in 1791 to become chief justice of the South Carolina supreme court. President George Washington made a recess appointment of Rutledge in 1795 to succeed John Jay as chief justice, and Rutledge presided over the Court's August term but the Senate subsequently rejected his appointment. Johnson, a former military commander, served on the Court from November 1791 to February 1793.

Q 168. Which justice wrote the most decisions?

A Justice William O. Douglas wrote the most decisions. He penned 1,164 decisions from 1939 to 1975.

Q 169. Has any justice ever been the subject of an assassination attempt?

A Justice Stephen J. Field, who served on the Supreme Court of the United States from 1863 to 1897, survived an alleged assassination attempt by the husband of a disgruntled litigant. While Field was holding circuit court in California, he invalidated a marriage contract between Sarah Althea Hill and William Sharon, a wealthy mine owner. Sharon was already dead and Hill had remarried David S. Terry, who had served with Field on the California supreme court.

When Field returned to California to hold circuit court in 1889, Terry spotted him eating breakfast at a railroad station restaurant. Terry struck Field two or three times in the face. Some observers felt that Terry, who was unarmed, was about to challenge Field to a duel. A federal deputy marshal accompanying Field shot Terry twice, killing him. California authorities arrested the marshal, David Neagle, and charged him with murder. Field also was arrested and charged as an accomplice, but the case against him was later dismissed.

Neagle argued the state could not detain him for actions taken in the performance of his duties under federal law. The Supreme Court of the United States agreed, concluding that Neagle "had just reason to believe that the attack would result in the death of Mr. Justice Field unless he interfered, and that he did justifiably interfere. . . . " Justice Field recused himself from consideration of the matter. Sarah Althea Terry subsequently was committed to a state asylum for the insane, where she spent the remaining forty-five years of her life.

Q 170. Who were the most "disagreeable" justices?

A Justice Oliver Wendell Holmes (1841–1935) is known as the "Great Dissenter" because of the depth and quality of his dissents, but the justice who wrote the most dissents, 486 in all, was William O. Douglas (1898-1980). Holmes penned just 173 formal dissents.

Justice William Johnson, who was appointed to the Court by President Thomas Jefferson in 1804, is known as the "father of dissent" or "the first great Court dissenter." Although only thirty-two at the time of his appointment, he established a tradition of dissenting during an era in which Chief Justice John Marshall emphasized unity on the Court.

In defense of the dissent, Chief Justice Charles Evans Hughes (1862–1948) wrote: "A dissent in a court of last resort is an appeal to the brooding spirit of the law, to the intelligence of a future day, when a later decision may possibly correct the error into which the dissenting judge believes the court to have been betrayed."

See 123 What percentage of Court decisions involve dissent?

Q 171. What may be the greatest dissent of all time?

A In *Plessy v. Ferguson* (1896) the Court voted 8–1 to uphold a Louisiana statute requiring railroads to provide separate transportation for white and black passengers. It took more than fifty years for the dissent, written by Justice John Marshall Harlan, to prevail. Harlan said the Constitution is "color blind and neither knows nor tolerates classes among citizens. In respect of civil rights, all citizens are equal before the law."

Q 172. Which justice was once a member of the Ku Klux Klan?

A Justice Hugo L. Black, a native of Harlan, Alabama, admitted after his appointment to the Court that he had been a member of the Ku Klux Klan in the 1920s. In a nationwide radio address, he said he had resigned from the Klan after two years and harbored no racial animosity. Black was appointed to the Court by President Franklin D. Roosevelt in 1937. He became an articulate voice for the rights of the oppressed while on the Court, and authored a landmark decision, *Gideon v. Wainwright* (1963), in which the Court guaranteed the right to counsel to indigent defendants.

Q 173. What is the gender/racial breakdown of the Supreme Court?

A The Supreme Court, also known as the "Brethren," traditionally was a male, all-white, and largely Protestant institution.

Thurgood Marshall, the great-grandson of a slave, broke the color barrier on the Court in 1967 when he was appointed by President Lyndon B. Johnson. Marshall was the winning attorney in the landmark case that brought about school desegregation, *Brown v. Board of Education of Topeka.* He was succeeded by conservative Clarence Thomas, who was appointed by President George Bush in 1991.

Sandra Day O'Connor, a federal appeals court judge, became the first female justice in the Court's history when she was appointed by President Ronald Reagan in 1981. She was joined in 1993 by Ruth Bader Ginsburg, a pioneering advocate for women's rights who was appointed by President Bill Clinton.

See 80 What U.S. president appointed the most women and minorities to the federal bench? 81 What is the demographic profile of the federal judiciary?

Q 174. Who won the closest U.S. Senate vote for confirmation to the Court in the twentieth century?

A Clarence Thomas. A former director of the U.S. Equal Employment and Opportunity Commission, Thomas was charged with sexually harassing a former employee, Anita Hill. He won confirmation in 1991 by a vote of 52 to 48. The closest successful confirmation vote in the Court's history was the 24–23 vote confirming Stanley Matthews's nomination to the Court in March 1881 by President James A. Garfield. It was the second time Matthews had been nominated to the Court. He had been nominated in January 1881 by President Rutherford B. Hayes, but the Senate had refused to act on the nomination.

Q 175. What percentage of Supreme Court justices were born poor?

A The vast majority of all federal judges are from upper- or upper-middle-class families, and that is particularly true of the Court. About 10 percent of the justices appointed since the Court was formed in 1789 are of humble origins, either poor or lower-middle-class.

One example was Justice James F. Byrnes, born in Charleston, South Carolina, in 1879, the son of poor Irish immigrant parents. His father died shortly before his birth. Forced to leave school at the age of fourteen, he never graduated from high school. Byrnes read the law privately while he worked as a law clerk and a court reporter, and passed the bar in 1903. He became a newspaper owner/editor, district attorney, and member of both the U.S. House and the U.S. Senate. He was appointed to the Court in 1941 by President Franklin D. Roosevelt, resigning fifteen months later to serve as director of both the World War II Office of Economic Stabilization and the Office of War Mobilization. He then served as secretary of state and, finally, as governor of South Carolina. He died in 1972.

Q **176. How much is the chief justice paid?**

A In 1999, the chief justice of the United States was paid $175,400. In addition, the chief justice is allowed to accrue outside earnings of up to $20,505.

Q **177. How much are associate justices paid?**

A Associate justices of the Supreme Court were paid $167,900 in 1999. In addition, the associate justices are allowed to accrue outside earnings of up to $20,505.

Q **178. How many justices were impeached?**

A Samuel Chase, an associate justice of the Supreme Court, was impeached by the U.S. House of Representatives on March 12, 1804, by a vote of 73–32, but he was acquitted by the Senate in a vote that fell short of the two-thirds required for impeachment. More than a majority of the senators felt that Chase had acted improperly but that his behavior did not rise to the level of an impeachable offense.

Chase was appointed to the Court by President George Washington in January 1776. This appointment did not stop him from actively campaigning for Federalist president John Adams in 1880. In an impassioned speech to a Baltimore grand jury in 1803, Chase denounced the democratic "mobocracy." He also strongly supported the unpopular Sedition Act of 1798 and campaigned to indict newspaper editors who opposed the Federalist party.

Chase had a colorful past even before he got to the Court. He was dismissed as a delegate to the Continental Congress from Maryland for two years when it was discovered that he had attempted to corner the flour market through speculation. Chase became a fervent opponent of the adoption of the U.S. Constitution. Under the pen name "Caution" he argued that a federal constitution would give rise to an elitist government.

After his impeachment trial, Chase, who suffered from gout, was too ill to attend Court sessions. He died in Baltimore in relative obscurity on June 19, 1811.

See 84 Can federal judges be fired? 85 How many federal judges were impeached? 86 What is an impeachable offense? 87 Must an impeachable offense include criminal misconduct? 88 Is there any appeal from impeachment?

Other Court Personnel

Q 179. What are the duties of Supreme Court law clerks?

A Law clerks have no statutorily defined duties. They generally screen cases for the justices, conduct legal research, and draft opinions, bench memorandums, and orders. Along with secretaries, law clerks perform as many administrative tasks as possible to free the justices for the nondelegable aspects of judging. Each sitting justice can be assigned up to four law clerks, retired justices are assigned one each, and the chief justice may have up to five law clerks. Thirty-six law clerks worked for the Court in 1999, each earning a salary of $47,501.

Q 180. Where did the position of law clerk originate?

A Justice Horace Gray, a former chief justice of the Supreme Judicial Court of Massachusetts who was appointed to the Supreme Court of the United States in 1881, began the practice of hiring clerical assistance. He hired the first law clerk, an honor graduate of Harvard Law School, at his own expense. Justice Oliver Wendell Holmes, Gray's successor on the Court, continued the practice. In 1886, at the recommendation of the U.S. attorney general, Congress provided each justice with $20,000 a year to hire a "secretary or law clerk." Law clerks were assigned to judges of the U.S. circuit courts in 1930, to district court judges in 1936, to magistrate judges in 1979, and to bankruptcy judges in 1984.

Q 181. Where do law clerks come from?

A In the past decade, almost half of all Court law clerks have attended Harvard or Yale Law School, where they were top students, usually members of elite law reviews. As of 1998, less than 2 percent of the 428 law clerks hired by all sitting justices had been black. About one-quarter had been female; 4 percent, Asian American; and 1 percent, Hispanic. None had been Native Americans. Four of the current nine justices have never hired a black law clerk, including Chief Justice William Rehnquist, who joined the Court in 1972, and Justices Anthony Kennedy, Antonin Scalia, and David Souter. The Court espouses equal employment policies but is not covered by federal laws barring workplace discrimination.

182. What do the Court's secretaries do?

A Secretaries generally have primary responsibility for handling administrative matters in the chambers. They assemble documents, help maintain the chambers' library, monitor the justices' calendars, and run errands for the justices. Secretaries also direct visitors to the justices' chambers and shield the justices from unnecessary encroachments on their time. Each Supreme Court justice is authorized to hire a secretary and an assistant secretary.

183. What is the Supreme Court Bar?

A The Supreme Court Bar is the cadre of attorneys who are authorized to practice before the Court. To be eligible for admission, an applicant must have been qualified to practice in the highest court of a U.S. state, commonwealth, territory, or possession or in that of the District of Columbia for at least three years immediately before the date of the application. Also, the applicant cannot have been the subject of an adverse disciplinary action within the three prior years and "must appear to the Court to be of good moral and professional character."

The applicant must file the statements of two sponsors who are members of the Supreme Court Bar and who endorse the "correctness" of the applicant's claim to possess all the qualifications required for admission. Sponsors also must affirm that the applicant is of good "moral and professional" character. An attorney may be admitted through an oral motion in open court or by a written motion in lieu of a formal appearance. Attorneys take an oath in which they agree to conduct themselves "uprightly and according to law" and to "support the Constitution of the United States. So help you God."

184. How many attorneys are members of the Supreme Court Bar?

A About 230,000 attorneys are admitted to the Supreme Court Bar. An average of about 5,000 new admissions are granted per year.

185. How long do lawyers have to make their arguments to the Court?

A Unless the Court directs otherwise, each side is allowed one-half hour for argument. According to the Rules of the Supreme Court of the United States, "additional time is rarely accorded." Despite these time constraints, the justices do not hesitate to interrupt the advocate with questions. Until 1849 there was no time limit on arguments before the Court, and they sometimes lasted as long as ten days. Not only that, but the Court listened quietly, without interrupting the advocate.

Q 186. What "law firm" practices more than any other before the Court?

A The "government's lawyer" at the Court is the solicitor general, the number-three-ranking official in the U.S. Department of Justice who is responsible for all of the federal government's litigation before the Court. Government-related litigation constitutes about half of the Court's entire caseload. The Congress created the office of solicitor general in 1870 when the Justice Department was formed to represent the executive branch of the federal government in suits and appeals that involve the interests of the government. The solicitor general has a staff of about two dozen attorneys who prepare the government's briefs and argue the government's cases before the Court. The office submits amicus curiae ("friend of the court") briefs to the Court in cases in which it is not a party, sometimes at the Court's request.

Q 187. What does the clerk of the Court do?

A Appointed by the Court, the clerk receives documents for filing with the Court and maintains the Court's records.

The Judiciary Act of 1789 authorized the Court, as well as each district court, to appoint a clerk. The act required clerks to "solemnly swear, or affirm, that I will truly and faithfully enter and record all the orders, decrees, judgments and proceedings of the said court, and that I will faithfully and impartially discharge and perform all the duties of my said office, according to the best of my abilities and understanding. So help me God."

The U.S. Supreme Court's first formal act upon assuming office was to establish the clerk's position, underscoring its importance. The first clerk, John Tucker of Massachusetts, was appointed on February 3, 1790. In addition to managing the Court, Tucker was required to collect judicial salaries and find lodging for the justices when necessary.

Today, the clerk of the Court manages a twenty-five-member staff, oversees the Court's dockets and calendars, records all motions and rulings, and collects filing fees and Court costs. The clerk also supervises admissions to the Supreme Court Bar and answers questions from litigants regarding the Court's procedures.

Q 188. What does the marshal of the Court do?

A The marshal is appointed by the Court and serves as the timekeeper of the Court's sessions, signaling lawyers by white and red lights as to time limits. The marshal also is the Court's general manager, paymaster, and chief security officer and supervises the Supreme Court Building and grounds. The marshal calls the Court into session by pounding the gavel and crying, "Oyez, Oyez, Oyez" (French, "Hear ye") . . . All persons having business before the Honorable, the Supreme Court of the United States, are admonished to draw near and give their attention, for the Court is now sitting. God save the United States and this honorable Court."

The Judiciary Act of 1789 authorized the appointment of a marshal for each federal district for a term of four years. The marshal appointed in the district in which the Court sat also served as the Court's marshal. In 1867 Congress authorized the Court to appoint its own marshal, who is removable at will. Today, the Court's marshal manages a staff of two hundred employees.

Q 189. What does the reporter of decisions do?

A The reporter of decisions is appointed by the Court and edits the Court's opinions by checking citations, correcting errors, and adding information necessary to identify the Court's final vote in a case and the attorneys for the parties. The nine-member office of the reporter of decisions also supervises the publication of the Court's opinions in the *United States Reports*. The position of reporter evolved informally after Alexander J. Dallas, who published a volume of Pennsylvania court decisions, simply added the Court's decisions to the volume. Dallas, who served as the Court's first reporter from 1790 to 1800, reportedly took the position as a public service. Dallas was succeeded by William Cranch, a judge in Washington, D.C., who served from 1801 to 1815. The first reporter to be formally appointed by the Court was Henry Wheaton, who served from 1816 to 1827.

Q **190. What does the Court librarian do?**

A The librarian is appointed by the Court and maintains a library that is for the "appropriate personnel" of the Court, members of the Bar of the Court, members of Congress and their legal staff, and attorneys for the United States and for federal departments and agencies. The library holds more than three hundred thousand volumes and a sophisticated electronic information system. The books may not be removed from the Court building, except by a justice or a member of a justice's staff.

Q **191. Who are the other Court officers?**

A Other Court officers include the administrative assistant, the court counsel, the curator, the director of data systems, and the public information officer, who are all appointed by the chief justice to assist with the administrative aspects of the chief justice's position.

BUDGET

Q **192. What is the budget of the U.S. Supreme Court?**

A The budget of the Court in a recent year was $37,495,000.

SUPREME COURT FIRSTS AND RECORDS

Q **193. Who was the first chief justice?**

A John Jay was the first chief justice, appointed by President George Washington in 1789. He resigned from the Court in 1795 to accept the governorship of New York.

Q **194. Who was the first Roman Catholic on the Court?**

A Roger B. Taney, a Catholic, became the first non-Protestant on the Court in 1835 when he was appointed by President Andrew Jackson. All but sixteen Supreme Court justices have been Protestant. Today there are three Catholics on the Court: Anthony M. Kennedy, Antonin Scalia, and Clarence Thomas, who returned to the Catholic faith of his youth after joining the Court as an Episcopalian.

Q 195. Who was the first Jew on the Court?

A Louis D. Brandeis became the first Jew on the Court when he was appointed by President Woodrow Wilson in 1916. Today there are two Jews on the Court, Ruth Bader Ginsburg and Stephen G. Breyer.

Q 196. Who was the oldest associate justice when appointed?

A Horace H. Lurton, who was sixty-five years of age when appointed by President Howard Taft in 1910, was the oldest justice at the time of his appointment. The oldest associate justice to leave office was Oliver Wendell Holmes, who was almost ninety-one when he retired in 1932.

Q 197. Who was the youngest associate justice when appointed?

A Joseph Story, who was appointed to the Court in 1811 by President James Madison at the age of thirty-two, is the youngest justice (by about a month) to ever be appointed to the Court.

Q 198. Who had the longest tenure on the Court?

A Justice William O. Douglas set the record when he retired on November 12, 1975, having served 36 years and 209 days.

See 165 Has any justice ever died on the bench? 168 Which justice wrote the most decisions?

Q 199. Who was the first woman lawyer to be admitted to the Supreme Court Bar?

A Belva A. Lockwood was admitted to the Supreme Court Bar in 1879, just four years after the Court had issued an opinion in which it refused to recognize women as the constitutional equals of men. In that case, *Minor v. Happersett* (1875), the Court said the Fourteenth Amendment didn't require Missouri to allow women the right of suffrage.

Lockwood had originally sought admission to the Supreme Court Bar in 1876, but, in an opinion written by Chief Justice Morrison R. Waite, the Court ruled, "As this court knows no English precedent for the admission of women to the bar, it declines to admit, unless there shall be a more extended public opinion or special legislation."

She successfully lobbied for passage of a bill in Congress to allow the admission of women. On February 7, 1879, the "Lockwood bill" was signed into law by President Rutherford B. Hayes.

Lockwood, who was known for riding a tricycle from her office to court, subsequently ran for president of the United States in 1888 on the Equal Rights party ticket. She polled 4,149 votes in six states, no small feat given the fact that women were not permitted to vote in the election. Early in her career, Lockwood made numerous attempts to represent clients in the U.S. Court of Claims, only to be prohibited from speaking in the courtroom upon the threat of contempt.

Q 200. Who was the first African American to be admitted to the Supreme Court Bar?

A Dr. John Sweat Rock, a lawyer and abolitionist, was admitted to practice law before the Bar of the Supreme Court of the United States on February 1, 1865. His admission was a major step toward a negation of the Court's *Dred Scott* decision of 1857, which denied the rights of citizenship to blacks. At the time, the Thirteenth Amendment, banning slavery, was still in the process of ratification.

Rock was born of free parents in Salem, New Jersey, a free state, on October 13, 1825. After a successful career as a dentist, he began to practice law. Rock wrote to Massachusetts senator Charles Sumner in mid-1864 asking for help in his efforts to gain admission to the Supreme Court Bar. Sumner responded that nothing could be done as long as Roger B. Taney, author of the *Dred Scott* decision, was chief justice. Taney died on October 12, 1864, and President Abraham Lincoln appointed as chief justice Salmon P. Chase of Ohio, an antislavery advocate. After prodding by Sumner, Chase admitted Rock to the Court's bar. The *New York Tribune* wrote of Rock's admission ceremony, "This inky hued African stood, in the monarchical power of recognized American Manhood and American Citizenship, within the bar of the Court which had solemnly pronounced that black men had no rights which white men were bound to respect; stood there a recognized member of it, professionally the brother of the distinguished counsellors on its long rolls, in rights their equal, in the standing which rank gives their peers." The inscription on Rock's tombstone reads: "John S. Rock, Oct. 13, 1825, Died Dec. 3rd, 1866. The 1st colored lawyer admitted to the Bar of the United States Supreme Court at Washington; On motion made by Hon. Charles Sumner, Feb. 1st, 1865."

U.S. COURTS OF APPEALS: INTERMEDIATE APPELLATE COURTS

IN GENERAL

Q **201. What is a U.S. court of appeals?**

A The U.S. courts of appeals were created by Congress as intermediate appellate courts in 1891 to relieve the Supreme Court of the burden of considering all appeals in cases decided by the federal trial courts. Today these appellate courts are, in effect, the courts of last resort for the vast majority of federal cases. They review all final decisions and certain final orders of district courts as well as orders of many federal administrative and regulatory agencies. Appeals filed in courts of appeals are generally heard by three-judge panels. Their decisions are subject to discretionary review by all of the judges of the respective circuits sitting together "en banc" (with all members of the court presiding) or by the Supreme Court.

Like the Supreme Court, the intermediate appellate courts articulate the rule of law for lower federal courts, attorneys, and the public, ensuring uniformity in the treatment of federal cases. The appeals courts determine whether the first decision maker correctly applied the law to the facts of the case and, if not, whether the verdict or decision should be set aside. Generally, appeals are heard only after a final judgment in a case. The court may order a variety of remedies, including a new trial.

There are thirteen federal judicial circuits, in which sit eleven numbered regional courts of appeals, the U.S. Court of Appeals for the District of Columbia Circuit, and the U.S. Court of Appeals for the Federal Circuit. The smallest of the regional courts of appeals is in the First Circuit, which has six judgeships, and the largest is in the Ninth Circuit, which has twenty-eight.

In addition to its regular appellate caseload, the U.S. Court of Appeals for the District of Columbia Circuit is authorized by Congress to hear appeals from certain administrative agency decisions, the U.S. Tax Court, and the Alien Terrorist Removal Court.

The U.S. Court of Appeals for the Federal Circuit has exclusive nationwide jurisdiction over a large number of diverse subject areas, including appeals in all cases involving patents, international trade, government contracts and personnel claims, and certain monetary claims against the government. The court was created in 1982 with the merging of the U.S. Court of Claims and the U.S. Court of Customs and Patent Appeals. It hears appeals from decisions of federal district courts, the U.S. Court of Federal Claims, U.S. Court of International Trade, U.S. Court of Appeals for Veterans Claims, and several federal agencies. The court consists of twelve circuit judges who sit in panels of three or more and may also hear or rehear a case en banc.

The court sits primarily in Washington, D.C., but may hold court wherever any court of appeals sits.

See 217 When does the court sit en banc?

Q **202. Where are the U.S. courts of appeals?**

A *Federal Circuit (twelve authorized judgeships)*
209 National Courts Bldg.
717 Madison Pl., N.W.
Washington D.C. 20439
(202) 633-6550

District of Columbia Circuit (twelve authorized judgeships)
E. Barrett Prettyman U.S. Courthouse
333 Constitution Ave. N.W.
Washington, D.C. 20001-2866
(202) 216-7000

First Circuit (six authorized judgeships)
1606 J. W. M. Post Office & Courthouse
90 Devonshire St.
Boston, MA 02109
(617) 223-9057
Jurisdiction: Maine, Massachusetts, New Hampshire, Rhode Island, and Puerto Rico.

Second Circuit (thirteen authorized judgeships)
U.S. Courthouse
40 Foley Sq.
New York, NY 10007
(212) 857-8500
Jurisdiction: Connecticut, New York, and Vermont.

Third Circuit (fourteen authorized judgeships)
21400 U.S. Courthouse
Independence Mall West
601 Market St.
Philadelphia, PA 19106
(215) 597-2995

Jurisdiction: Delaware, New Jersey, Pennsylvania, and the Virgin Islands.

Fourth Circuit (fifteen authorized judgeships)
U.S. Courthouse Annex
1100 E. Main St., 5th Floor
Richmond, VA 23219
(804) 771-2213
Jurisdiction: Maryland, North Carolina, South Carolina, Virginia, and West Virginia.

Fifth Circuit (seventeen authorized judgeships)
U.S. Court of Appeals, Room 109
600 Camp St.
New Orleans, LA 70130
(504) 589-6514
Jurisdiction: Louisiana, Mississippi, and Texas.

Sixth Circuit (sixteen authorized judgeships)
532 U.S. Post Office & Courthouse
100 E. Fifth St.
Cincinnati, OH 45202-3988
(513) 564-7000
Jurisdiction: Kentucky, Michigan, Ohio, and Tennessee.

Seventh Circuit (eleven authorized judgeships)
U.S. Courthouse & Federal Office Building
219 S. Dearborn St.
Chicago, IL 60604
(312) 435-5850
Jurisdiction: Illinois, Indiana, and Wisconsin.

Eighth Circuit (eleven authorized judgeships)
1114 Market St.
St. Louis, MO 63101-2077
[(314) 539-3609]
Jurisdiction: Arkansas, Iowa, Minnesota, Missouri, Nebraska, North Dakota, and South Dakota.

Ninth Circuit (twenty-eight authorized judgeships)
95 Seventh St. (94103)
P.O. Box 193939
San Francisco, CA 94119-3939

(415) 556-9800

Jurisdiction: Alaska, Arizona, California, Hawaii, Idaho, Montana, Nevada, Oregon, Washington, Guam, and the Northern Mariana Islands.

Tenth Circuit (twelve authorized judgeships)
Byron White U.S. Courthouse
1823 Stout St.
Denver, CO 80257
(303) 844-3157
Jurisdiction: Colorado, Kansas, New Mexico, Oklahoma, Utah, and Wyoming.

Eleventh Circuit (twelve authorized judgeships)
Tuttle Court of Appeals Bldg.
56 Forsyth St., N.W.
Atlanta, GA 30303
(404) 335-6100
Jurisdiction: Alabama, Florida, and Georgia.

Q 203. What factors influenced the geographic formation of the circuits?

A The Judiciary Act of 1789 established thirteen federal districts roughly along state lines, each with a trial court of general jurisdiction. The thirteen districts were combined into three regional circuits—eastern, middle, and southern—each with a court that had limited jurisdiction and special trial court jurisdiction. The circuits were grouped into regional entities because it was felt that credibility and accountability are fostered when appellate judges are drawn primarily from the region they serve. As the country grew, so did the number and size of the circuits. The size, alignment, and composition of the circuits have changed at least eleven times since 1789. Early in the nation's history, for example, the New England states and New York constituted a single circuit, whereas these states today are grouped into two different circuits. Some of the districts in the circuits today have little in common, either geographically or in terms of shared regional identity.

See 26 What was the Judiciary Act of 1789?

Q 204. What circuit stretches from the Arctic Circle to the Mexican border . . . and beyond?

A The Ninth Circuit. When California became a state, it was so far from Washington, D.C., that even Congress agreed that it would too burdensome for a U.S. Supreme

Court judge to "ride circuit" there. In 1850 Congress established an unnumbered federal circuit for California, containing two districts. President Franklin Pierce appointed Georgia lawyer Matthew Hall McAllister to serve as the circuit judge of the Circuit Court of California, the only full-time circuit judge assigned to one court. McAllister arrived in California in 1856, amid an outbreak of vigilante violence in San Francisco. After six years he resigned and returned, exhausted, to Georgia. Congress abolished the California Circuit Court and formed a new Tenth Circuit that included California, Oregon, and Nevada.

After the Civil War Congress realigned the states into nine circuits, and the Tenth Circuit was designated as the Ninth Circuit. The circuit grew incrementally as the country grew, and it came to include Montana, Idaho, Washington, Arizona, Alaska, and Hawaii, as well as the U.S. territories of Guam and the Northern Mariana Islands. It now serves a population of more than 49 million people, almost 60 percent more than the next-largest circuit.

Former chief justice Warren E. Burger once described the Ninth Circuit Court of Appeals as "an unmanageable administrative monstrosity." In 1997 Congress passed a bill establishing a Commission on Structural Alternatives for the Federal Courts of Appeals, which will study the structure and alignment of the circuits, particularly the Ninth Circuit.

Q 205. When did Congress create the U.S. court of appeals?

A The modern-day U.S. court of appeals was created in 1891 to alleviate the appellate burden of the Supreme Court and to ensure greater uniformity in the interpretation of federal laws across the country.

The Judiciary Act of 1789, which established the nation's judicial system, initially created the Supreme Court, three circuit courts, and thirteen federal district courts. The circuit courts had limited appellate jurisdiction, serving mainly as trial courts for major federal offenses and certain civil suits in which the government, an alien, or citizens from different states were parties.

The early circuit courts had no judiciary of their own. Congress required two Supreme Court justices to sit with a local federal district court judge in each district of the circuit. The justices continually complained about the rigors and perils of "riding circuit." To mitigate the hardships, Congress reduced the number of justices required to hold circuit court to one, and then decreed that circuit court could be convened in the absence of any justice by the federal district judge assigned to the circuit. Finally, in the Judiciary Act of 1869, Congress authorized the appointment of one circuit judge for each circuit.

The modern-day U.S. court of appeals was created in 1891 when Congress passed the Circuit Court of Appeals Act, otherwise known as the Evarts Act after its sponsor, Sen. William M. Evarts of New York.

The Evarts Act established a new level of federal courts, the "circuit court of appeals," between the existing circuit and district courts and the Supreme Court. Under the law, nine circuits were created, and an additional circuit judge was hired to sit alongside the existing circuit and district judges assigned to each circuit. The new circuit court was authorized to hear appeals from decisions of district courts and the original circuit courts, and its trial court jurisdiction was removed. In 1911 Congress abolished the old circuit courts altogether.

There were forty-four states in 1891 when Congress created the new circuit courts of appeals. As new states were added, Congress increased the number of courts to a total of thirteen in 1892. Congress created the U.S. Court of Appeals for the District of Columbia in 1893, split the Rocky Mountain states from the Eighth Circuit and created a new Tenth Circuit in 1929, and divided the Fifth Circuit into the Fifth and Eleventh Circuits in 1981. Congress in 1982 created the Federal Circuit, a jurisdictional rather than geographical circuit, out of the Court of Claims and the Court of Customs and Patent Appeals.

See 29 What was the Circuit Court of Appeals Act of 1891?

Q 206. What was "circuit riding"?

A When Congress created the original circuit courts in 1789, it failed to create any separate judgeships for the courts. Instead, Congress assigned two Supreme Court justices to sit in each circuit alongside a local federal district judge. The circuit court met twice yearly in cities within the districts, forcing the justices, many of whom were aged, to make long and arduous journeys, over muddy roads and bridgeless streams, sometimes on horseback. The justices complained that they were being asked, as justices, to review decisions they made as circuit judges.

The demands of "circuit riding" caused Justice James Iredell to refer to his life as that of a "traveling postboy." Iredell traveled an estimated one thousand miles between his home in North Carolina and Philadelphia, where Supreme Court sessions were held, in addition to making two trips each year to the states in his circuit—Georgia, North Carolina, and South Carolina .

Nevertheless, Congress resisted pleas to halt circuit riding, ostensibly to keep the justices from becoming isolated in Washington. Congress did enact a statute in 1862 that allowed one justice, instead of two, to be assigned to each circuit and which permitted the district judge assigned to the circuit to convene court even if that justice did not attend.

Circuit riding ended in 1891 when Congress passed the Circuit Court of Appeals Act, also known as the Evarts Act, which established a new intermediate appellate court called a circuit court of appeals. This court was run by two circuit judges and a district court judge.

A vestige of "circuit riding" still remains, however. Each justice is still assigned to a circuit. That designation is significant only occasionally when the Court receives a petition for a stay of execution, for extraordinary procedures in an appeal, or for rulings in national security cases.

Q 207. At what point may a ruling be appealed to the U.S. court of appeals?

A The U.S. court of appeals may hear only certain appeals from U.S. district courts. The court can hear an appeal on a final judgment in a case. A judgment is final when it "ends the litigation on the merits and leaves nothing for the court to do but execute the judgement" (*Callin v. U.S.*, 1945). The appeals court may also hear an "interlocutory appeal," or an appeal of a ruling on a matter that must be addressed before the case can proceed.

Q 208. What is an appellee/appellant?

A The appellant is the party who is appealing the lower court ruling. The appellee, the party against whom the appeal is brought, generally but not always won the lower court judgment.

Q 209. How many appeals are filed each year in the U.S. court of appeals?

A A total of 53,805 appeals were filed in the twelve regional courts of appeals in 1998, an all-time high. That figure compares with 52,319 appeals in 1997, 51,991 in 1996, 50,072 in 1995, 48,322 in 1994, 50,224 in 1993, 40,898 in 1990, and 3,899 in 1960.

Because of the increase in appeals, many federal appeals courts are deciding more cases based solely on the trial court record, and are sharply limiting the number of cases in which they agree to hear oral arguments.

Of the 53,805 appeals filed in 1998, there were 20,100 appeals in civil cases, 17,422 from prisoner petitions, 10,535 in criminal cases, 1,203 in bankruptcy cases, 3,793 from administrative agency decisions, and 752 from original proceedings.

With respect to the U.S. Court of Appeals for the Federal Circuit, a total of 1,454 appeals were filed with that body in 1998. The largest number of appeals, 462, were from decisions by the Merit Systems Protection Board.

Q **210. How does the U.S. court of appeals dispose of appeals?**

A U.S. courts of appeals terminated 52,002 cases during the year ending September 20, 1998. Of these, 24,910 were decided on the merits (after full consideration of the arguments). These mid-level appellate courts reversed 10.4 percent of lower court decisions. Of the appeals that were decided on the merits,

- 19,414 were affirmed or enforced,
- 1,903 dismissed,
- 2,558 reversed,
- 608 remanded, and
- 427 constituted other dispositions.

In 1998 the Seventh and the Fifth Circuit appellate courts were most likely to reverse a lower court, with reversal rates of 13.1 percent and 19.6 percent, respectively. The Second Circuit was least likely to reverse a lower court, with a reversal rate of 2.3 percent.

Q **211. What type of appeal is most and least likely to result in a reversal?**

A A total of 15.2 percent of appeals of civil cases filed by private parties (as opposed to the U.S. government) resulted in reversal in 1998, the highest proportion of any category of appeals. The next-highest category was bankruptcy appeals, which were reversed 14.4 percent of the time.

Only 6.5 percent of criminal appeals resulted in a reversal, the lowest proportion of any category of appeals. The next-lowest category was administrative appeals, which resulted in a reversal only 6.6 percent of the time.

Q **212. Why have the number of appeals skyrocketed?**

A Some observers attribute the tremendous growth in the number of appeals filed to the revolution in criminal procedure that occurred during Earl Warren's tenure as chief justice of the Supreme Court (1954–1969). During this time the Court extended most of the Bill of Rights to the states and expanded the rights of prisoners to attack convictions and conditions in federal prisons. In addition, Congress has spurred the growth of appeals through bail reform, speedy trial laws, and laws mandating the right to government-subsidized counsel in criminal cases. The role of the federal judiciary has increasingly expanded in the areas of civil rights enforcement, social welfare enhancement, and consumer and environmental protection, among other societal issues.

Q 213. What group files the most appeals in the U.S. court of appeals?

A Prisoners. In 1996 and 1997 prisoner petitions constituted almost half of all of the civil appeals filed in the U.S. court of appeals. There were 16,996 prisoner petitions filed in 1996 and 16,188 in 1997. Many alleged civil rights violations. The almost 5 percent decline in prisoner appeals in 1997 is attributed to the enactment of the Prison Litigation Reform Act in April 1996, which was intended to reduce frivolous petitions by imposing filing fees. In 1998 prisoners filed 17,422 petitions, an increase of 7.6 percent over the prior year.

Q 214. What class of criminals files the most appeals?

A The largest number of criminal appeals in 1998—4,749—were filed by defendants in drug cases.

Q 215. How does the U.S. court of appeals decide a case?

A Each court of appeals consists of six or more judges, depending on the caseload of the court. Appeals are heard by panels of three judges. Approximately one month before an appeal is scheduled for oral argument, judges in the circuit are asked to review the list of pending appeals and report to the chief judge any cases in which they have a potential disqualification or conflict of interest. The judges are then randomly assigned by the circuit executive to sit on various panels. The identities of the judges on any panel are typically kept secret until the days on which the cases are argued.

Unlike a federal district judge, an appeals court panel does not hear the testimony of witnesses or accept new factual evidence in a case. The appeals court bases its decision on the record of the lower court proceeding. The record includes items introduced into evidence, pleadings and motions, the judge's instructions to the jury, and transcripts of the testimony of witnesses. In addition, attorneys for both sides present briefs, or written arguments, that focus on the legal authority for their arguments, including decisions in prior similar cases. The attorneys also appear before the panel to make brief oral presentations or arguments, during which the judges frequently ask questions about relevant laws or raise any concerns they have.

The court also may consider arguments by the U.S. government or outside parties who have no direct stake in the case but who have an interest in its outcome. Outside parties must obtain permission from the litigants or the court to file an amicus curiae, or "friend of the court," brief. The U.S. government is not required to obtain permission to file an amicus curiae brief.

Immediately after the oral arguments, the judges meet privately to discuss the case. Each judge presents his or her views in reverse order of seniority. To reach a decision, two of the three judges must agree. The most senior, or presiding, judge then assigns a judge to write the opinion in the case. A judge who disagrees with the majority may write a dissenting opinion. Select opinions of the judges of the U.S. Courts of Appeals are published in bound volumes, or reporters, and can be found at most law libraries. The federal appellate courts' decisions also are regularly published at Web sites maintained by the individual courts on the Internet.

Q 216. How important is oral argument in an appeal?

A J. Edward Lumbard, a former chief judge of the U.S. Court of Appeals for the Second Circuit in the 1960s, put it this way: "The importance of oral argument is emphasized by the fact that in about 75 percent of the arguments the case is finally decided in accordance with the impression which the judges have as they leave the bench. Probably 20 percent is a fair estimate of the proportion of cases in which our judges have no firm impression one way or the other at the conclusion of the argument. In the remaining 5 percent of the cases the decision finally arrived at is contrary to the impression after oral argument."

Q 217. When does the court sit *en banc*?

A A party who is dissatisfied with the decision of a three-judge panel of the appeals court may ask the court to rehear the case *en banc* in the hope of winning a more favorable decision. Typically, when an appeals court sits en banc, all of the judges of the court convene together. However, in the Ninth Circuit, which has the largest court of appeals, with twenty-eight judges, an en banc court consists of eleven judges. Parties dissatisfied with the decision of the limited en banc court in the Ninth Circuit may petition to convene the full court en banc. A judge may request a ballot vote of the whole court on the issue of whether the case should be reheard en banc by the full court. Full-court sessions are most frequently called to overrule prior decisions, settle panel conflicts within a circuit, correct error, or ensure majority control of policy issues of exceptional importance.

Once the matter is settled, a final judgment, or mandate, is entered in the record, and the case is closed in the court of appeals. A losing party may then seek review by the U.S. Supreme Court.

Q 218. What percentage of cases filed in the U.S. court of appeals are heard by the court?

A All of them. Unlike the U.S. Supreme Court, the appeals court has no discretionary jurisdiction.

Q 219. What is the median time from filing to resolving an appeal?

A In 1998 the median time from the filing of a case in lower court to its final disposition in the U.S. court of appeals was twenty-seven months.

Q 220. Are appeals resolved faster with or without an attorney?

A Without. A 1995 study by the Administrative Office of the U.S. Courts found that "pro se" cases, in which litigants are not represented by counsel, are generally resolved faster than those in which counsel is retained. A larger percentage of these cases are decided procedurally, rather than on the merits after arguments and briefs.

Q 221. Do circuits have to follow the law in other circuits?

A The circuit courts are free to accept—or not—each other's decisions so long as the Supreme Court is silent on the matter. The Supreme Court is the sole arbiter of conflicting precedents among the courts of appeal. Within a circuit, however, the decision of one panel is binding on other panels unless it is reversed by the court en banc.

See 217 When does the court sit en banc?

Q 222. Do appeals courts ever reverse themselves?

A Occasionally. A party is entitled to petition the court for a rehearing of a case within two weeks after a decision has been issued. According to one estimate, rehearings are sought in up to half of all cases. Most petitions are summarily denied. A small number lead to changes to eliminate ambiguity or correct a mistake, particularly in bankruptcy cases.

Q 223. What appellate courts had a policy of omitting the names of district court judges whom they criticized in their opinions?

A Most appellate courts include the names of the trial judges—the chief judges of the district courts whose decision are being appealed—in the headnotes to their opinions. Until the 1950s, however, the U.S. Courts of Appeals for the Second Circuit and the District of Columbia Circuit omitted the names of trial judges from their opinions to avoid publicly embarrassing those whose decisions had been reversed or remanded. Decisions in these circuits occasionally piqued public curiosity with references to unnamed judges who displayed "outbursts of petulant irritation" or "discourtesy and prejudice." The matter became a subject of running dispute between Chief Justice Learned Hand and Judge Charles E. Clark of the Second Circuit appellate court. Shortly after Hand retired, at Clark's insistence and with the support of law professors and others, the court altered its practice in 1952. It was followed by the District of Columbia's circuit court of appeals.

PERSONNEL

Judges

Q 224. What do judges on the U.S. Courts of Appeals do?

A Appellate court judges sit in panels, usually of three judges, and decide appeals of decisions made by a judge or jury in federal district court. An appellate court judge's decision is made on the basis of the written record of a case and the oral arguments by attorneys for both parties. As with other federal judges, appeals court judges are appointed for life by the president and are subject to confirmation by the Senate. The president customarily consults the attorney general and the deputy attorney general. The president also allows U.S. senators of the president's political party— specifically, those from the states that make up the appellate circuit in which the vacancy exists—to have significant input into the appointment process. A candidate typically undergoes a background check by the FBI, and his or her qualifications are reviewed by a committee of the American Bar Association. The Senate Judiciary Committee reviews the candidate's fitness for the position and may conduct hearings to question the nominee. If its vote is favorable, the candidate's nomination is placed before the full Senate, which accepts or rejects the nomination by a simple majority vote.

Each court of appeals has six or more judges, depending on the caseload of the court. As with other Article III judges, who serve on courts established in Article III of the U.S. Constitution, circuit court judges hold office "during good Behaviour" and may be impeached after a trial in the Senate for "Treason, Bribery, or other High Crimes and Misdemeanors."

Q 225. How many appeals court judges are there?

A At present each court of appeals has from 6 to 28 permanent circuit judgeships (179 in all), depending on the amount of judicial work in the circuit. Ninety-one "retired" senior judges also serve on the court, handling a reduced caseload.

Q 226. What is the average caseload of an appeals court panel?

A The number of cases decided per three-judge panel on the U.S. Courts of Appeals in 1998 (not including those decided by the Federal Circuit Court of Appeals) was 934, compared with 940 in 1997, 934 in 1996, 899 in 1995, 868 in 1994, and 902 in 1993.

Q 227. What does the chief judge of the circuit do?

A The chief judge presides over the circuit's judicial council, which oversees the administration of justice in the federal courts of the circuit and implements policy directives received from the Judicial Conference of the United States, the chief policy-making body within the federal judiciary. The chief judge is a member of the judicial conference. The size of the council is determined by a vote of each judge of the circuit. The council must include an equal number of circuit and district judges.

The chief judge calls an annual judicial conference of all circuit and district judges in the circuit, and sometimes members of the bar, to discuss the state of the circuit's federal courts. The chief judge assigns judges to temporary duty on other courts in the circuit, informs the chief justice of the United States when the temporary assistance of judges from other circuits is needed, and reviews complaints of misconduct.

A chief judge must have at least one year of service on the court, cannot have served as chief judge previously, must have the greatest seniority among active judges on the court, and must be under the age of sixty-five at the time of the appointment. A judge may serve as chief judge beyond the age of seventy unless a younger judge is eligible to become chief judge or acting chief judge. The term of the chief judge is seven years.

Q 228. Who was the first female appeals court judge?

A Florence E. Allen, a justice of the Ohio supreme court, became the first woman to serve on a federal court of appeals when Franklin D. Roosevelt appointed her to the Sixth Circuit in 1934. Many thought Allen would be the first woman appointed to the Supreme Court. However, Allen did not. She wrote, "When my friends delightfully tell me that they hope to see me upon the Supreme Bench of the U.S., I know two things: first, that will never happen to a woman while I am living, and second, that perhaps it is just as well not to mention that possibility at the present time because there is a certain type of lawyer that immediately becomes fighting mad when that possibility is mentioned."

Q 229. What is the salary of an appeals court judge?

A In 1999, judges of the U.S. circuit court of appeals earned $145,000, plus up to $20,505 in outside earnings, including income from teaching but not including royalties.

Q 230. What corrupt appellate judge came within a hair of being appointed to the Supreme Court of the United States?

A Martin T. Manton, presiding judge of the U.S. Court of Appeals for the Second Circuit, was a prominent Democrat from New York City who was one of three leading candidates to fill a vacancy on the Court in 1922. He received the strong backing of the Roman Catholic Church in New York City. However, Chief Justice William Howard Taft vehemently objected to Manton's appointment, and the Judiciary Committee of the Association of the Bar of the City of New York "voted unanimously to do all in its power to stop Manton's drive for the Court." Manton, who resigned from the appellate court, borrowed heavily from litigants and accepted outright payments from them.

Q 231. What does the circuit executive do?

A The judicial council of each circuit, the chief administrative body of the circuit, may appoint a circuit executive to carry out its administrative duties. The circuit executive typically also serves as the administrator for the court of appeals. He or she serves at the pleasure of the council, which is composed of equal numbers of appellate judges and district judges, with the circuit's chief judge presiding. The circuit executive's duties vary from circuit to circuit. In many circuits the circuit executive administers the budget and personnel systems, including the appointment of magistrates and bankruptcy court judges, the temporary reassignment of district court judges to meet staffing needs, and the implementation of attorney discipline procedures. The circuit executive also conducts studies and prepares reports on the work of the federal courts within the circuit, serves as the circuit's liaison with state courts, bar groups, the media, and the public, and arranges circuit judicial council and judicial conference meetings. The circuit executive frequently is assisted in his or her administrative duties by a clerk, circuit librarian, and staff attorneys.

Q 232. What does the appellate clerk do?

A Each court of appeals appoints a clerk who serves at the pleasure of the court. The clerk appoints deputies and clerical assistants. The primary duties of the clerk are maintaining the files and records of the court, ensuring compliance with federal and court rules, entering orders and judgments of the court, scheduling cases for hearings, distributing case materials needed by the court, collecting required fees, disseminating the court's opinions, giving procedural assistance to attorneys and litigants, and maintaining a roster of attorneys admitted to practice before the court.

Q 233. What does a "crier" do?

A The crier announces the opening of court, recesses, and adjournments. Each court of appeals is authorized to employ criers, who may also serve as bailiffs and messengers. A bailiff maintains order in the courtroom under the direction of the presiding judge.

Q 234. What is the budget of the U.S. courts of appeals?

A The budget for the twelve regional U.S. courts of appeals in fiscal year 1999 was $272 million. The budget for the U.S. Court of Appeals for the Federal Circuit in 1999 was $16,101,000.

DISTRICT COURTS: FEDERAL TRIAL COURTS

In General

Q 235. What is a U.S. district court?

A U.S. district courts are the general trial courts of the federal system, where civil and criminal cases are filed and trials are held. District courts also have exclusive jurisdiction over bankruptcy cases, and each district court has a bankruptcy unit. Technically, district courts are courts of limited jurisdiction, as are all Article III federal courts—that is, those courts established in Article III of the U.S. Constitution—because their jurisdiction is explicitly conferred on them by the Constitution and Congress.

There are ninety-four district courts in the fifty states, the District of Columbia, the Commonwealth of Puerto Rico, and the territories of Guam, the U.S. Virgin Islands, and the Northern Mariana Islands. Most states comprise a single judicial district, but some have up to four districts.

District courts hear criminal cases when a federal statute is alleged to have been violated and civil cases in which the value of the dispute exceeds $75,000 and the action falls within the district court's jurisdiction.

Q 236. What is the jurisdiction of a federal district court?

A District courts have jurisdiction over cases that present a question of federal law and over those involving citizens of different states where the amount in dispute is over $75,000.

Federal question jurisdiction appears under Article III, Section 2, of the U.S. Constitution, which says the "judicial power" of the federal courts should extend to cases "arising under this constitution, the Laws of the United States, and Treaties made, or which shall be made under their Authority."

A number of federal statutes confer authority upon district courts to hear cases involving civil actions arising under the laws of the United States and cases involving postal, patent, copyright, internal revenue, and civil rights matters.

As authorized by Article III and a federal statute (28 U.S.C., Section 1332), federal courts also have "diversity jurisdiction," or jurisdiction over cases involving citizens of different states. Diversity jurisdiction entitles federal courts to hear cases and controversies involving the following parties:

1. citizens of different states,
2. citizens of a state and citizens or subjects of a foreign state,
3. citizens of different states in which citizens or subjects of a foreign state are additional parties, and
4. a foreign state, acting as plaintiff, and citizens of a state or of different states.

See 67 What is the jurisdiction of federal courts? 345 What is diversity jurisdiction?

Q 237. Can a civil case be removed from federal to state court?

A No. It only happens the other way around. A lawsuit originally filed in a state court may be removed to federal court before trial if the defendant demonstrates the federal court has either federal question or diversity jurisdiction (for definitions of these types of jurisdiction, see previous question).

Q 238. Can a federal court decline to accept a state case that is properly before it?

A Yes. Under abstention doctrines, a federal court abstains from hearing a case that involves a question of state law and is properly within the federal court's jurisdiction when a decision would disrupt an important state policy, the federal litigation would duplicate pending state litigation, or the federal court wishes to avoid a question of constitutional law.

Q 239. What are territorial courts?

A Acting under its authority to govern the territories of the United States, Congress established district courts in the territories of Guam and the Virgin Islands. Congress also created a district court in the Northern Mariana Islands that is administered by the United States under a trusteeship agreement with the United Nations. There is one judge each in Guam and the Northern Mariana Islands, and two in the Virgin Islands.

Territorial courts serve essentially the same function as district courts and also preside over many local matters that, in the states, are decided in state courts.

Territorial courts were the first "legislative courts" created by Congress under Article I of the Constitution. Unlike judges of "constitutional courts," created under Article III, territorial court judges are appointed to fixed, ten-year terms, and their salaries are not protected under the Constitution during their terms in office.

Q 240. What ship served as a floating courthouse in the nineteenth century?

A *The Bear*, a U.S. revenue cutter, served as a territorial courthouse in southern Alaska during the nineteenth century, delivering mail and justice. Territorial district judge James Wickersham conducted many trials and other court proceedings aboard *The Bear*.

Q 241. How are the size and location of a district determined?

A A major consideration in the formation of a federal district is its adherence to state boundaries. Only one of the ninety-four federal districts includes the territory of more than one state. The District of Wyoming includes parts of Yellowstone National Park that are located in Idaho and Montana. Similarly, the District of Hawaii includes Pacific Island territories that are not part of the state. Some states are so large that several districts are located in them. California, New York, and Texas have the most districts, four each. Congress authorizes judgeships for each district based in large part on the caseload.

See 203 What factors influenced the geographic formation of the circuits?

Q 242. How many cases are filed annually in U.S. district courts?

A A total of 314,478 cases were filed in U.S. district courts in 1998, a decrease of about 2.4 percent from the total for the year before.

Federal caseload has more than quadrupled in the past twenty-five years, partly because Congress continues to pass new laws that "federalize" crimes previously prosecuted on the state level and create new civil causes of action over matters previously resolved in state courts. It is estimated the district courts' annual caseload will reach more than one million cases by 2020. Court officials have expressed concern that uncontrolled growth in the federal court system will lessen the quality of the federal judiciary and its ability to dispense justice swiftly, inexpensively, and fairly.

The U.S. district court caseload was 322,390 in 1997, 317,021 in 1996, 294,123 in 1995, 281,875 in 1994, and 276,636 in 1993.

Q 243. What is the breakdown of criminal and civil cases heard in U.S. district courts?

A Four times more civil than criminal cases were filed in 1998. There were 256,787 civil cases, compared with 57,691 criminal cases.

The largest number of filings on the civil docket—146,827—were "federal question" cases which required the courts to interpret compliance with the U.S. Constitution, federal law, or treaties. There were also 57,852 cases in which the United States was a plaintiff or defendant and 51,992 cases filed by citizens of different states. Cases involving the United States included breach of contract claims and actions to recover defaulted student loans or Social Security disability benefits.

The 57,691 cases on the criminal docket included 16,281 drug cases and 9,339 cases involving smuggling of illegal aliens or attempted reentry into the country by deported aliens or aliens previously convicted of felonies.

Q 244. How long does it take to resolve a case filed in U.S. district court?

A The median time in 1998 from the filing of a criminal case in U.S. district court to sentencing was 5.6 months . The median time from the filing of a civil case to its disposition was eight months.

Q 245. How many cases go to trial in U.S. district court?

A The vast majority of cases are resolved by such means as settlement, default, and dismissal. In 1998 federal district judges accepted pleas from 46,708 felony defendants in criminal cases and terminated 215,354 civil cases before or during pretrial proceedings. Judges completed 6,847 criminal trials and 9,349 civil trials in 1998.

See 431 What is a trial?

Q 246. How long do trials take in U.S. district court?

A Forty-five percent of the trials completed in federal court in 1998 were completed within one day. Twenty-six percent of all trials lasted four days or longer, the longest being a securities, commodities, and exchange case that lasted 152 days.

Q 247. How much in damages do federal juries award in civil cases?

A Federal juries awarded $1.318 billion in tort (personal injury) cases in 1992 and $1.771 billion in contract cases. The total amount awarded in all general civil cases in federal court was $1.8 billion, compared with $5.8 billion in state courts. State courts handle the vast majority of civil and criminal litigation in the United States.

Q 248. What percentage of federal criminal cases involve drugs, fraud, and immigration?

A Sixty percent of all criminal cases filed in federal courts in 1998 involved a combination of drugs, fraud, and immigration. Defendants in these cases accounted for 65 percent of all of the criminal defendants before the court. The Western District of Texas led the nation in drug cases (1,593), with the Southern District of California coming in second (1,564).

Q 249. Has the nation's drug epidemic affected the federal courts?

A Federal courts began to be inundated with cases involving illegal drugs in the late 1980s. The number of drug defendants in 1998 was 24,181. That figure compares with 22,276 in 1997, 18,502 in 1995, 19,217 in 1990, 11,208 in 1985, and 1,846 in 1960.

The vast majority of drug defendants plead guilty or enter a plea of *nolo contendere*, in which they do not admit guilt but do not contest the charge. In 1998 a total of 1,487 defendants were convicted after entering not guilty pleas, and 241 were acquitted.

Q 250. What percentage of federal criminal defendants are convicted?

A Eighty-eight percent, or 59,885 criminal defendants, were convicted in 1998. Of these, 55,913 entered guilty pleas, 343 entered a plea of *nolo contendere*, or no contest, 601 were convicted after a court trial, and 3,028 were convicted after a jury trial. A total of 8,049 defendants were not convicted. Of these, charges were dismissed against 6,968 defendants, 594 were acquitted after a court trial, and 487 were acquitted after a jury trial.

Q 251. What is the average prison sentence meted out to federal criminal defendants?

A The average prison sentence given to the 59,885 defendants who were convicted in federal court in 1998 was 58.8 months.

Q 252. How is a judge assigned to a case?

A The chief judge of each district court is responsible for enforcing the court's rules on case assignments, which are typically set forth in a written plan. The rules are designed to ensure equitable distribution of caseload and to prevent litigants from "judge shopping." Most courts use a random drawing to assign new cases. Another method rotates the names of available judges. Judges with special expertise may be assigned cases requiring such expertise, for example, asbestos-related cases or prisoner cases.

Q 253. How many cases do federal judges have at one time?

A The federal judiciary measures caseload by weighting filings according to the time required for a judge to resolve various types of civil and criminal actions. A bankruptcy fraud case is weighted as five times more difficult than a case involving a defaulted student loan. The number of weighted filings per judgeship in 1998 was 484, a decrease from 1997's total of 519.

Q 254. How does a federal judge know what sentence to mete out in a criminal case?

A Judges must follow sentencing guidelines for criminal cases promulgated by the United States Sentencing Commission. These guidelines are intended to avoid sentencing disparities among similarly situated criminals who are convicted of the same crime. The guidelines allow a judge some discretion to adjust a sentence upward or downward depending on unique factors in the case. In addition, Congress has adopted numerous mandatory minimum sentencing laws that limit a judge's discretion. Many of these laws involve illegal drugs.

See 301 What is the U.S. Sentencing Commission?

Q 255. How often are the decisions of federal district court judges appealed?

A Roughly 15 percent of the time. There were 48,057 appeals from U.S. district courts in 1998, including 37,522 civil appeals and 10,535 criminal appeals.

Q 256. What role does arbitration play in federal court?

A Under the Alternative Dispute Resolution Act of 1998, all federal district courts are required to have an alternative dispute resolution program, though how the program is structured is left up to individual courts. Forms of alternative dispute resolution include, but are not limited to, mediation, early evaluation of a case by a neutral party, minitrials, and voluntary arbitration. The court may refer a case to arbitration if both parties consent or may order arbitration for a case in which a plaintiff seeks no more than $150,000 in damages. In both instances arbitration is not binding. The parties may still request a trial, and the case is treated as if it never went through arbitration. The arbitrator is a neutral party or panel that evaluates the case and presents the parties with an opinion of the likely outcome of a trial. Most cases referred to arbitration in federal court involve personal injury claims, contract actions, labor suits, and civil rights actions.

Q 257. How are federal jurors selected?

A Each judicial district has a written plan for the random selection of jurors from a fair cross-section of the community. This plan prohibits discrimination in the selection process. Lists of registered and actual voters, as well as other lists, such as those of licensed drivers, are the sources of potential jurors' names.

To be eligible, jurors must be at least eighteen years of age and citizens of the United States who have resided for at least one year in the judicial district. They must be able to read, write, and understand English with the degree of proficiency required to fill out a juror qualification form. Persons who are incapable by reason of mental or physical infirmity are ineligible to serve, as are persons who have felony charges pending against them or were convicted of a felony.

Exempted from jury service are members of the armed forces on active duty; professional firefighters and police officers; and "public officers" of federal, state, or local governments who are actively performing public duties. Courts are authorized by statute to temporarily or permanently excuse a juror from service for reasons of "undue hardship or extreme inconvenience."

See 436 What is a petit jury?

258. What is bankruptcy court?

A Bankruptcy courts are legislative courts, created by Congress according to Article I of the U.S. Constitution. They decide petitions by individuals and corporations seeking protection under the nation's federal bankruptcy laws. The U.S. court of appeals in the circuit in which the district is located appoints bankruptcy judges to fourteen-year terms. Each federal district court has a bankruptcy unit.

President Jimmy Carter signed the Bankruptcy Reform Act in 1978, requiring that bankruptcy cases be filed in bankruptcy court rather than in district courts. In 1982 the Supreme Court ruled in *Northern Pipeline Construction Co. v. Marathon Pipe Line Co.* that a portion of the law was unconstitutional. The Court held that Congress could not grant broad jurisdiction over federal and state law claims to a corps of bankruptcy "judges" who lacked the benefits guaranteed to federal judges under Article III, including life tenure and salary protections. In 1984 Congress passed a new law limiting the scope of bankruptcy court jurisdiction to core bankruptcy issues and requiring that bankruptcy court rulings be subject to review by a district judge.

Appeals from bankruptcy court can be made to a district judge or to a bankruptcy appellate panel if one exists in the circuit. Final orders in either of these forums are appealable to the Supreme Court at its discretion.

Of the 326 authorized bankruptcy judge positions in 1998, a total of 314 were filled and there were 12 vacancies. Bankruptcy judges are paid $125,764 annually. The budget for bankruptcy courts in fiscal 1999 was $627,605,000.

Q **259. How many bankruptcy cases are filed each year?**

A A record 1,436,964 petitions were filed in U.S. bankruptcy court in fiscal year 1998, an increase of 5 percent over the number filed in 1997. The vast majority of all bankruptcy cases—about 97 percent—are nonbusiness cases or cases filed by individual debtors. The surge in nonbusiness cases is blamed on the greater availability of consumer credit, which has led to record levels of debt as a percentage of personal income. There were 1,389,839 nonbusiness cases filed in 1998, compared with 47,125 business cases. The largest numerical increases in bankruptcy filings occurred in California, New Jersey, and Maryland.

About 71 percent of all bankruptcy cases filed since 1994 were filed under Chapter 7, which allows a debtor to retain certain exempt property while the remaining property is sold to repay creditors. About 28 percent of cases were filed under Chapter 13, which permits creditors to be repaid, in full or in part, in installments over a three-to-five-year period. About 0.6 percent of filings were under Chapter 11, which enables a business to continue operating while formulating a plan to repay its creditors. Nonbusiness cases rose by 77 percent between 1994 and 1998, while business cases declined by 13 percent.

Q 260. Has there ever been a U.S. district court in a foreign country?

A Yes. Congress created the U.S. Court of China in 1906 to serve the large number of Americans living and working there. The court handled diverse matters, from admiralty cases to divorce actions. One judge was assigned to the court, which sat in fourteen cities. The court ceased to function at the start of World War II.

PERSONNEL

Judges

Q 261. What does a federal district judge do?

A U.S. district court judges preside over pretrial, trial, and posttrial proceedings involving civil and criminal cases filed with the court. Only one judge is usually required to hear and decide a case in district court. A few federal statutes require three-judge panels. The judge maintains order in the courtroom, decides if the evidence offered is illegal or inadmissible, instructs the jury (if there is one) about how the law applies to the case, and determines the facts and makes a decision in nonjury trials. Each district court has from two to twenty-eight federal district judgeships, depending on the amount of judicial work within the district. District judges are nominated by the president, and their nominations are subject to confirmation by the Senate. In choosing a nominee, the president typically extends great deference to the wishes of the senator from the president's political party who represents the state where the judge is going to sit. This practice is known as "senatorial courtesy." Federal court judges hold their offices during good behavior as required by Article III, Section 1, of the Constitution. Each district court also has one or more U.S. magistrate judges and bankruptcy judges.

Q 262. How many federal district judges are there?

A Of the 646 authorized U.S. district court judgeships in 1998, a total of 591 were filled. In addition, there were 276 "retired" or senior judges, who accept a reduced workload. Senior judges handle about 15 percent of the federal courts' annual workload.

Q 263. What percentage of appointees for federal judgeships are from the same party as the appointing president?

A The vast majority of them. A total of 90.5 percent of Democratic president Bill Clinton's appointees for U.S. district court judgeships from 1993 to 1998 were Democrats, 2.4 percent were Republicans, 6.5 percent were independents or had no party affiliation, and 0.6 percent were listed as "other."

The most partisan president in recent years was Ronald Reagan (1981–1988). During his first term, 96.9 percent of his appointees were Republicans, and 4.1 percent were Democrats. He appointed no independents or unaffiliated voters. During his second term, 90.7 percent of Reagan's appointees were Republicans, 6.2 percent were Democrats, and 3.1 percent were independents or had no party affiliation.

Q 264. How many federal district judges went to private or Ivy League law schools?

A A total of 57.4 percent of Clinton's appointees obtained their law degrees from private or Ivy League law schools, as did President Bill Clinton, who attended Yale Law School.

Of the appointees of Clinton's predecessor, Republican George Bush, 47.3 percent obtained law degrees from private or Ivy League institutions. Bush, who attended Yale University as an undergraduate, was not a lawyer.

Q 265. How often does Congress reject a judicial nominee?

A The U.S. Senate, responsible for confirming the judicial nominations submitted by the president, seldom rejects outright a candidate for a low-level federal court judgeship. If a candidate's qualifications are challenged, the Senate simply delays acting on the nomination, or the candidate, facing certain defeat, asks the president to withdraw his or her nomination. The Republican-controlled Senate was criticized during the presidency of Democrat Bill Clinton for its slow pace in acting on judicial nominations. According to the Alliance for Justice, the average time from judicial nomination to confirmation for the past twenty years was ninety-one days. In 1998, reports the Alliance, it took 232 days. Critics blamed the delays on conservative Republicans who were ideologically opposed to Clinton.

One nominee who withdrew in 1998 on the eve of her confirmation vote was Philadelphia Court of Common Pleas judge Frederica Massiah-Jackson, whom Clinton had nominated to the U.S. district court in the Eastern District of Pennsylvania. She would have been the first African American woman to sit on a federal court in Pennsylvania. She faced certain defeat after being accused of, among other things, being soft on crime.

The Senate is more willing to reject a nominee to the nation's highest court, possibly because of the importance and visibility of these nominees. About 20 percent of nominees for the Supreme Court either are rejected by the Senate or withdraw their nominations.

The closest rejection occurred when President James Buchanan nominated his secretary of state, Jeremiah S. Black, to the Supreme Court in 1861. Black failed to win confirmation by one vote. Republicans were reluctant to fill the Court vacancy, which would otherwise be filled by incoming Republican president Abraham Lincoln. Also, Black's nomination was criticized in the northern antislavery press because he was not an abolitionist.

Q 266. What does the chief judge of the district do?

A The chief judges of district courts supervise the district court clerk's office, the probation office, the pretrial services office, and the administration of the magistrate judge system. They also help oversee the bankruptcy court. The chief judge also may specially assign a case to a judge if the case is one of unusual length or complexity. Moreover, the chief judge appoints magistrate judges when a majority of judges in a district cannot agree on a candidate.

Q 267. Who is the "meanest" federal judge in history?

A This record may go to Willis Ritter, a Salt Lake City, Utah, lawyer appointed to the federal bench in 1949. Ritter is said to have hissed at a lawyer he didn't like while the lawyer was attempting to present his case. "Like a snake, he was going 'ssss' all the time I was speaking," recalled the advocate. One observer said Ritter was "ecumenically mean, which is to say he seems to dislike most persons who come into his court, be they defendant, government lawyer, private trial attorney, or ordinary citizen." He apparently didn't like his fellow judges any more than the lawyers who practiced before him. In fact, he wouldn't ride on the same elevator with one of them, and court clerks had to schedule their appearances in the courthouse on different days.

268. What is the salary of a U.S. district court judge?

A In 1999, a U.S. district judge earned $136,700. Full-time magistrates and bankruptcy judges earned $125,764. Judges in district court may earn up to $20,505 in outside earnings, such as salary from teaching, not including royalties.

Q **269. How many citizen complaints against federal judges are upheld?**

A A total of 1,002 complaints against judges were resolved in 1998. Of these, chief judges dismissed 734, and judicial councils dismissed 258. Most complaints were dismissed because they were perceived as going to the merits of a case or as involving procedural rulings not relevant to the complaint process. "Corrective" action was taken by chief judges in three cases and five complaints were withdrawn. Judicial councils took unspecified action on two complaints.

A total of 1,051 complaints were filed against federal judges in 1998. The most-often-cited allegation was prejudice and bias and abuse of judicial power.

Under federal law (Section 372 [c] of Title 28 of the U.S. Code) any person may complain about a federal judge or magistrate judge who the person believes "has engaged in conduct prejudicial to the effective and expeditious administration of the business of the courts" or "is unable to discharge all the duties of office by reason of mental or physical disability." Prohibited judicial conduct includes using the judge's office to obtain special treatment for friends and relatives, accepting bribes, and improperly engaging in discussions with lawyers or parties to a case. The law does not prohibit making the wrong decision in a case. "Mental or physical disability" may include temporary conditions as well as permanent disability.

Complaints can be filed with the clerk of the governing circuit's court of appeals or with the applicable national court. Complaints are typically reviewed first by the chief judge of the circuit, who determines whether the complaint raises an issue that should be investigated.

U.S. Magistrates

Q **270. What is a U.S. magistrate judge?**

A A magistrate judge is a judicial officer who performs a wide array of judicial functions authorized under the Federal Magistrates Act of 1968.

The duties of magistrate judges vary according to the needs of the federal district in which they work. They hear minor criminal matters and some civil cases. They issue arrest warrants or summonses, conduct preliminary hearings in criminal cases, and, if the district court permits and the defendants agree, preside at trials of defendants who face no more than one year's imprisonment. Magistrate judges conduct civil trials when both litigants consent. In 1998 magistrates terminated 10,339 civil cases with the litigants' consent and disposed of 96,832 criminal misdemeanor and petty offense cases.

A magistrate judge is appointed by majority vote of the active district judges. A full-time magistrate serves an eight-year term, and a part-time magistrate serves a four-year term. Of the 508 authorized magistrate judge positions in 1998, a total of 491 were filled, and there were 17 vacancies.

Congress created the office of magistrate to assist federal district judges in dealing with increased workloads. In 1990 Congress changed the title from "magistrate" to "magistrate judge."

An appeal of the magistrate's judgment may be made directly to the circuit's court of appeals or, if the litigants agree, to a district judge, whose decision is followed by discretionary review in the court of appeals.

As of January 1, 1998, full-time magistrate judges were paid $125,746 per year.

Court-Related Personnel

Q 271. What does a district court executive do?

A A half-dozen federal district courts employ a district court executive to serve as a court administrator. These districts include four of the largest federal district courts (Eastern District of New York, Southern District of New York, Northern District of Georgia, and Southern District of Florida) and the Eastern District of Michigan. The district court executive performs management duties that otherwise would be assigned to the clerk of court, so that the clerk can focus on managing cases filed with the court.

Q 272. What does the clerk of court do?

A The clerk of court is an officer appointed by the district court who is responsible for the administrative and clerical operations of the court. The clerk's office oversees the intake, processing, and maintenance of court records, manages the courtroom, handles public inquiries and requests, processes all pleadings and other court documents, and prepares financial and statistical documents necessary to the operation of the court. The clerk works closely with the chief judge to manage the flow of cases through the district.

Q 273. What do U.S. marshals do?

A The U.S. Marshals Service was created along with the federal judiciary in the Judiciary Act of 1789. Marshals and deputy marshals protect the federal judiciary, transport federal prisoners, protect endangered witnesses, and manage assets seized from criminal enterprises. They pursue and arrest 55 percent of all federal fugitives, more than those arrested by all other federal agencies combined. The first federal law enforcement officer in the United States to be killed in the line of duty was Robert Forsyth, U.S. marshal for the District of Georgia, who was shot and killed while attempting to serve civil papers on January 11, 1794.

The first marshals were appointed by President George Washington to carry out all lawful orders issued by judges, Congress, and the president. In the early days, marshals served court papers and disbursed federal funds, paying the court clerks, U.S. attorneys, jurors, and witnesses. They also rented the courtrooms and jail space and hired the bailiffs, criers and janitors. Until 1870 marshals took the national census every ten years. Marshals have also been called on to carry out extraordinary missions, including registering enemy aliens in time of war, capturing fugitive slaves, and carrying out spy swaps between the United States and the Soviet Union.

Q 274. What does a pretrial release officer do?

A A pretrial services officer is a district court employee who screens criminal defendants for pretrial release. The officer provides information on which the court can base release and detention decisions while a criminal case is pending. In 1998 pretrial services officers screened 78,603 defendants.

The courts released half of all defendants pending trial, including 34.9 percent at initial hearings and 14 percent at detention hearings in which risk of flight was assessed. The most frequently ordered restrictive condition on release concerned substance abuse. A total of 16,697 defendants were ordered to stay away from alcohol and drugs.

House arrest and electronic monitoring were ordered for 5,063 defendants awaiting trial. A total of 2,968 defendants were placed in a pretrial diversion program, which is an alternative to prosecution of criminal charges.

Q **275. What do probation officers do?**

A Probation officers provide the district court with reliable information about the offender, the victim, and the offense committed, allowing the court to make an informed and impartial judgment with respect to sentencing.

The probation officer collects information about the history and characteristics of the defendant and compiles a presentence investigation report for the court. The officer also gathers information necessary to classify the defendant's offense and the defendant under guidelines promulgated by the U.S. Sentencing Commission. Another responsibility of the officer is to collect victim impact statements.

Finally, the probation officer monitors convicted offenders who are released under court supervision. In 1998 a total of 93,737 persons were under the supervision of the U.S. probation system, including 54,819 persons serving terms of supervised release following their discharge from prison.

The judiciary estimated that in 1997 an average of 4,700 federal offenders were under home confinement on a daily basis. If placed in prison, these individuals would have cost the government $69 million to $106 million.

See 301 What is the U.S. Sentencing Commission? 538 What is probation?

Q **276. What do courtroom deputies do?**

A A courtroom deputy (also known as "minute law clerk" or "case manager") is an employee of the clerk of court's office who records the minutes of the court and assists the judge with scheduling trials and hearings on motions. The deputy also administers oaths to jurors, witnesses, and interpreters, maintains custody of trial exhibits, records a description of all relevant actions taken in open court or in the judge's chambers, and serves as a liaison between the judge's chambers and the clerk of court's office.

See 272 What does the clerk of courts do?

Q **277. What does a court reporter do?**

A Some courts use court reporters to create a word-for-word record of every court session, as required by federal law. Other courts maintain their official record on tape recordings. The court reporter also produces a written transcript of the proceedings at the request of either plaintiff or defendant or if either of them appeals the case. Official reporters are court employees who receive an annual salary but must provide their own supplies and equipment. They are allowed to charge fees for certain work performed in the course of their official duties, such as preparing transcripts at the request of litigants. Fees for these services are established by the U.S. Judicial Conference.

Q 278. What is a special master?

A A special master is an impartial expert appointed by a district judge to hear and consider evidence or to make an examination with respect to some issue in a pending action. For example, the district court may appoint a certified public accountant as a special master in a case involving complicated financial issues. The special master makes a report to the court, which is used to assist the court in deciding the merits of the issue. The fee paid to the special master, who may be called to testify in the case, is determined by the court and taxed to the parties as costs.

Q 279. What do staff attorneys and law clerks do?

A They help judges research and draft opinions.

U.S. Attorney

Q 280. What does a U.S. attorney do?

A U.S. attorneys are the nation's principal litigators under the direction of the U.S. attorney general. They conduct most of the federal court trial work in which the United States is a party. The Office of the U.S. Attorney was created by the Judiciary Act of 1789, which required the president to appoint a person "learned in the law to act as attorney for the United States" in each federal district and to prosecute "all delinquents for crimes and offenses cognizable under the authority of the United States, and all civil actions in which the United States shall be concerned. . . ."

The ninety-three U.S. attorneys are the chief federal law enforcement officers of the United States within their respective jurisdictions. They have wide latitude to determine the priorities of their office, and how its resources are allocated to meet the needs of their districts. Each federal district has one or more assistant U.S. attorneys, with large urban areas having more than a hundred. In 1997 U.S. attorneys and their assistants filed 39,291 criminal cases in federal court, including 11,935 cases involving drug offenses. U.S. attorneys prosecuted 58,906 defendants, of whom 23,542 were defendants in drug cases.

One U.S. attorney is assigned to each judicial district, with the exception of Guam and the Northern Mariana Islands, where a single U.S. attorney serves in both districts. By statute, U.S. attorneys are responsible for the prosecution of cases brought by the federal government, the prosecution and defense of civil cases in which the United States is a party, and the collection of debts owed to the federal government that could not be collected by administrative agencies. They have full authority and control for their office in the areas of personnel management, financial management, and procurement.

Q 281. How are U.S. attorneys selected and appointed?

A U.S. attorneys are appointed by the president, with the advice and consent of the Senate. They are appointed to serve a term of four years but are subject to removal at the president's discretion. The position is generally considered a political plum awarded to a supporter who is an attorney and a member of the president's political party. Assistant U.S. attorneys are formally appointed by the attorney general, who may also fire them.

Public Defender

Q 282. What does the federal public defender do?

A Federal public defenders represent indigent defendants in criminal matters. Congress makes federal courts responsible for administering public defender programs for defendants with limited financial resources. Each district has a plan to provide such representation either by a private panel of attorneys or by a federal public or community defender office. A total of 101,133 appointments of counsel were made for indigent defendants in 1998 in accordance with the Criminal Justice Act of 1964.

There are about sixty federal public defender organizations that include a staff of attorneys who are specialists in criminal law and receive regular training by the Administrative Office of the U.S. Courts and the Federal Judicial Center.

Civil litigants who are indigent are not entitled to a court-appointed lawyer in federal court. These *pro se* (parties without counsel) litigants face many obstacles, including unfamiliarity with procedural and substantive law. Many state and local bar associations and law schools operate programs that provide civil counsel to low- and moderate-income litigants at no charge. These lawyers work pro bono, or without compensation.

See 70 What is the Administrative Office of the U.S. Courts? 71 What is the Federal Judicial Center?

Q 283. Who nominates and appoints federal public defenders?

A Judges of the U.S. courts of appeals appoint public defenders in most of the sixty districts that have public defender organizations. This system has been criticized because defenders, though insulated from federal trial judges, must, in effect, practice before their employer when they file an appeal. A 1993 proposal to establish an independent center for federal criminal defender services was rejected by the Committee on Defender Services of the Judicial Conference of the United States, the judicial body that sets policy for public defenders, ostensibly because a majority of federal public defenders wanted to keep the existing system.

BUDGET

Q 284. What is the annual budget for the U.S. district court?

A The budget for the U.S. district courts in fiscal year 1999 was $1.553 billion, compared with $1.384 billion in 1998, and $1.304 billion in 1997. The budget for bankruptcy courts was $344 million in 1999, and the budget for federal probation and pretrial services was $635 million.

COURTS OF SPECIAL JURISDICTION

U.S. COURT OF APPEALS FOR THE ARMED FORCES

Q 285. What is the U.S. Court of Appeals for the Armed Forces?

A This court serves as the final appellate tribunal to review court-martial convictions of all of the armed forces. Its decisions are subject to review only by the Supreme Court. The court is staffed with civilian judges to emphasize the principle of civilian control of the military. Congress established a military justice system in 1950 when it enacted the Uniform Code of Military Justice and created the U.S. Court of Military Appeals. The name of the court was changed in 1994 to the U.S. Court of Appeals for the Armed Forces. It is located for administrative purposes within the Department of Defense.

The court has jurisdiction to review the record in all cases extending to death (those potentially involving the death penalty), cases certified to the court by a judge advocate general of an armed force or by the general counsel of the Department of Transportation (acting for the Coast Guard), and petitions filed by the accused persons themselves if they have received a sentence of confinement for one year or more and/or a punitive discharge.

Because they serve on a legislative court, created by Congress according to Article I of the U.S. Constitution, judges on the U.S. Court of Appeals for the Armed Forces do not have life tenure and are not protected by the Constitution from salary reduction while in office.

The court can be reached at:

U.S. Court of Appeals for the Armed Forces
450 E Street, N.W.
Washington, D.C. 20442-0001
(202) 761-1448
http://www.armfor.uscourts.gov/

See 91 What is the chief difference between federal constitutional and legislative courts?

286. Who staffs the U.S. Court of Appeals for the Armed Forces?

The U.S. Court of Appeals for the Armed Forces is staffed by five civilian judges who are appointed to fifteen-year terms by the president and whose nominations are subject to confirmation by the Senate.

287. What is the annual budget for the U.S. Court of Appeals for the Armed Forces?

The budget for the U.S. Court of Appeals for the Armed Forces in fiscal year 1999 was $7,324,000.

U.S. COURT OF FEDERAL CLAIMS

288. What is the U.S. Court of Federal Claims?

The U.S. Court of Federal Claims has nationwide trial jurisdiction over a broad array of monetary claims against the United States. It is located for administrative purposes within the U.S. Department of Commerce.

From 1982 to 1992 the court was named the U.S. Claims Court. To be valid, a claim either must be authorized by the U.S. Constitution, an act of Congress, the regulation of an executive department, or a contract with the United States; or must involve damages in cases not concerning a tort, or personal injury. Federal district courts have exclusive jurisdiction over tort actions that allege a civil wrong or breach of duty, and concurrent or shared jurisdiction over tax claims with the U.S. Court of Federal Claims.

Half of the cases filed before the court involve tax refund suits and claims by federal government contractors suing for breach of contract. The court also hears cases involving the federal taking of private property for public use, civilian and military pay questions, backpay demands from civil servants claiming unjust dismissal, and appeals of decisions of the Indian Claims Commission.

Congress occasionally grants the court jurisdiction over specific types of claims against the United States, such as those arising under the National Vaccine Injury Compensation Program. Congress may refer any claim to the court for which there is no apparent legal remedy and may request a recommendation about whether there is an equitable basis on which to compensate the claimant.

A total of 1,105 cases were filed with the court in 1998, including 264 contract actions and 313 tax cases. During that period the court terminated 1,179 cases. It awarded $1.7 billion in money judgments to claimants.

The U.S. Court of Federal Claims is a legislative court, created by Congress according to Article I of the Constitution. As such, its judges do not have lifetime tenure and have no constitutional protection against salary reduction while in office.

Judgments of the court are final and binding on both the claimant and the United States. However, they are subject to appeal to the U.S. Court of Appeals for the Federal Circuit.

The court can be reached at:

U.S. Court of Federal Claims
717 Madison Place, N.W.
Washington, DC 20005
(202) 219-9657

See 91 What is the chief difference between federal constitutional and legislative courts?

Q 289. Who staffs the U.S. Court of Federal Claims?

A The court is composed of a chief judge, designated by the president, and fifteen associate judges. All of these judges are appointed by the president for fifteen-year terms, and their nominations are subject to Senate confirmation. A judge of the U.S. Court of Federal Claims earns $135,700 per year.

Q 290. What is the annual budget of the U.S. Court of Federal Claims?

A The fiscal 1999 budget allotment for the U.S. Court of Federal Claims was $2,303,000. The allotment did not include certain major costs (judges' salaries and travel expenses, for example), which came out of the budget of the Administrative Office of the U.S. Courts.

U.S. COURT OF INTERNATIONAL TRADE

Q 291. What is the U.S. Court of International Trade?

A The U.S. Court of International Trade handles cases involving international trade, customs duties, and unfair import practices by trading partners. This court was originally established in 1890 as the Board of United States General Appraisers, with jurisdiction over tariff acts that had been held previously by the district and circuit courts. The board was superseded by the U.S. Customs Court in 1926. Congress changed the name of the court and significantly expanded its jurisdiction when it passed the Customs Courts Act of 1980.

Today, the court has exclusive nationwide jurisdiction to decide any civil action against the United States, its officers, or its agencies arising out of any law pertaining to international trade. The court also reviews administrative actions of government agencies dealing with importations.

The court is a constitutional court, established by Congress according to Article III of the Constitution. Its judges receive lifetime appointments, and their salary cannot be reduced. The court has the same powers as a district court and can hold hearings and trials anywhere in the nation, and even in foreign countries. Trials are held in U.S. courthouses, and the court is equipped with conference telephones to hear oral arguments and conduct conferences with parties at other places, should the need arise. The court may grant any relief appropriate to the case before it, including injunctive relief (commanding that a party engage in or desist in a certain action) and money judgments.

In 1998 the U.S. Court of International Trade reported 3,575 cases filed, compared with 2,275 in 1997. The court terminated 936 cases in 1998, compared with 711 in 1997.

The U.S. Court of International Trade can be reached at:

U.S. Court of International Trade
One Federal Plaza
New York, N.Y. 10007
(212) 264-2800

Q 292. Who staffs the U.S. Court of International Trade?

A The U.S. Court of International Trade is staffed by a chief judge and eight judges who are appointed by the president and whose nominations are subject to Senate confirmation. The chief judge normally assigns a single judge to hear a case but may assign a three-judge panel if the matter involves the constitutionality of an act of Congress, a presidential proclamation, or an executive order. Judges also may be assigned temporarily by the chief justice of the United States to perform judicial duties in a U.S. court of appeals or a U.S. district court.

The chief judge of the U.S. Court of International Trade is a statutory member of the Judicial Conference of the United States, the principal policy-making body of the federal judiciary.

A judge of the U.S. Court of International Trade earns $135,700 per year.

Q 293. What is the annual budget of the U.S. Court of International Trade?

A The budget for the U.S. Court of International Trade for fiscal year 1999 was $11,804,000.

U.S. COURT OF APPEALS FOR VETERANS CLAIMS

Q 294. What is the U.S. Court of Appeals for Veterans Claims?

A The U.S. Court of Appeals for Veterans Claims is an independent judicial body that has exclusive jurisdiction to review decisions of the Board of Veterans Appeals. However, the court may not review the schedule of ratings for disabilities or the actions of the secretary of the Department of Veterans Affairs in adopting or revising that schedule. Decisions of the court may be appealed to the U.S. Court of Appeals for the Federal Circuit.

The U.S. Court of Appeals for Veterans Claims can be reached at:

U.S. Court of Appeals for Veterans Claims
625 Indiana Ave., N.W.
Suite 900
Washington, D.C. 20004
(202) 501-5970

See 91 What is the chief difference between federal constitutional and legislative courts?

Q 295. Who staffs the U.S. Court of Appeals for Veterans Claims?

A The court consists of a chief judge and at least two, but not more than six, associate judges. All judges are appointed by the president with the advice and consent of the Senate for terms of fifteen years.

Q 296. What is the annual budget of the U.S. Court of Appeals for Veterans Claims?

A The budget for the U.S. Court of Appeals for Veterans Claims was $10,195,000 in fiscal year 1999.

U.S. TAX COURT

Q 297. What is the U.S. Tax Court?

A The U.S. Tax Court is an independent judicial body in the legislative branch that decides disputes between the Internal Revenue Service and taxpayers. The court was originally called the U.S. Board of Tax Appeals when it was created by Congress in 1924. At that time, it was an independent agency in the executive branch. The court's name was changed to Tax Court of the United States in 1942 and then to U.S. Tax Court in 1969. Congress changed the court's status in 1969, making it an Article I, or legislative, court. As such, its judiciary does not have lifetime tenure and is not protected by the Constitution from salary reduction. The nineteen judges of the tax court are experts in federal taxation and travel to eighty cities around the country.

The court adjudicates disputes involving deficiencies or overpayments in income, estate, gift, and generation-skipping transfer taxes when deficiencies have been determined by the commissioner of internal revenue. It also hears cases initiated by persons to whom taxes have been transferred and by those who have received notices of liability from the IRS. The court can make declaratory judgments relating to the qualifications of retirement plans, including pension, profit-sharing, stock bonus, annuity, and bond purchase plans; the tax-exempt status of a charitable organization, qualified charitable recipient of a gift, private foundation, or private operating foundation; and the status of interest on certain governmental securities. Approximately 26,000 cases were filed in the U.S. Tax Court in 1998, compared with 25,955 in 1997. The court's decisions may be appealed to a U.S. court of appeals and, if necessary, to the U.S. Supreme Court.

The U.S. Tax Court can be reached at:

U.S. Tax Court
400 Second St., N.W.
Washington, D.C. 20217
(202) 606-8754

See 91 What is the chief difference between federal constitutional and legislative courts?

Q 298. Who staffs the U.S. Tax Court?

A The court is composed of nineteen judges who are appointed to fifteen-year terms by the president and whose nominations are subject to confirmation by the Senate. These judges elect one of their peers to serve a two-year term as chief judge, with overall responsibility for the administration of the court. The chief judge may call on senior judges, those over age sixty-five who have several years of experience on the federal bench and handle reduced caseloads, to perform further judicial duties. The chief judge also appoints fourteen special trial judges who serve at the pleasure of the court.

See 90 What is the "Rule of 80"?

Q 299. What is the annual budget of the U.S. Tax Court?

A The budget for the U.S. Tax Court was $34,490,000 in fiscal year 1999.

OTHER FEDERAL JUDICIAL BODIES

Q 300. What is the Judicial Panel on Multidistrict Litigation?

A If a case involves one or more questions of fact and is pending in more than one district, either the plaintiff or the defendant may petition the Judicial Panel on Multidistrict Litigation to transfer the case to a single district and consolidate the multiple legal actions into a single action for pretrial proceedings. A federal judge may also invoke the intervention of the panel.

The panel was created by an act of Congress on April 29, 1968, in response to the judiciary's struggle to coordinate almost 2,000 related cases involving twenty-five thousand claims pending in thirty-six districts around the country. All of the cases nationwide are transferred temporarily to a single district for coordinated or consolidated pretrial proceedings.

The panel consists of seven federal judges who are selected by the chief justice of the United States from the courts of appeals and district courts. The panel acted on 16,594 civil actions in the year ending September 30, 1998. It transferred 15,735 cases originally filed in ninety-three different districts to forty districts for coordinated or consolidated pretrial proceedings. Most cases centralized by the panel involved asbestos and silicone gel breast-implant litigation and contraceptives. The panel refused to centralize 181 actions. The panel can be reached at:

Judicial Panel on Multidistrict Litigation
Thurgood Marshall Federal Judiciary Building
Room G-255
One Columbus Circle, N.E.
Washington, D.C. 20002
(202) 273-2800

Q 301. What is the U.S. Sentencing Commission?

A In 1984 Congress created the U.S. Sentencing Commission as an independent agency in the federal judicial branch to formulate sentencing guidelines and practices for the federal courts. Congress, the criminal justice community, and the public had long been concerned about sentencing disparities. Guidelines issued by the seven-member commission prescribe the appropriate form and severity of punishment for offenders convicted of federal crimes. In assessing the seriousness of an offense, the guidelines take into account the nature of the defendant's criminal conduct and the offense for which the defendant was convicted. The guidelines are intended to avoid sentencing disparities among similarly situated criminals who are convicted of the same crime. The commission, which has a staff of about one hundred, also advises Congress and the executive branch on the development of effective crime policy and collects information on federal crime and sentencing issues. The budget for the U.S. Sentencing Commission in fiscal year 1999 was $9,487,000. The commission can be reached at:

U.S. Sentencing Commission
1 Columbus Circle, N.E.
Suite 2-500 South
Washington, D.C. 20002

(202) 273-4500

http://www.ussc.gov/

See 254 How does a federal judge know what sentence to mete out in a criminal case?

Q 302. What is the Foreign Intelligence Surveillance Court?

A The Foreign Intelligence Surveillance Court is a highly secret body that was created in 1978 when Congress passed the Foreign Intelligence Surveillance Act (FISA) in an attempt to control domestic surveillance activities by federal intelligence agencies. This court has the sole authority to hear applications for and grant orders approving electronic surveillance and physical searches of foreign agents, including suspected terrorists, in the United States. The court consists of seven federal district court judges, each from a different district, who are appointed by the chief justice of the Supreme Court. It meets twice yearly in Washington, D.C., in a secure conference room at the Department of Justice.

In 1998 a total of 796 applications were made for orders and extensions of orders approving electronic surveillance or physical searches under FISA. The court granted all of them. In what is believed to be a first, the court declined in 1997 to approve an application for reasons that it did not disclose. The government subsequently withdrew the case, rendering the matter moot. In 1997 a total of 796 applications were granted by the court.

The FISA also provides for an appeals court, but none has ever met because no appeal has ever been filed. The chief justice appoints three judges from U.S. district courts or courts of appeals to the appeals court, one of whom is designated as the presiding judge.

Judges on the Foreign Intelligence Surveillance Court serve a maximum term of seven years and are not eligible for reappointment. One judge is typically from a district court in Washington, D.C., and the other six judges rotate through Washington.

Q 303. What is the Alien Terrorist Removal Court?

A This court was created in the Antiterrorism and Effective Death Penalty Act of 1996 to hear applications from the office of the U.S. attorney general to deport foreign nationals suspected of being alien terrorists. The chief justice of the Supreme Court appointed five U.S. district court judges from different judicial circuits to serve staggered five-year terms on the court. The court had not yet become operational in mid-1999.

Special procedures allow the court to protect information that is classified for national security reasons. The government must provide the defendant with an unclassified summary of the evidence against him or her but is not required to reveal classified information. The court determines whether the summary is sufficient to allow the foreign national to prepare a defense. If not and the government fails to provide a satisfactory summary within fifteen days, the case is dismissed. The government is required to prove its case by a "preponderance of the evidence," or by showing that it is more probable than not that the alien is a terrorist.

V

STATE CONSTITUTIONS

IN GENERAL

Q **304. What are state constitutions?**

A Under the Tenth Amendment of the U.S. Constitution, power that the Constitution does not specifically delegate to the federal government resides with the states. Every state has a constitution to limit the residual power of the state over its citizens and to articulate their fundamental rights and liberties, often providing greater protection for individuals than that afforded by the U.S. Constitution. Nineteen state constitutions explicitly prohibit discrimination on the basis of sex, for example, a safeguard that is not spelled out in the text of the U.S. Constitution. Other state constitutions extend certain rights to persons with disabilities or to victims of crime, mandate a balanced budget, and set term limits for legislators. Most constitutions also address a variety of other issues, including the education of children in the state, impeachment of elected officials, and taxation.

Before the ratification of the Fourteenth Amendment in 1868, federal courts could not compel states to enforce any of the provisions of the U.S. Constitution's Bill of Rights. Therefore, state constitutions were initially the citizenry's major source of protection against governmental abuse.

State constitutions also provide a framework of government for the states and set forth the division of powers between the various branches of government and their political subdivisions. All state constitutions call for the creation of three branches of government—an executive, legislative, and judicial branch.

In all but two states, the executive branch is led by a governor who is popularly elected to a four-year term. In New Hampshire and Vermont, the governor serves a two-year term.

All states except Nebraska specify that the legislative branch should consist of a bicameral legislature, with a house and senate. Nebraska's constitution of 1875 was amended by voters in 1934 to establish a unicameral legislature.

A state constitution is the highest expression of law in the state. It is superseded only by the U.S. Constitution as that document is interpreted by the Supreme Court. The Court can invalidate a state constitution or any of its provisions deemed to conflict with the U.S. Constitution.

State constitutions are more easily amended than the U.S. Constitution and, as a result, serve as a source of innovation and experimentation. They had a profound influence on the formation of the U.S. Constitution, the Bill of Rights, and, ultimately, the movement toward democratic government in many foreign nations. Concepts initially set forth in state constitutions, including the principle that all people are created equal, inspired citizens in this century who marched for greater freedoms in South Africa, China, and Eastern Europe.

See 31 What is a constitution? 41 What type of court system does the U.S. Constitution envision?

Q 305. What came first? The U.S. Constitution or state constitutions?

A State constitutions. The Continental Congress urged the colonies to adopt their own constitutions on December 21, 1775. Eleven of the thirteen colonies wrote new constitutions; Connecticut and Rhode Island transformed their colonial charters into republican charters by deleting all references to the king. Many of the ideas espoused in these documents were influential in the 1781 drafting of the U.S. Constitution's predecessor, the Articles of Confederation.

All of the states had adopted written constitutions by 1787, the year of the adoption of the U.S. Constitution.

HISTORY AND NOTABLE CONSTITUTIONS

Q 306. What was the first colony to adopt a written constitution declaring its independence from England at the urging of the Continental Congress?

A New Hampshire was the first colony to declare its independence from England and, on January 6, 1776, became the first one to adopt a constitution without the prior approval of the crown or English Parliament. A provincial congress composed of wealthy landowners convened in violation of British law to ratify the 911-word constitution. Delegates expected the constitution to be in effect only until the conflict with England was resolved. The group planned to form a two-chamber legislature, declared itself the house of representatives, and then elected a second, twelve-member chamber called a council. However, a motion to adopt an oath of loyalty to the new state government failed.

Q 307. How did state constitutions influence the making of the U.S. Constitution?

A The Framers of the U.S. Constitution used as a starting point for the national document many of the ideas and concepts contained in state constitutions.

Historians say fear of tyranny led Americans to limit the power of state government by requiring in state constitutions the formation of bicameral legislatures and an intricate system of governmental checks and balances. Early state constitutions emphasized the direct, continuing consent of popular majorities. These features were incorporated into the U.S. Constitution. Most state constitutional congresses also adopted declarations of individual rights, and others specified inviolable rights in the texts of their constitutions. These documents were the prototypes for the U.S. Constitution's Bill of Rights.

One of the most influential state constitutions was the Massachusetts Constitution of 1780. It was drafted by John Adams, who went on to become the nation's first vice president and second president. It called for a bicameral legislature, free exercise of religion, and a "government of laws, and not of men." This document influenced both the U.S. Constitution and other state constitutions.

Early state constitutions were fluid documents, often amended or superseded. Between 1776 and 1798 the first fourteen states ratified an estimated twenty-five constitutions.

Q 308. What state has the oldest written constitution still in effect?

A Massachusetts's constitution, adopted in 1780. Earlier constitutions, including New Hampshire's (1776), were superseded by newer state constitutions.

Q 309. What colonial constitution barred lawyers?

A The Fundamental Constitutions of Carolina, adopted in 1669. This constitution also established a system of "hereditary Nobility" over the province by landed gentry, guaranteed religious tolerance of "Jews, Heathens, and other Dissenters from the purity of Christian Religion," and ensured that "every Freeman of Carolina shall have absolute Power and Authority over his Negro Slaves. . . ."

Q **310. Do all state constitutions contain a bill of rights?**

A All state constitutions have either a statement or bill of rights. A bill of rights is an extended declaration of the individual rights of citizens.

Q **311. What was the first state to adopt a declaration of rights?**

A The Virginia Declaration of Rights of 1776 was the first constitution to contain a separate "declaration of rights" as the "foundation of government."

The Convention of Delegates of the Counties and Corporations in the Colony of Virginia endorsed the declaration on June 12, 1776. The document was written primarily by George Mason, later a delegate to the Constitutional Convention of 1787 and a leader in the effort to add a bill of rights to the U.S. Constitution. Mason, of Williamsburg, Virginia, was influenced by notions of natural rights espoused by English philosopher John Locke (1632–1704), who believed that all people are born free with certain natural rights.

Section 1 of the Virginia Declaration of Rights declares that "all men are by nature equally free and independent, and have certain inherent rights, of which, when they enter into a state of society, they cannot by any compact deprive or divest their posterity; namely, the enjoyment of life and liberty, with the means of acquiring and possessing property, and pursuing and obtaining happiness and safety."

The declaration guaranteed citizens the right to trial by jury, protection against cruel and unusual punishment, freedom of the press, and free exercise of religious beliefs. It also permitted state religious establishments and allowed tax money to be spent to support the Protestant religion.

This document was influential in the drafting of other state constitutions, the Bill of Rights to the U.S. Constitution, the Declaration of Independence, and France's 1789 Declaration of Rights of Man and the Citizen.

See 45 What colony's declaration of rights became the model for the Bill of Rights to the U.S. Constitution?

Q **312. Which state constitution ruled out officeholding for all but about 10 percent of its white adult population?**

A South Carolina's constitution of 1778 required candidates for governor to have a debt-free estate of £10,000 (about $450,000), senators to be worth £2,000, and assemblymen to have property worth about £1,000. This constitution was a flagrant example of the use of property qualifications to maintain a power elite. However, most state constitutions restricted voting and officeholding to propertied white men, excluding women, blacks, Native Americans, and propertyless whites. By the 1820s most states had eliminated the requirement that voters be property holders.

Q **313. Why was the Pennsylvania constitution of 1776 considered the most radical of its time?**

A The Pennsylvania constitution of 1776 was the most democratic of its time. It abolished property ownership as a qualification for political participation and gave all men over the age of twenty-one who had paid taxes and resided in the state for at least a year the right to vote and hold office.

The Pennsylvania constitution, which was adopted amid reports of the impending invasion of Philadelphia by British troops, replaced the post of governor with that of a president and a supreme executive council. It established a unicameral (one house) state legislature that had complete legislative power and required that sessions of the legislature be public. One of its most unique features was the establishment of a Council of Censors to ensure that the "constitution has been preserved inviolate in every part; and whether the legislative and executive branches of government have performed their duty as guardians of the people, or assumed to themselves, or exercised other or greater powers than they are entitled to by the constitution."

Pennsylvania's constitution alarmed politicians in other states, who feared popular rule would lead to the tyranny of legislative majorities. John Adams of Massachusetts denounced Pennsylvania's unicameral legislature as "so democratical that it must produce confusion and every evil work." Adams warned of the dangers of too immediate and powerful popular control over government.

Ironically, Pennsylvania's innovative constitution was unpopular throughout its sixteen-year existence and was annulled in 1790 and replaced with a document that conformed more closely to those of other states.

Q **314. What state constitution empowered a Council of Revision to revise the acts of the legislature?**

A New York's constitution of 1777 empowered a Council of Revision, consisting of the governor and judicial officers of the state, to review and to revise acts of the legislature. If a proposed bill "should appear improper to the said council, or a majority of them, that the said bill should become a law of this State, that they return the same, together with their objections thereto in writing, to the senate or house of assembly" for reconsideration. Thereafter, the proposed bill would require the approval of two-thirds of both the house and the senate to become law.

Q **315. What happens when a state constitution conflicts with the U.S. Constitution?**

A The U.S. Constitution takes precedence over any conflicting state constitution, state law, or federal law. The national document's Article VI, Section 2, states that the U.S. Constitution is the supreme law of the land "and the Judges in every State shall be bound thereby, any Thing in the Constitution or Laws of any State to the contrary notwithstanding." The Supreme Court determines whether a provision of a state constitution conflicts with the U.S. Constitution.

The case that has been called the "keystone" to the federal judiciary's power is *Martin v. Hunter's Lessee* (1816), in which the Court decided in favor of a British claim to a parcel of land in Virginia, rejecting the claim of a Virginia resident. The Virginia courts refused to recognize the Court's jurisdiction, claiming the U.S. Constitution gave the Court no right to tell a state court what to do. The Court upheld the constitutionality of Section 25 of the Judiciary Act of 1789, which authorized the Court to review a decision of a state's highest court when the case involved the Constitution or federal laws or treaties and when it had been decided against the federal government.

See 55 What is the supremacy clause?

Q **316. Which state has adopted the most constitutions?**

A Louisiana has adopted eleven, the most recent having been approved on December 31, 1974. Georgia is a close second, having enacted ten constitutions, the latest on July 1, 1983.

Q **317. What are the longest and shortest state constitutions?**

A Alabama's constitution is believed to be the longest constitution in the world. The state's sixth constitution, adopted on November 28, 1901, has been amended 618 times. Roughly the size of *Moby Dick,* it contains an estimated two hundred twenty thousand words, compared with an average of about thirty thousand for other state constitutions. The shortest state constitution is Vermont's at eighty-three hundred words. Even Vermont's constitution is lengthy compared with the U.S. Constitution, which has about thirty-five hundred words.

The archaic language of the Alabama Constitution, and the reluctance of Alabama's citizens to adopt a new constitution, are blamed for the extensive modification of the document. Critics say Alabama's constitution is an obstacle to better government and progress in the state. For example, to take advantage of modern federal highway funding programs and urban renewal projects, Alabama was forced to amend the constitution more than forty times. The constitution says the state cannot "engage in works of internal improvement, nor lend money for its credit in aid of such." When the constitution was first drafted, the framers feared that the collapse of the State Bank in 1837 and the heavy spending of the government during the Reconstruction era after the Civil War would lead to higher taxes that could bankrupt the state. At that time, carriages and buggies traversed the state's roadways.

Q 318. What state constitution limited the state's total debt to $750,000?

A The Ohio Constitution of 1851, like many constitutions of its time, severely limited state economic activity. Early state constitutions were mostly silent on economic development issues. Therefore, some state legislatures began providing direct cash subsidies to select industries and investing directly in private corporations, a practice that incurred public suspicion and protest. The Ohio Constitution effectively put an end to these practices in Ohio.

Q 319. Which state constitution was the first to abolish slavery?

A The Vermont Constitution, written in 1777, was the first state constitution to abolish slavery. This constitution does not specifically mention blacks but contains a general antislavery clause. Chapter 1, Article 1, of the Vermont Constitution declares that

> all persons are born equally free and independent, and have certain natural, inherent, and unalienable rights, amongst which are the enjoying and defending of life and liberty, acquiring, possessing and protecting property, and pursuing and obtaining happiness and safety; therefore no person born in this country, or brought from over sea, ought to be holden by law, to serve any person as a servant, slave or apprentice, after arriving to the age of twenty-one years, unless bound by the person's own consent, after arriving to such age, or bound by law for the payment of debts, damages, fines, costs or the like.

By omitting any reference to the payment of taxes or property qualifications, Section 7 of the Vermont Constitution was also the only state constitution to give the vote to every adult male.

It was not until 1865, after the Civil War, that the Thirteenth Amendment to the U.S. Constitution was adopted, prohibiting slavery. The Thirteenth Amendment declares: "Neither slavery nor involuntary servitude, except as punishment for crime whereof the party shall have been duly convicted, shall exist within the United States, or any place subject to their jurisdiction."

State constitutions contained various discriminatory provisions. For example, Article XI, Section 12, of the Tennessee Constitution in 1870 provided that no public school "shall allow white and negro children to be received as scholars together."

See 44 Did the U.S. Constitution address the issue of slavery?

Q **320. What constitution prohibited the passage of any law impairing "the right of property in negro slaves"?**

A The Constitution of the Confederate States of America, adopted by the Congress of Confederate States, including South Carolina, Georgia, Florida, Alabama, Mississippi, Louisiana, and Texas, contained this provision. It was adopted at a constitutional convention in Montgomery, Alabama, on March 11, 1861. Many southern state constitutions contained provisions upholding the institution of slavery. The Mississippi Constitution of 1832, for example, states, "The legislature shall have no power to pass laws for the emancipation of slaves without the consent of the owners. . . . " After the Civil War the confederate states were forced to amend their constitutions to abolish slavery.

Q **321. What common tactic was used by constitution writers to disenfranchise minority voters after the Civil War?**

A A poll tax was written into the constitutions of several southern states to circumvent the Fifth Amendment to the U.S. Constitution, which was adopted in 1870 and prohibited states from denying the right to vote on the basis of race.

The Twenty-fourth Amendment, ratified in 1964, abolished the poll tax in federal elections. Two years later, in *Harper v. State Board of Elections,* the Supreme Court held the poll tax violated the equal protection clause of the Fourteenth Amendment in state or local elections.

Another common tactic used by states to disenfranchise black voters was requiring voters to pass literacy tests. The Supreme Court upheld in 1898 a requirement adopted by Mississippi that voters pass an "understanding" test on the provisions of the state and federal constitutions. Literacy tests were finally abolished with the passage of the Voting Rights Act in 1965.

Q 322. What state constitution restricted the right of leaders of the "late rebellion" to vote or hold office?

A The post–Civil War constitution adopted by Arkansas in 1868. It was revised in 1874 to provide that "no power, civil or military," could interfere "to prevent the free exercise of the right of suffrage."

Q 323. Which state constitution denied the right to hold public office to bank officers, clergymen, and anyone who had ever fought a duel?

A Florida's first constitution, adopted in 1845.

Q 324. Which was the first state constitution to give women the vote?

A It is unclear whether the committee that drafted the New Jersey Constitution of 1776 intended to grant women the vote, but that constitution granted suffrage to all free adult inhabitants who were "worth" £50 and resided in the "place of voting for one year." Records showed that election officials interpreted the provision literally to allow propertied single women to vote. Women were encouraged to exercise their vote in a series of fierce electoral battles in the late 1790s. New Jersey politicians voted in 1807 to disfranchise women, as well as African Americans and non-tax-paying whites. Legislators used traditional biological and social arguments of "women's inferiority" to justify their exclusion from suffrage. The Wyoming Territory in 1869 became the first government anywhere to specifically allow women the right to vote.

Q 325. How are state constitutions amended?

A State constitutions spell out how they should be amended. Typically, a state constitution allows the state legislature to propose amendments, often by a three-fourths vote of both houses. Most states also allow amendments to be proposed at constitutional conventions and include directions for the election of delegates. All states, except Delaware, require that constitutional amendments be submitted to the voters for ratification.

Eighteen states also allow voter initiatives to place proposed amendments on the ballot. These initiatives usually require the collection of petitions signed by a percentage of voters who cast ballots for governor in the last state election.

State constitutions are amended more frequently than the U.S. Constitution. One reason for this is that the amending process at the state level is generally easier than that at the national level—only one state need ratify the proposed amendment. At least thirty-eight states must ratify a proposed amendment to the U.S. Constitution, either through state legislatures or state conventions, a process that usually takes at least seven years to complete.

See 51 How is the U.S. Constitution amended?

Q 326. What effort to amend a state constitution became known as the "Magnificent Failure"?

A The unsuccessful effort to amend Maryland's constitution in 1968 is known as the "Magnificent Failure." Proponents of constitutional reform worked painstakingly for two years to write a new constitution in plain and simple language, including a declaration of rights. A last-minute campaign to win public support for the document failed in a climate of racial unrest, after rioting in Baltimore.

Q 327. Which state amended its constitution to allow suffrage for Mormons in 1982?

A Idaho. The state adopted an amendment in 1982 by a vote of 191,474 to 99,713 to allow Mormons to vote, serve as jurors, and hold public office, even though these rights had been acknowledged by the state legislature since the turn of the century.

An anti-Mormon provision was placed in Idaho's constitution in 1890 during a period of widespread anti-Mormon sentiment. It barred from "voting, serving as a juror or holding any public office" an individual "who is a bigamist or polygamist, or is living in what is known as patriarchal, plural or celestial marriage . . . or who, in any manner, teaches, advises, counsels, aids or encourages any person to enter into bigamy." The terms *celestial* and *patriarchal* referred to marriage in the Mormon Church. The constitutional provision was intended to deter the political influence of Mormons, who tended to vote as a political block.

Q 328. Which constitution includes a war song?

A The Constitution of the Iroquois Nations, also known as "The Great Binding Law, Gayanashagowa." If an "obstinate" nation refused to accept the "Great Peace," this constitution, believed to be at least five hundred years old, instructed the war chief of the Iroquois Confederacy of upstate New York to sing the following song as his troops approached the enemy:

Now I am greatly surprised
And, therefore, I shall use it—
The power of my War Song.
I am of the Five Nations
And I shall make supplication
To the Almighty Creator.
He has furnished this army.
My warriors shall be mighty
In the strength of the Creator.
Between him and my song they are,
For it was he who gave the song,
This war song that I sing!

Q 329. Which state constitutions contain anti-abortion amendments?

A The constitutions of Arkansas, Rhode Island, and Colorado. Arkansas and Colorado both prohibit using public funds to pay for abortions except to save the mother's life. Article 1, Section 2, of the Rhode Island Constitution declares, ". . . No person shall be deprived of life, liberty or property without due process of law, nor shall any person be denied equal protection of the laws. No otherwise qualified person shall, solely by reason of race, gender or handicap be subject to discrimination by the state, its agents or any person or entity doing business with the state. Nothing in this section shall be construed to grant or secure any right relating to abortion or the funding thereof."

Q 330. Which state constitutions establish English as the states' official language?

A Arizona, California, Florida, and Nebraska have all adopted constitutional provisions making English their official language. Section 6 of Article III of California's constitution was amended after the passage of a popular initiative in 1986 to say that "(a) English is the common language of the people of the United States of America and the State of California. This section is intended to preserve, protect and strengthen the English language, and not to supersede any of the rights guaranteed to the people by this Constitution. (b) English is the Official Language of the State of California."

Louisiana's first constitution was drafted in French with a "duly authenticated English translation," even though it stipulated that English was Louisiana's official language. Louisiana's current constitution, adopted in 1974, contains no language clause.

331. Does any state constitution protect gays and lesbians from discrimination?

The California Constitution was interpreted by the state's supreme court as prohibiting discrimination against gays and lesbians in *Gay Law Students Association v. Pacific Telephone and Telegraph Company* (1979). California's constitution states that its provisions do not depend on those rights guaranteed in the U.S. Constitution.

The Hawaii Supreme Court ruled in *Baehr v. Lewin* in 1993 that barring same-sex couples from marrying discriminates on the basis of sex and may violate the equal protection clause of that state's constitution. Hawaii's constitution says that no person may be denied equal protection of the law on the basis of religion, sex, ancestry, or race. The court ruled that denying gays access to the rights and benefits of marriage is unconstitutional unless the ban is justified by compelling state interests and is narrowly drawn to avoid unnecessary abridgments of constitutional rights.

Conversely, Colorado's constitution was amended in 1993 to prevent the state from passing laws to protect gays and lesbians from discrimination on the basis of sexual orientation. The U.S. Supreme Court in *Romer v. Evans* (1996) declared this amendment to be in violation of the equal protection clause of the Constitution's Fourteenth Amendment because it infringed on the fundamental right of gays and lesbians to participate in the political process.

332. Which state constitution establishes a right of citizens to review public documents?

Section 9 of Montana's constitution, adopted in 1973, states, "No person shall be deprived of the right to examine documents or to observe the deliberations of all public bodies or agencies of state government and its subdivisions, except in cases in which the demand of individual privacy clearly exceeds the merits of public disclosure." Montana's progressive constitution also imposes term limits on politicians and guarantees the right of a speedy legal remedy "for every injury of person, property, or character."

Q **333. Which state constitution is dedicated to fulfilling the philosophy "Ua mau ke ea o ka aina i ka pon"?**

A Hawaii's constitution of 1959. The state's motto, the phrase translates as "The life of the land is perpetuated in righteousness."

Q **334. What do most state constitutions have in common?**

A Unlike the U.S. Constitution, all but thirteen state constitutions contain a preamble that expresses gratitude to God for the state's civil, political, and religious liberties. Of the states that do not acknowledge God, seven mention a higher power. The constitutions of Colorado, Maine, Missouri, and Washington honor the "Supreme Ruler of the Universe"; Delaware's honors "Divine goodness" and the "Creator"; Hawaii's mentions "Divine Guidance"; and Iowa's acknowledges a "Supreme Being."

States that do not pay homage to either God or a higher power in their constitution preambles include Massachusetts, Oregon, Tennessee, and Virginia. The constitutions of New Hampshire and Vermont do not contain preambles.

VI
THE STATE COURT SYSTEM

IN GENERAL

Q 335. What is a state court system?

A State court systems are the primary means of adjudicating disputes in the United States. Each state has a court system that operates independently according to the constitution and laws of that state. As a result, every state court system is different. However, the basic structure of court systems among the fifty states is similar. Most states have three levels of courts: appellate courts, courts of general jurisdiction, and courts of limited jurisdiction.

All states have at least one state court of last resort that has final jurisdiction over appeals of judgments emanating from lower state courts and jurisdiction where granted by the state constitution and state legislature. Two states, Texas and Oklahoma, are unique in that they each have two courts of last resort, which hear criminal and civil matters, respectively.

Thirty-nine states and Puerto Rico also have intermediate appellate courts. These mid-level courts are typically the first to hear appeals within their jurisdiction, and decide most appeals within the state. Their jurisdiction is limited by law or the court of last resort to specific types of cases or to those arising from particular lower courts.

All states have at least one court of general jurisdiction, the trial court in which the most serious civil and criminal trials are conducted. Most states are divided into judicial districts or circuits to determine the territory of their general jurisdiction courts, with each unit consisting of one or more counties. The names and jurisdictions of these courts vary from state to state. For example, whereas the major trial court in Pennsylvania is called the court of common pleas, in New York it is known as the supreme court, in California as the superior court, and in Massachusetts as the district court. There are approximately twenty-five hundred general jurisdiction courts in the United States.

Forty-four states and Puerto Rico have courts of limited jurisdiction, courts that handle less serious criminal offenses, such as misdemeanors and traffic infractions, and civil cases in which the monetary damages are limited to a specified amount. In criminal cases judges generally are limited to imposing a maximum fine and a jail sentence of twelve months or less. Some states have several different "lower" courts, including small claims, magistrate, and municipal courts. For example, Georgia has nine such courts, Indiana has eight, and Massachusetts has seven. There are approximately 13,900 courts of limited jurisdiction in the United States.

Many states also have courts of special jurisdiction, which may be either courts of general jurisdiction or courts of limited jurisdiction. The jurisdiction of these courts is limited by subject matter. Courts of special jurisdiction include family, domestic violence, juvenile, and probate courts.

Apart from some basic similarities, there is enormous diversity among state court systems. In fact, the organization of a state's court system may differ among counties within the same state. Since the 1980s an increasing number of states have formed a "unified court structure" in which trial courts are consolidated into a single general jurisdiction court level to achieve greater uniformity and enhanced efficiency.

Q 336. Where is the source of state power?

A Governmental authority that is not specifically delegated to the federal government by the U.S. Constitution belongs to the states and to the people. The Tenth Amendment to the Constitution, ratified in 1791 as part of the Bill of Rights, states:

"The powers not delegated to the United States by the Constitution, nor prohibited by it to the States, are reserved to the States respectively, or to the people."

Each state has adopted its own constitution, bill of rights or declaration of rights, and various state statutes that outline the parameters of its authority over its citizens. States cannot impinge on basic rights that are guaranteed to all citizens by the Constitution as interpreted by the Supreme Court.

Q 337. In terms of caseload, how do federal and state courts compare?

A State courts handle the vast majority of all litigation filed in the United States. There were 89.2 million filings in state courts in 1997, compared with 2.3 million filings in federal courts. One study shows that state courts of general jurisdiction handled approximately ninety times as many criminal and twenty-six times as many civil cases as did U.S. district courts in 1994.

Q 338. What is the breakdown of cases filed in state courts?

A In 1997 the following cases were filed in state courts:

- Traffic, 52.6 million
- Civil, 15.4 million
- Criminal, 14.1 million
- Domestic, 5.1 million
- Juvenile, 2.0 million

Q 339. What is the price tag for the nation's justice system?

A The most recent federal study showed that direct expenditures for the nation's justice system totaled $97.5 billion, including all federal, state, and local spending for police, judicial and legal services, and corrections (jails and prisons).

Police protection accounted for $44.04 billion of the total. This category included police departments and buildings, medical examiners, school crossing guards and animal wardens, and so on. Corrections, including prisons and jails, represented $31.96 billion, and judicial and legal services, including courts, prosecutors, and public defenders, represented $21.56 billion.

Of the justice system's total cost, local government paid the largest share: municipalities paid $26.305 billion, and counties, $23.672 billion. The states contributed $30.271 billion, while the federal government paid about $13.529 billion.

Q 340. How has spending for our nation's justice system changed over time?

A Total direct spending on the justice system by the federal, state, and local government from 1982 to 1993 rose by 172.1 percent.

Following are the year-by-year totals:

Year	Total government spending on justice system ($ millions)	Year	Total government spending on justice system
1982	$35,842	1988	$65,231
1983	39,680	1989	70,949
1984	43,943	1990	79,434
1985	48,563	1991	87,567
1986	53,500	1992	93,777
1987	58,871	1993	97,542

Source: Bureau of Justice Statistics, *Sourcebook of Criminal Justice Statistics, 1997* (Washington, D.C.: GPO, 1998).

A In 1993, the most recent year for which statistics are available, the cost of the justice system per capita was $378.39. This cost includes $162.05 for police, $83.63 for judicial and legal services, and $123.93 for corrections (prisons and jails).

A 1990 study showed that courts receive less than a penny of every dollar spent by the state and federal government in the nation. Of the total, 0.7 cents went to judicial and legal services, including courts, prosecutors, and public defenders. This expense compares with 1.4 cents for police protection and 1.1 cents for correctional programs such as jails, prisons, probation, and parole.

In 1990 the nation spent six times as much on social insurance programs as on justice activities, almost five times as much on national defense and international relations, four times as much on education and libraries, and more than three times as much on interest on debt. Social insurance programs include Social Security and Medicare.

Q **342. Who governs the state court system?**

A In forty-three jurisdictions the chief justice of the state court of last resort is the designated head of the judicial branch in that state. The court of last resort governs the state judicial branch in Iowa, Massachusetts, Missouri, Pennsylvania, Texas, Vermont, and Washington. In Utah the Judicial Council is the designated head of the state court system. Chaired by the chief justice of the state supreme court, it consists of fourteen state appellate and lower court judges. It is the policy-making body for the judiciary and has the constitutional authority to adopt uniform rules for the administration of all courts in the state. Governance of the Utah judicial branch generally is determined by the state constitution, state statutes, and rules of the judicial branch.

As with the federal court system, the executive and legislative branches of government have tremendous impact on the state judiciary. Either or both of these branches of government confirm and reject judicial nominees; create judgeships; determine the structure, jurisdiction, and substantive laws of the courts; pass laws affecting judicial discipline and sentencing policy; and determine appropriations and compensation for judges.

Q **343. What is the state court "unification" movement?**

A Historically, new courts were created on both the state and local levels as the need arose, often with their own administration and rules. This resulted in a hodgepodge of courts with overlapping jurisdictions that were incomprehensible to laypersons and many lawyers. In 1906 legal scholar Roscoe Pound, in a speech before the American Bar Association, called the American court system archaic "in its multiplicity of courts, in preserving concurrent jurisdictions, and in the waste of judicial manpower it involves." Pound's comments sparked movements to reform the court system, including the state court unification movement, which has the goal of consolidating trial courts into a single set of trial courts with jurisdiction over all cases and procedures.

In 1997 Puerto Rico, the District of Columbia, and the following eight states had unified court systems: Connecticut, Illinois, Iowa, Kansas, Minnesota, North Dakota, South Dakota, and Wisconsin. Several other states are moving toward establishing a unified court system, including New Jersey and Indiana.

Q 344. How is it determined which cases a state court may hear?

A Federal court jurisdiction is established by the U.S. Constitution and federal law. Everything else, by default, is within the jurisdiction of state courts. Many factors determine which state court is the appropriate forum for a particular case.

The jurisdiction of the highest court in the state is generally determined by the state's constitution and by various legislative enactments. In response to population and economic growth in the 1960s, for example, many states created intermediate appellate courts to relieve the caseload burden on the states' highest appellate courts. These intermediate courts now hear appeals formerly heard by the states' highest courts.

The jurisdiction of lower courts is chiefly determined by the state legislature, which can pass laws creating new crimes or expanding the supervisory authority of the court over noncriminal behavior. In recent years, for example, many states passed laws criminalizing family violence and entitling victims to a wide range of civil remedies. Legislatures also created new tiers of lower courts, such as family, juvenile, and drug courts, for public policy reasons or to handle caseload increases.

The federal government also influences the jurisdiction of state courts by adopting new federal laws that govern behavior once within the realm of state courts or by limiting or expanding the types of cases which can be heard in federal courts.

Q 345. What is diversity jurisdiction?

A The U.S. Constitution gives federal courts jurisdiction over certain cases that would otherwise be heard in state court. This jurisdiction, known as diversity jurisdiction, was originally intended to protect out-of-state citizens from possible prejudice in state courts.

Diversity jurisdiction may be invoked if the parties to the litigation are citizens of different states or if one of the parties is from a different nation, provided the "amount in controversy" is greater than $75,000. Congress has steadily increased the amount-in-controversy requirement in recent years. The requisite amount was $10,000 until 1989, when it was raised to $50,000. Congress raised the requirement again in 1997—to $75,000. There is no amount-in-controversy requirement for cases involving the Constitution, treaties with other nations, and federal statutes or for cases in which the federal government is a party.

Diversity jurisdiction is derived from Article III, Section 2, of the Constitution, which provides that the "judicial power" of the federal courts shall extend to "controversies . . . between citizens of different states" and between citizens of a state and "foreign States, Citizens or Subjects."

Critics say diversity jurisdiction allows lawyers to shop for judges who favor their clients. Proponents say the right to have a case heard in federal court is vital in states dominated by corporate interests that are parties in litigation.

See 67 What is the jurisdiction of federal courts?

Q 346. Where is the dividing line between state and federal court jurisdiction?

A The jurisdictional divide between state and federal courts is constantly shifting. For example, Congress effectively changed the dividing line when it raised the amount-in-controversy requirement—the minimum disputed amount necessary for a case to be considered in federal court—for diversity jurisdiction by a third, to $75,000 in 1997. In one fell swoop, Congress narrowed the caseload of federal courts and expanded that of state courts. More than half of the states have established a state-federal judicial council to address issues of jurisdictional overlap and matters of common concern to state and federal courts.

Q 347. Do state courts make public policy?

A State courts often establish new policy when they review questions involving the state or federal constitution or general legislation and administrative rules, when they exercise discretion in interpreting precedents, and when they innovate when fashioning a ruling. For example, there was no governmental policy in existence governing whether terminally ill citizens have a right to die until the case of *In the Matter of*

Karen Quinlan (1976). The New Jersey Supreme Court, at the request of the family of a permanently comatose patient, ordered hospital officials to remove a respirator that was helping the young woman breathe. Since then, many states have made similar rulings and enacted new legislation that allows people to specify in advance of a terminal illness what kind of treatment they wish to receive. Other areas in which state supreme courts have forged new policy include the equity of school funding systems, land use and low-cost housing, public access to judicial proceedings, the right of free speech on private property, criminal procedure, and gender discrimination.

Q 348. What is merit selection of judges?

A The majority of states use elections to select judges. However, since the 1930s, a growing number of states have adopted a system for selecting judges on the basis of merit. The movement was spearheaded by the American Bar Association to combat the corruption of elected judges controlled by political machines.

Missouri in 1937 became the first state to amend its constitution and establish a statewide nominating committee to select judges. Its citizens were outraged when a barely qualified opponent waged a successful campaign to unseat one of Missouri's most respected jurists after he had incurred the wrath of state political party leaders. Under the Missouri plan, panel members are appointed by the governor and include judges, lawyers, and citizens. The panel nominates a pool of qualified candidates for gubernatorial appointment. The appointee then faces a "retention election" at regular intervals. In a retention election, the candidate is unopposed. Voters are asked simply whether the judge should be retained for another term.

The following eighteen jurisdictions use a system in which the candidates are recommended by a judicial nominating commission and then appointed by the governor, legislature, or both:

Alaska	Hawaii	New Mexico
Arizona	Iowa	Rhode Island
Colorado	Kansas	South Carolina
Connecticut	Maryland	Utah
Delaware	Massachusetts	Vermont
District of Columbia[a]	Nebraska	Wyoming

[a] Presidential appointment, U.S. Senate confirmation.

The following seven states combine a merit selection system with other methods of judicial selection:

Florida	New York	South Dakota
Indiana	Oklahoma	Tennessee
Missouri		

Q **349. What methods of judicial selection, besides the merit system, are used by states?**

A In addition to merit selection, states use the following methods to choose judges: gubernatorial appointment without a nominating commission, nonpartisan and partisan elections, and election by the state legislature.

The following five states use gubernatorial appointment without a nominating commission:

California
Maine
New Hampshire (with approval of elected executive council)
New Jersey (with consent of state senate)
Puerto Rico (with confirmation by Puerto Rico senate)

The following eighteen states use a system of nonpartisan election that formally excludes the participation of political parties:

Florida [a]	Mississippi	Oklahoma [a]
Georgia	Montana	Oregon
Idaho	Nebraska [a]	South Carolina [a]
Kentucky	Nevada	Tennessee
Michigan	North Dakota	Washington
Minnesota	Ohio [b]	Wisconsin

[a] For courts of general jurisdiction.
[b] Candidates are nominated in partisan primaries.

The following twelve states use partisan election, in which candidates run as members of a political party:

Alabama	Louisiana	Pennsylvania
Arkansas	Missouri [a]	Tennessee [a]
Illinois	New York [a]	Texas
Indiana [a]	North Carolina	West Virginia

[a] For courts of general jurisdiction.

In Virginia, the state legislature elects judges. Those in the District of Columbia are appointed by the president.

In virtually every state, the governor fills judicial vacancies that occur before the end of judges' terms of office.

Q 350. How much do judicial elections cost?

A The cost of state judicial election contests has increased dramatically in recent years, and they now resemble the "dashes for cash" of legislative contests, with funds going primarily to pay for expensive advertising campaigns. Public cynicism toward judicial fundraising and the role of money in judicial races has prompted reform movements in several states, including Pennsylvania, North Carolina, Kentucky, and Ohio. A study commission appointed by the Supreme Court of Pennsylvania recommended in 1998 that judicial campaign expenditures be *limited* to $1 million for supreme court office. That's small change in some other states. Candidates spent $4.3 million in an election for a single seat on the Texas Supreme Court in 1996.

Q 351. What limits are placed on candidates in a judicial election?

A Every state has adopted a code of judicial ethics that includes broad statements, called canons, which set forth rules governing the conduct of judges. Candidates for judicial office are generally prohibited from making:

1. pledges or promises of conduct in office other than the faithful and impartial performance of the duties of the office
2. statements that commit or appear to commit the candidate with respect to cases, controversies, or issues likely to come before the court
3. statements that knowingly misrepresent the identity, qualifications, present position, or other fact concerning the candidate or an opponent.

Judicial candidates also may not personally solicit or accept campaign contributions. They must establish committees to secure and manage campaign funds and to obtain public statements of support. Incumbents in states that use merit selection to choose judges can conduct only limited campaigning in retention elections (elections in which voters decide whether a judge should be retained for another term) unless there is active opposition to their retention.

Q 352. How do states police the integrity of judges on the bench?

A Since 1960 every state has formed a judicial conduct organization to review complaints of judicial misconduct and disability. In most states, the state court of last resort reviews the decisions of the judicial conduct organization.

Many states have a two-tier system in which a separate inquiry board, composed of lawyers, judges, and nonlawyers, investigates judicial complaints. If the complaint has merit, the board files it with a judicial conduct commission, composed of judges, to impose sanctions. In some states, such as Illinois, the inquiry board and commission are independent from the judiciary, though members of the judiciary serve on these bodies.

Misconduct charges have been filed against members of state courts of last resort in at least eight states in recent years. Several states create substitute supreme courts to investigate and adjudicate the complaints against justices on the states' highest courts. In California the members of the substitute court are appeals court judges selected by lottery. Other states that have provisions for a substitute supreme court are Alaska, Florida, Georgia, Indiana, Massachusetts, Minnesota, Mississippi, North Carolina, Pennsylvania, and Wyoming.

A judge found guilty of willful or persistent conduct that is inconsistent with a judge's duties is subject to a variety of sanctions, including expulsion, suspension, censure, or private reprimand. A study of judicial disciplinary actions in forty states found that more than a hundred state judges were privately sanctioned, thirty-seven were publicly censured or reprimanded, ten were suspended from office, and sixteen were removed from office. Seventy-five judges were allowed to resign or retire after complaints were lodged against them.

A judicial conduct organization is not an appellate court and therefore lacks the authority to consider or reverse a judicial decision tainted by alleged misconduct. Judicial conduct panels go by many names, including Judicial Supervisory Commission, Judicial Investigation Commission, Judicial Conduct Board, and Commission on Retirement, Removal, and Discipline, among others.

See 84 Can federal judges be fired?

Q 353. What type of judicial conduct is "misconduct"?

A Improper conduct violates the state code of judicial conduct. Generally, improper conduct includes rude, improper, and abusive treatment of parties, counsel, witnesses, jurors, and court staff; conflict of interest; giving or receiving bribes, loans, gifts, or favors; and communicating improperly with one party to a proceeding. Many, if not most, of all complaints involve judicial demeanor.

Among those judges forced to step down was New York chief justice Sol Wachtler, who was convicted and sent to prison in 1992 for threatening to kidnap the teenage daughter of his former, socialite lover and for demanding $20,000 and mailing a condom to the girl.

Pennsylvania Supreme Court justice Rolf Larsen was reprimanded by his fellow justices in 1994 for using court employees to obtain prescription tranquilizers as part of a scheme to keep his psychiatric treatment a secret. Larsen, then in line to become the state's chief judge, accused two benchmates of judicial misconduct, calling them "fix artists." Larsen subsequently was impeached by the Pennsylvania state senate for misbehavior in office and convicted on two counts of conspiring to illegally obtain antidepressants. A grand jury found no credible evidence that Larsen's peers had fixed cases.

Q 354. Do state court judges possess the power of judicial review?

A Yes, state judges frequently are called on to decide whether a state law complies with the state and/or federal constitutions. One study found that the fifty state courts of last resort reverse approximately 23 percent of laws challenged, including 9 percent of laws that involve criminal appeals and 34 percent of those that involve civil liberties. State judges also regularly rule on issues concerning the civil rights and liberties of state citizens, and are free to set standards more protective of individual rights than those guaranteed by the U.S. Constitution.

See 101 What is judicial review? 102 What is the significance of Marbury v. Madison? *103 Was* Marbury v. Madison *the first case to assert the power of judicial review?*

Q 355. Must a state defer to the law of another state?

A In some circumstances. Article IV, Section 1, of the U.S. Constitution requires states to give "Full Faith and Credit . . . to the public Acts, Records, and judicial Proceedings of every other State."

This clause requires, with some exceptions, that states recognize the laws, public records, and judicial decrees of other states. Thus a lawbreaker in one state cannot flee to another state to evade judgment. However, a state has no power to enact laws or decrees governing the conduct of "foreign citizens" in other states or to regulate the territory of other states. Before a person is subject to the authority of a court, the court must have jurisdiction over both the person and the subject matter coming before it.

Q 356. What state court system evolved differently from other state court systems?

A Because its population was predominately of Spanish and French origin, Louisiana followed the legal precedents of these continental countries rather than those of England. Its civil law system is based on the Code Napoleon of 1804. France initially adopted the code to safeguard civil victories won during the French Revolution, including individual liberty, equality before the law, and the lay character of the state. Many parts of the code are traceable to Roman law. The code regulates private law matters such as property, wills, contracts, liabilities, and obligations. It is divided into three "books": "Of Persons," "Things and the Different Modifications of Ownership," and "Of the Different Modes of Acquiring the Ownership of Things." Perhaps the most important part of the code was the fact that the law was written (as opposed to made by judges) in a nontechnical way that was accessible to the public. Under the code, the legislature is viewed as the primary lawmaking body, and it is the duty of judges to apply the law in an equitable fashion. Time has blunted many of the differences between Louisiana's civil code and the civil law of other states.

Q 357. What prominent state court system was once called the worst in the nation, with features reminiscent of medieval England?

A Many state court systems were slow to enter the twentieth century, but New Jersey's achieved notoriety. Before 1947 New Jersey had seventeen distinct classes of courts which operated autonomously, including separate courts for law and equity. Sixteen justices sat on New Jersey's then–court of last resort, derisively referred to as "a little larger than a jury, a little smaller than a mob." New Jersey's governor, in 1938, appointed the twenty-eight-year-old son of a powerful Jersey City mayor to the state's highest court despite the young man's lack of experience and the fact that it had taken him five tries to pass the state bar exam. The American Judicature Society, which promotes national judicial reform, said New Jersey had "the nation's worst court system."

The process of reform of New Jersey's court system began when the state amended its constitution in 1947. New Jersey has unified its court system to include a state court of last resort, an intermediate appellate court, a single court of general jurisdiction, and two courts of limited jurisdiction. Former chief justice Arthur

Vanderbilt (1948–1957) is credited with transforming the state's supreme court into one of the best in the nation. The New Jersey Supreme Court today includes seven members.

Q 358. How many states allow cameras in the courtroom?

A Forty-seven states allowed cameras in trial and/or appellate courts in 1994. In some states, certain types of cases are exempt, such as juvenile and adoption cases, and the permission of the parties and/or the court is required. Jurisdictions that do not allow cameras in the courtroom are the District of Columbia, Indiana, Mississippi, and South Dakota.

Q 359. Do states require judges to participate in ongoing legal education?

A About half of the states require judges to undergo some form of legal education each year.

Q 360. How many states have established a state court gender bias task force?

A Forty-one states and the District of Columbia had established a state court gender bias task force in 1996. Many of these task forces were formed by the state court of last resort or the state bar association. These bodies are working to eliminate gender bias in state courts. Some of the activities the task forces have undertaken include judicial education programs, domestic violence projects, gender bias complaint procedures, amendments to codes of judicial conduct, and increased judicial appointments of women and other minorities. A few states, such as North Carolina and Tennessee, elected not to form a gender bias task force. Instead, North Carolina established an advisory committee on gender fairness and minority concerns within the state's Administrative Office of the Courts, and Tennessee's state bar association conducted open meetings and educational programs on gender bias issues. The other jurisdictions without gender bias task forces are Alabama, Mississippi, Oklahoma, Pennsylvania, South Carolina, Virginia, and Wyoming.

Q 361. How are state court systems funded?

A In 1995 twenty-seven jurisdictions reported that their state provides greater than 60 percent of the funding for the state's courts. The balance of the funding comes from the local (county or municipality) governments. Eight states reported their court systems receive 30 percent to 60 percent of their funding from state sources, and sixteen reported receiving less than 30 percent of their court funding from these sources. (One state, Illinois, did not provide an estimate.)

A few states also rely on court fees to fund or partially fund individual courts of limited jurisdiction, including Connecticut's probate court and Louisiana's justice of the peace and mayor's courts.

Q **362. How are state court costs and fees determined?**

A In most jurisdictions the state legislature is the sole authority for setting the level of state court costs and fees, and mandates the return of some or all of revenues generated by the courts to state coffers. In a few jurisdictions fees are set or subject to approval by the state supreme court. Revenues generated by state court systems, including court costs and fees, can be considerable. Indiana, for example, reported that its court system generated almost $123 million through the operation of all the courts in 1997. Of that amount, 49 percent went to the state, 43 percent to the county, and 8 percent to local government. A total of $31,370,965, or 26 percent, was directed to special programs and funds not related to court operations.

Q **363. Who prepares the budget for state trial courts?**

A Individual courts typically prepare their own budgets and submit them for approval to the chief justice of the state court of last resort, to a budget committee, or to the budget office of the court of last resort and/or the state's administrative office of the court. The budget the judiciary submits to the executive or legislative branch is usually prepared by the court of last resort with the assistance of the administrative office or by the administrative office under the direction of the chief justice of the court of last resort.

The administrative office recommends new positions based on workload and population formulas, purchases and distributes supplies for the courts, collects and reports on statistical information, and oversees the implementation and evaluation of pilot programs such as court-ordered mediation. It also advises the state legislature on the need for judges, prosecutors, magistrates, and clerical employees. Appropriations for those positions and other expenses of the court system go through the administrative office.

Despite its influence in budgetary matters, the administrative office cannot dictate how clerks, district attorneys, or other local court officials use their personnel and cannot discipline judges or others for inadequate performance.

Q 364. What is the state court system's budget process?

A In about half the states, the judiciary's budget is submitted to the executive branch by the chief justice of the state court of last resort or by the state administrative office of the court. The judiciary's budget then may be presented to the legislature by the governor as part of a general appropriations bill or as part of several other bills. In a few states, including Florida, the budget is submitted to both the executive and legislative branches. Florida's governor may only make recommendations to change the judiciary's budget; the legislature has the final word. In some states the judiciary's budget goes directly to the legislature or to the appropriate funding source for approval.

The annual budget period for the judiciary is typically one year, from July to June. In a few states it is October to September. A handful of states have a biennial, or two-year, budget span, which is usually also from July to June.

Q 365. What percentage of a state's budget goes to the judiciary branch?

A In 1993 the state-funded portion of the judicial budget represented from 0.0075 percent (South Carolina) to 2.5 percent (Alabama) of the total state budget. The state-funded portion of the judicial budget of Puerto Rico represented 3.5 percent of that jurisdiction's total budget.

Q 366. Where is the most and least expensive state justice system, per capita?

A The District of Columbia had the most expensive justice system per capita in 1993. It cost $1,257.10 per capita, including $461.28 for police, $245.60 for judicial and legal services, and $550.22 for corrections. Alaska ranked second, at $634.86 per capita.

West Virginia had the least expensive justice system per capita in 1993. It cost $122.88 per capita, including $53.19 for police, $37.35 for judicial and legal services, and $32.34 for corrections. Mississippi ranked second lowest, at $138.54 per capita.

Q 367. How many workers are employed by the state and local justice systems?

A The latest federal study shows that in 1993 a total of 1,825,953 employees worked in the state and local (county and municipality) justice system. Employees include all police, court, and corrections personnel. Of the total, 570,934 employees worked for the state, and 1,093,233 worked for local government. That total compares with 161,786 employees working in the federal justice system. The total number of federal, state, and local employees working in the justice system increased by 41.5 percent from 1982 to 1992.

Q 368. What state spends the most and least on judicial and legal services?

A According to the latest federal study, California spent the most in 1993, $3.28 billion, and North Dakota spent the least, $22.33 million. These figures include direct expenditures for the courts, prosecution, public defense, and legal services. The range of spending reflects, among other things, differences in population and the degree of urbanization in the state.

Q 369. What type of case is filed most frequently in state court systems?

A More traffic cases are filed in state courts than any other type of case. In 1997, 52.6 million traffic cases were filed in state courts.

See 429 Why have traffic filings declined in courts of general jurisdiction?

Q 370. How many states have laws against "frivolous lawsuits"?

A In 1998 at least twenty-nine states had passed laws to penalize litigants who file frivolous or worthless lawsuits. The phrase "frivolous lawsuit" is derived from the Federal Rules of Civil Procedure, which govern the conduct of attorneys in the federal court system. The federal rules are not binding on state court practitioners but serve as a model for similar laws in many states.

The federal rules authorize judges to penalize the filing of a frivolous suit. When filing pleadings, motions, and other papers, attorneys practicing in federal court implicitly indicate that they have conducted a reasonable inquiry and have concluded the action is not frivolous. Sanctions range from monetary penalties to an order to pursue additional legal education. The definition of "frivolous" varies widely among the states but generally includes litigation that is conducted in bad faith for the purposes of harassment or delay, causing needless increase in the cost of litigation, and which is not supported by any reasonable basis in law or equity.

Q 371. How litigious is the U.S. population?

A In 1997 the median number of civil suits filed per one hundred thousand people in the United States was between 5,099 and 5,197. The median represents the middle score. Half of the states had higher rates and half lower.

372. Where are civil suits most and least likely to occur?

A The District of Columbia stood out in 1997 with the largest number of civil filings per one hundred thousand people, 19,648. Almost 90 percent of these filings stemmed from either small claims or landlord disputes. Also, the district is inundated daily with workers from Virginia and Maryland, who become involved in litigation there but are not reflected in the population count.

The district was followed by Maryland, with 17,662 civil filings; Virginia, 15,867; New Jersey, 8,520; New York, 7,527; and South Dakota, 7,397.

The state with the fewest civil filings was Tennessee, which recorded 1,343 per one hundred thousand people for a total of 72,108 lawsuits. Other jurisdictions with low numbers of civil filings were Nevada, with 1,474 per one hundred thousand people; Mississippi, 2,360; Maine, 2,657; Puerto Rico, 2,729; and Texas, 2,992. (The totals for Tennessee and Nevada underrepresented the states' actual filings in that they omitted filings from state courts of limited jurisdiction.)

California, the most populous state, ranks twenty-fourth among the fifty states in terms of the number of civil filings per one hundred thousand people, whereas Delaware, the forty-seventh-most-populous state, ranks tenth because thousands of companies maintain headquarters there.

STATE APPELLATE COURTS

STATE COURTS OF LAST RESORT

In General

373. What is a state court of last resort?

A A state court of last resort is typically established under a state constitution to serve as the highest court in a state, subject to review only by the Supreme Court of the United States in cases involving the interpretation of federal laws or the U.S. Constitution. The state court of last resort generally has final jurisdiction over appeals from decisions of state intermediate appellate and trial courts. It also interprets the state's constitution and determines the constitutionality of state laws.

Most state courts of last resort have exclusive jurisdiction over appeals of final orders imposing the death penalty, appeals of district court decisions declaring invalid provisions of the state constitution, and statewide election contests. These courts generally have broad discretion to consider petitions involving substantial questions of law or public importance. This is especially true in states that have an intermediate appellate court level to handle the bulk of routine appeals. State courts of last resort typically resolve conflicting interpretations of law by lower state courts and questions of law certified to it by state intermediate appellate courts and federal district courts. The decisions of a state court of last resort are published and become the law of the state.

State courts of last resort also have original jurisdiction over a narrow range of matters, which means they handle the case from the beginning. Original proceedings include extraordinary writs or petitions for court orders, such as a writ of habeas corpus by a prisoner seeking release from custody or confinement that he or she considers unlawful.

In 1997 a total of 93,190 appeals were filed in state courts of last resort, compared with 202,085 filed in intermediate appellate courts. However, state courts of last resort do not merely decide appeals. They typically promulgate rules governing the operations of their state's entire court system, including rules of appellate, civil, and criminal procedure. A state's highest court generally has exclusive jurisdiction over who is admitted to the practice of law in the state, what constitutes unauthorized practice of law, and whether an attorney who practices law in the state should be disciplined or disbarred. The court may also administer the oath of office to public officials.

Q 374. Does every state have a court of last resort?

A Yes, and Texas and Oklahoma have two. These states split jurisdiction for final appellate review between separate civil and criminal courts of last resort. In both states the courts of last resort are called the supreme court and the court of criminal appeals. The supreme court handles matters of a civil nature, and the court of criminal appeals decides all criminal matters.

Q 375. What are state courts of last resort called?

A The state court of last resort is called the state supreme court in most states. However, it is called the court of appeals in New York, Maryland, and the District of Columbia; the supreme judicial court in Maine and Massachusetts; and the supreme court of appeals in West Virginia. In both Texas and Oklahoma, the state courts of last resort are called the supreme court and the court of criminal appeals.

Q 376. Where do state courts of last resort generally sit?

A At the state capital. However, many state courts of last resort convene, at the court's discretion, at other locations in the state. For example, West Virginia's supreme court convenes yearly at West Virginia University School of Law. In two states, Idaho and Tennessee, the court of last resort is located in the state capital but is required by state law to sit in other cities. Tennessee's supreme court also sits in Knoxville and Jackson, while Idaho's supreme court also sits in six locations around the state.

Q 377. How large are state courts of last resort?

A Most state courts of last resort contain seven members. The largest courts of last resort have nine members and are located in Alabama, District of Columbia, Iowa, Mississippi, Texas, and Washington. The smallest courts of last resort, each with five members, are located in Alaska, Arizona, Delaware, Hawaii, Idaho, Indiana, Nevada, New Hampshire, New Mexico, North Dakota, Rhode Island, South Carolina, South Dakota, Tennessee, Utah, Vermont, West Virginia, and Wyoming. Oklahoma has a nine-member supreme court and a five-member court of criminal appeals. Louisiana has an eight-member supreme court.

Q 378. What percentage of all cases are appealed to state appellate courts?

A A tiny fraction of the cases disposed of in lower state courts are appealed. In 1997 state courts of general jurisdiction disposed of about 13 million cases. The number of appeals filed in state appellate courts that year totaled 295,275.

The vast majority of cases cannot be appealed because they are disposed of by negotiated settlements or plea bargains. One study showed that in 1988 only 6.1 percent of criminal cases and 9.2 percent of civil cases in trial courts of general jurisdiction concluded with a jury or nonjury trial. In addition, many litigants cannot afford the cost of an appeal, including filing fees, attorneys' fees, and photocopying expenses. Finally, there must be an appealable issue, such as a wrong jury instruction, before a case can be appealed, and most cases do not meet this requirement.

Q 379. What types of appeals are considered by a state court of last resort?

A A state's highest court considers mandatory and discretionary appeals. A mandatory appeal is an appeal of right, or an appeal that the court must hear and decide "on the merits" (after considering legal arguments), such as an appeal of a death penalty sentence. A discretionary appeal is a petition to the court requesting court review that, if granted, will result in the case being heard by the court and decided on its merits.

Mandatory appeals are the smallest segment of caseload in most state courts of last resort. The court hears more discretionary petitions because they often involve important matters of public policy. State courts of last resort reviewed 60,841 discretionary petitions in 1997, compared with 32,349 mandatory petitions, which the court is required to consider.

Q 380. What factors determine the caseload of a state court of last resort?

A The jurisdiction of a state court of last resort is generally set forth in the state's constitution or by state law. A court may have complete discretion over the cases it accepts, no discretion, or a combination of both. A major factor in determining caseload is whether an intermediate appellate court exists in the state to accept routine appeals and free up the state court of last resort to handle matters deemed to have greater impact in the state.

The highest appellate court in Illinois, for example, has virtually complete discretion over its caseload, except that it is required to accept death penalty appeals. Mandatory appeals in Illinois are heard by the state's intermediate appellate court. By contrast, the Supreme Court of Nevada, which has no intermediate appellate court, has little discretion over its caseload because it is the first and only court of appeal in its state court system.

Caseload shifts also occur because of trends in society, such as economic downturns that result in more bankruptcy actions, and as a result of state and federal legislation. For example, in 1995 the Indiana legislature adopted a law raising the sentence for murder to fifty-five years. A pre-existing amendment to the state constitution allows murder defendants who are sentenced to more than fifty years in jail to bypass the state's intermediate appellate court and file appeals directly with the state supreme court. These provisions acting in concert caused the number of mandatory appeals in the state supreme court to double.

From 1987 to 1996, the number of criminal petitions filed in fourteen state courts of last resort that reported statistics to the government increased by 24 percent and the number of civil petitions by 18 percent.

Q 381. Which states receive the largest and smallest number of appellate filings?

A Ten states accounted for a majority of all appellate filings in state courts in 1997: California, 33,361; Florida, 25,005; Texas, 20,096; New York, 18,891; Pennsylvania,

17,770; Ohio, 15,218; Louisiana, 13,319; Illinois, 12,906; New Jersey, 11,395; and Michigan, 11,260.

Eleven states had fewer than 1,000 appeals filed in their appellate courts in 1997: Hawaii, 913; Alaska, 872; New Hampshire, 915; Montana, 872; Maine, 724; Rhode Island, 686; Vermont, 582; Delaware, 551; South Dakota, 432; North Dakota, 402; and Wyoming, 380.

These figures reflect cases filed in both state courts of last resort and intermediate appellate courts.

Q **382. How do state courts of last resort decide whether to accept a discretionary case?**

A The vast majority of state courts of last resort meet *en banc,* or in their entirety, to review petitions for appeal. The exceptions are Iowa, New Mexico, Virginia, and Washington, where a panel of justices decides which cases the entire court will consider. In all but about fifteen states, a majority of the full court or the panel must vote to grant review. In a few states, including New Hampshire, Rhode island, and Virginia, approval by a single justice can grant review.

See 217 When does the court sit en banc?

Q **383. How often do state courts of last resort accept a discretionary appeal?**

A State courts of last resort accepted, on average, 10 percent of the discretionary petitions filed in 1997.

Forty-four percent of discretionary petitions accepted by state courts of last resort in 1997 involved criminal appeals; 34 percent, civil appeals; 11 percent, original proceedings; and 6 percent, other (including disciplinary matters concerning the conduct of judges and attorneys). Five percent were appeals from administrative agency decisions. Original proceedings involve cases the court hears from beginning to end, such as election disputes and petitions for sentence review. In 1997 state courts of last resort denied 39 percent of all discretionary petitions.

Q **384. How many cases are disposed of annually by state courts of last resort?**

A State courts of last resort typically have small backlogs, as these courts have greater control than other courts over their own caseload. Of the 93,190 cases and petitions filed in state courts of last resort in 1997, a total of 89,524 cases and petitions were resolved.

Q 385. How many full opinions are written by justices on state courts of last resort?

A In 1997 state courts of last resort published written opinions in 14 percent of case dispositions. In states without an intermediate appellate court, where the state court of last resort is the only appellate court, the median number of opinions per justice was thirty-seven in 1996. In states that have an intermediate appellate court, which accepts most routine appeals, the median number of opinions per justice was twenty-three in 1996. Full written, published opinions can be cited as precedent in future litigation, clarify the meaning of new laws, and achieve uniformity by resolving conflicting opinions among lower tribunals.

Q 386. What state supreme court devised the "market share" theory of liability?

A In 1980 the California Supreme Court was confronted with a lawsuit by a woman who had developed cancer as a result of a prescription drug taken by her pregnant mother decades earlier. She was unable to ascertain which of the two hundred manufacturers of the drug, DES, a synthetic estrogen, was responsible for her injuries. The court devised an innovative new theory which divided liability for the woman's injuries among the manufacturers according to their market share for the drug. Thus the plaintiff was not required to identify the single manufacturer of the drug used by her mother. The manufacturers could escape liability by showing they could not have produced the dosages consumed by the plaintiff's mother. Several other state courts adopted all or part of the "market share" theory espoused by the California Supreme Court in *Sindell v. Abbott Laboratories.*

Q 387. What percentage of cases decided by state courts of last resort include dissents?

A A high percentage of the decisions of state courts of last resort are unanimous, an indication of the collegiality of these courts. Most state courts report dissent rates below 10 percent, though about a dozen courts report rates above 25 percent.

Q 388. How often is a decision by a state court of last resort appealed to the U.S. Supreme Court?

A State courts of last resort almost always live up to their name. In one study of six thousand state supreme court decisions, only 2 percent were appealed to the U.S. Supreme Court and, of these, only a few were actually considered by the Court.

Some decisions by state courts of last resort cannot be appealed to the Supreme Court. A state's highest court, for example, is the final arbiter for questions that involve only state law. Also, the Supreme Court cannot overturn an opinion of a state court of last resort when it is based on the state's constitution and when the constitution affords more rights than those available under the U.S. Constitution.

However, the Supreme Court may review a state-constitution-based decision if the constitution affords fewer rights than those available under the U.S. Constitution. It also may review all cases that involve substantial questions of federal law. The Supreme Court has virtually complete discretion in determining whether a question of federal law is "substantial."

Litigants must exhaust all proper remedies in the state court system to have "standing" before the Supreme Court.

See 118 What is a federal question?

Q 389. How much does it cost to file a case in a state court of last resort?

A A 1995 study by the National Center for State Courts found that all but two states impose fees to file lawsuits in their respective state courts of last resort. These filing fees varied from a low of $6 in Tennessee to a high of $250 in California, Connecticut, Delaware, Florida, Indiana, Minnesota, New York, and Washington. The average fee was $123.05. North Carolina and Puerto Rico did not impose filing fees for their courts of last resort.

Q 390. Do state courts of last resort strictly adhere to precedents handed down by the U.S. Supreme Court?

A State courts of last resort are bound by the Supreme Court's interpretation of the U.S. Constitution but have been known to evade unpopular decisions, occasionally by open defiance.

In the 1820s the state of Georgia enforced increasingly stringent laws against the Cherokee Indians, prompting the Cherokees to ask the Supreme Court to invalidate these laws. In 1830 the Court ordered a stay of execution in the case of a Cherokee

Indian, Corn Tassles, who had been convicted of murder. Georgia ignored the order and executed Tassles. The Court subsequently decided it had no jurisdiction over the suit in the first place because it had been filed by the Cherokee tribe, technically a foreign nation.

The power struggle between the Court and Georgia reignited in 1832 when Georgia convicted and jailed two missionaries for violating a state law that forbade white persons to live in Indian territory without a state license. The missionaries, Samuel Worcester and Elizur Butler, appealed to the Court, arguing the state lacked the power to impose such a requirement. The Court ruled in *Worcester v. Georgia* (1832) that the state law was an unconstitutional usurpation of federal jurisdiction over Indian matters. However, Georgia refused to release the missionaries. The flap prompted President Andrew Jackson to quip, "Well, John Marshall has made his decision, now let him enforce it." A few months later, South Carolina claimed the right to nullify a federal tariff that it deemed to be unconstitutional. Jackson's sympathies quickly shifted. He asked for, and Congress agreed to grant, an expansion of federal judicial power. Realizing that his state's case had been irreparably damaged, the governor of Georgia pardoned and freed the missionaries.

Appellate courts routinely exercise discretion in the application of federal precedents and may select those that are either more or less expansive. Courts may also creatively interpret the situation at issue in the case under review or give a narrow, literal interpretation of the applicable Supreme Court precedent.

See 4 What is stare decisis?

Q **391. What state supreme court allowed the execution of an "innocent" man?**

A In 1955 the U.S. Supreme Court ordered Georgia to provide a new trial for Aubry Lee Williams, a black man convicted of murdering a white liquor store clerk in Atlanta by a jury chosen using racially discriminatory procedures. The Georgia Supreme Court took the position that the U.S. Supreme Court had no jurisdiction in the matter and that it would not be bound by the Court's judgment. Despite this challenge to its authority, the Court refused to consider the case a second time. Williams was executed on March 30, 1956. Some commentators argue that Williams was "innocent" because a criminal defendant must be considered innocent if his or her conviction is improperly secured.

To select the jurors in Williams's case, a superior court judge drew tickets from a wooden box containing the names of all qualified men in the jurisdiction. The names of white prospective jurors were written on white tickets and the names of nonwhite men on yellow tickets. This practice allowed the state to monitor the number of minorities serving on juries.

Some commentators believe Georgia's defiance sent an unfortunate message throughout the South that the cost of noncompliance with U.S. Supreme Court civil rights rulings was likely to be low.

Just two years later, the Alabama Supreme Court defied a 1958 U.S. Supreme Court order to throw out a temporary injunction issued by a lower court that barred the NAACP from conducting further activities in the state until it produced its membership list. The U.S. Supreme Court said the order violated the U.S. Constitution's guarantee of freedom of association. The Alabama Supreme Court did not comply with the high court's order to remand the case until 1961, earning it a reputation among state supreme courts for having "a particularly notable record for cynical disregard of the law."

Q 392. Why did the Texas Supreme Court recuse itself, en masse, in a 1925 case involving a discriminatory club?

A All members of the Texas Supreme Court of 1925 were forced to recuse themselves in the case of *Johnson v. Darr*, which involved a trust and title dispute between several parties and a fraternal organization known as Woodmen of the World. All justices were members of Woodmen of the World. Texas governor Pat Neff appointed a special three-member court composed of women attorneys—the only attorneys in the area who were not Woodmen of the World. The special chief justice of the panel was Hortense Ward, Texas's first woman lawyer, and Ruth Brazzil and Hattie L. Henenberg were special associate justices. The oath of office required the women to swear that they had never fought a duel. The special all-women court affirmed the ruling of the lower court by deciding in favor of the Woodmen of the World.

Q 393. Which state supreme court was transformed virtually overnight from a conservative bastion of "old stock" Republicans to an activist "prolabor" Democratic majority?

A From the Civil War to 1978, the Ohio Supreme Court was dominated by a succession of conservative WASP Republicans reputedly deferential to big business and insurance companies. In 1978 Democrats obtained a 4–3 majority, and then a 6–1 majority, on the court. The Democratic-majority court, led by a populist Irish Catholic, Frank Celebrezze, proceeded to undo a long line of precedents that had restricted suits against state and local governments, limited medical malpractice claims, and barred compensation for workers injured on the job. Celebrezze subsequently became enmeshed in a dispute with the Ohio Bar Association. He was also embarrassed by an ill-fated bid for the governor's office and began feuding with Republicans on the court, creating what the press called a "circus atmosphere." Ohio's electorate transferred control of the court back to Republicans in 1986. Then, as now, Ohio selected judges through "nonpartisan elections" following nomination in partisan primaries.

Q **394. Why did California voters oust three state supreme court justices in 1986?**

A Judicial retention elections rarely generate any political heat, let alone voter interest, but that was not the case in California in 1986. Three state supreme court justices, including Chief Justice Rose Elizabeth Bird, were denied their bid for retention by voters who considered them weak on the death penalty. The justices had voted to overturn death penalties imposed by California trial courts in 95 percent of the cases the court was asked to review. Bird voted to overturn death penalty cases 100 percent of the time. These justices were replaced by new justices who proved much more willing to sustain death sentences.

Q **395. How many jurisdictions impose time limitations on oral arguments in state courts of last resort?**

A Unlike the U.S. Supreme Court, slightly more than half of all state courts of last resort impose no time limit on oral arguments. Those states that have no limitations are:

Arkansas	Missouri	Rhode Island
California	Nebraska	South Carolina
Connecticut	New Hampshire	Tennessee
Hawaii	New Jersey	Utah
Kansas	New York	Virginia
Louisiana	North Dakota	Washington
Maryland	Ohio	West Virginia
Massachusetts	Oregon	Wisconsin
Mississippi	Pennsylvania	

JUSTICES

Q 396. What do justices on a state court of last resort do?

A All of the justices who sit on a state court of last resort typically hear and decide appeals argued before the court. They decide the appeal after reviewing the written record made during the lower court proceeding, including the trial transcript, as well as written arguments submitted by attorneys with respect to the legal issue in dispute in the appeal. Sometimes attorneys are allowed to make oral arguments buttressing their written arguments. Appellate court judges determine whether the trial court erred by allowing inadmissible testimony, improperly instructing the jury about the law, or misinterpreting the meaning of a statute or the state and/or federal constitution. If the error is serious enough, the court may reverse the lower court's judgment and remand the case for rehearing. Generally, a majority of the court must agree on decisions before they are binding on other state courts.

Q 397. What is the term of office for justices on state courts of last resort?

A Most are elected to fixed terms that range between six and fourteen years (fifteen years in the District of Columbia). Massachusetts and Rhode Island offer appellate court judges lifetime appointments.

Q 398. What is the salary of a justice on a state court of last resort?

A As of January 1, 1997, the salary of an associate justice on a state court of last resort ranged from $68,874 to $133,600, with an average salary of $101,782.

Q 399. What role does the chief justice play on a state court of last resort?

A The role of the chief justice on a state court of last resort is not unlike that of the chief justice on the U.S. Supreme Court. The chief justice serves as the head of the entire state judicial system, oversees statewide judicial administrative and policy-making bodies, and presides over the court of last resort itself.

The duties of the chief justice may include assigning justices and judges to duty in courts that require temporary assistance, supervising the compilation and presentation of the judicial budget to the state legislature, presiding over impeachment proceedings in the legislature, and swearing in state officers, including the state governor.

The chief justice frequently presides over one or more judicial councils or conferences that serve in a policy-making or advisory capacity. These bodies, which often include judges from each level of the court system, conduct studies to improve the system and propose rules and methods of practice and procedure.

The vote of the chief justice has no greater weight on the court than those of other justices, but he or she may exert influence indirectly through administrative functions and the assignment of opinion writing duties.

Q 400. How is the task of writing a majority opinion assigned on state supreme courts?

A In most state supreme courts, cases are assigned randomly, by rotation or by lot, when the appeal is filed or prior to scheduled oral arguments in the case. In these courts, the judge assigned to write the opinion generally has a special responsibility to study the written briefs and to question counsel at oral arguments.

In some states, as with the U.S. Supreme Court, the chief justice assigns a justice to write the opinion after holding a decision conference on the appeal. The decision conference is held as soon as practicable after attorneys present oral arguments to the court. At the decision conference the justices exchange views and tentatively agree on a decision unless a justice requests more time, in which case the decision is made at a later conference.

In most states there is no constitutional or statutory requirement that all cases submitted to the court be decided by a written opinion stating the reasons for the court's ruling. In these states, a cases may be decided with an oral ruling from the bench at the close of oral argument. Many courts dispose of cases by issuing "short orders," which merely say "affirmed" or "denied," or by issuing short, written decisions with a summary one-paragraph explanation of the reason for the court's actions.

All but a handful of state supreme courts publish regular decisions of the court in official reports. Increasingly, state supreme court decisions also may be found at Internet sites maintained by the respective state court systems.

Q 401. How is the chief justice selected on a state court of last resort?

A The most popular method of selecting a chief judge on a state court of last resort is by a vote of the other judges on the court. Other methods are by gubernatorial appointment, seniority, legislative appointment, and rotation of all of the judges on the high court. In two states, Texas and Ohio, the chief judge is elected directly by the people. Judges of the supreme and district courts select a chief judge in North Dakota, while a judicial nominating commission appoints the chief justice in the District of Columbia and Indiana. Many states limit the chief judge's term or require him or her to step down at the age of seventy.

Q 402. Do you have to be a lawyer to be a justice on a state court of last resort?

A All but two states require members of their court of last resort be licensed attorneys. Delaware and Maine require only that the candidate be "learned in the law." Many states also require candidates to have practiced law for at least five years, to be members of the state bar association, to be between thirty and seventy years of age, and to be state residents.

OTHER COURT-RELATED PERSONNEL

Q 403. What does the clerk of the state court of last resort do?

A In many states the state constitution authorizes the state court of last resort to appoint a clerk, who holds office at the pleasure of the court, to keep all papers, records, files, and the seal of the supreme court. The clerk receives all documents filed in cases, circulates that material to the justices, and releases orders and opinions of the court to the public. The clerk may appoint a chief deputy clerk to discharge the duties of the office in the clerk's absence.

Q 404. What does the state court administrator do?

A The state court administrator serves as the liaison among the court system and the legislative branch, the executive branch, the auxiliary agencies of the court, and the national court research and planning agencies. The administrator manages all nonjudicial aspects of the judiciary, including the preparation of the judiciary's budget request and its submission to the state legislature and/or the executive branch. The administrator's office collects data on court operations, oversees management of the court system's physical facilities, and administers alternative sanction programs. The administrator is typically appointed by the chief justice of the state court of last resort. In 1997 salaries of state court administrators ranged from $55,227 to $122,893, with a mean of $89,247 and a median of $86,960.

Q **405. What is the state board of bar examiners?**

A The state board of bar examiners is appointed by the state court of last resort to ensure that only qualified persons are admitted to the practice of law in the state. The board determines the professional competence of applicants for admission to practice by conducting written examinations in subjects determined by the court, investigates the character and other qualifications of applicants, and submits to the court the names of applicants deemed fully qualified for admission to practice. Admission to the bar of the state is finally accomplished by rule of the court.

Q **406. What do the law clerks of the state court of last resort do?**

A Every justice on a state court of last resort is authorized to hire at least one law clerk. Many of these clerks are recent graduates of law school who are serving a one or two-year clerkship. Others are experienced lawyers who are on a career track within the court. Law clerks provide direct legal assistance to the judge by, among other things, researching and drafting opinions. Justices also have a central administrative staff, including a secretary or administrative assistant.

STATE INTERMEDIATE APPELLATE COURTS

In General

Q **407. What are state intermediate appellate courts?**

A Most states have revised their constitutions to create intermediate appellate courts, often called courts of appeal, to handle the increasing workload of the state courts of last resort. In these states the intermediate courts handle the vast bulk of appeals from lower courts in the state. Appellants may ask to bypass the intermediate court and have their appeal heard directly by the state court of last resort, but these requests are usually denied.

The jurisdiction of intermediate appellate courts includes appeals from final judgments or orders of trial courts in cases that are not directly appealable to the state court of last resort. Intermediate appellate courts are generally the first avenue of appeal for all criminal and civil cases in the state court system, with the exception of criminal cases in which the death penalty was imposed and cases that present a question about the constitutionality of a state or federal law. Criminal appeals are brought by defendants convicted at trial, while civil appeals often arise from rulings on motions that dispose of a case prior to trial, such as the dismissal of a claim for lack of merit.

Many state intermediate appellate courts also have the power to review actions taken by state agencies in carrying out the duties of the executive branch of government.

A party who is dissatisfied with the decision of the intermediate appellate court may file a petition for review with the state court of last resort. As with the U.S. Supreme Court, the state court of last resort typically has wide discretion in deciding whether to consider the merits of an appeal. In reality the decision of the intermediate appellate court is the final decision for the vast majority of appeals filed in the state court system. Minnesota's court of appeals, for example, has the final say in about 95 percent of the appeals filed in that state every year.

Q 408. Which states have an intermediate appellate court?

A Thirty-nine states and Puerto Rico have at least one intermediate appellate court. Five states have two.

The following states have one intermediate appellate court:

Alaska	Kansas	New Mexico
Arizona	Kentucky	North Carolina
Arkansas	Louisiana	Ohio
California	Maryland	Oklahoma
Colorado	Massachusetts	Oregon
Connecticut	Michigan	South Carolina
Florida	Minnesota	Texas
Georgia	Mississippi	Utah
Hawaii	Missouri	Virginia
Idaho	Nebraska	Washington
Illinois	New Jersey	Wisconsin
Iowa		

The following states have two intermediate appellate courts. Their jurisdiction is determined either by case subject matter (criminal, civil, tax, and so on) or by which lower court is eligible to file an appeal.

Alabama	New York	Tennessee
Indiana	Pennsylvania	

The following states and the District of Columbia have no intermediate appellate court. In these states, predominately rural and sparsely populated, the state court of last resort hears all appeals.

Delaware	Rhode Island
Maine	South Dakota
Montana	Vermont
Nevada	West Virginia
New Hampshire	Wyoming
North Dakota	

Q 409. What are state intermediate appellate courts called?

A Most state intermediate appellate courts are called courts of appeals. However, the intermediate appellate court is called the appellate court in Illinois, the appellate division of superior court in New Jersey, and the court of special appeals in Maryland. In states with two intermediate appellate courts, the courts are called:

- Court of civil appeals and court of criminal appeals (Alabama)
- Court of appeals and tax court (Indiana)
- Appellate division of supreme court and appellate terms of supreme court (New York)
- Court of criminal appeals and court of civil appeals (Oklahoma)
- Superior court and commonwealth court (Pennsylvania)
- Court of appeals and court of criminal appeals (Tennessee)

Q 410. Where do state intermediate appellate courts sit?

A Most intermediate appellate courts sit in one location, often at the state capital, but may convene elsewhere in the state at the court's discretion. However, eighteen states required their intermediate appellate court to sit in multiple locations in 1993. Each location was a region within the state and usually had its own chief judge and a contingent of permanently assigned judges. These states were:

Arizona	Kentucky	Oklahoma
California	Louisiana	Tennessee
Florida	Michigan	Texas
Idaho	Minnesota	Virginia
Illinois	Missouri	Washington
Indiana (tax court only)	Ohio	Wisconsin

Q 411. What is the caseload of state intermediate appellate courts?

A A total of 202,085 cases and petitions were filed in state intermediate appellate courts in 1997. That total compares with 93,190 cases filed in state courts of last resort.

Q 412. How much of the caseload of intermediate appellate courts is discretionary?

A Very little. The vast majority of the caseload of an intermediate appellate court is represented by mandatory appeals, or appeals the court is required to hear. There were 170,728 mandatory appeals in the caseload of state intermediate appellate courts in 1997, compared with 31,357 discretionary petitions. These courts have far less discretion in determining their workload than do state courts of last resort. In fact, one reason that intermediate appellate courts exist is to handle routine and less consequential appeals so as to free the state court of last resort to handle the most weighty and important matters.

Q 413. What types of appeals are intermediate appellate courts required to hear?

A Criminal and civil appeals dominate the workload of intermediate appellate courts. In 1997 the composition of mandatory appeals in twenty-one intermediate appellate courts was: civil, 40 percent; criminal, 39 percent; administrative agency, 10 percent; original proceedings, 5 percent (postconviction remedy, sentence review, and so on); juvenile, 4 percent; and other, 2 percent.

Q **414. How has the mandatory caseload of intermediate appellate courts changed over time?**

A From 1987 to 1996, the number of mandatory appeals in intermediate appellate courts rose by about 47 percent. This includes a 32 percent increase in criminal appeals and a 15 percent increase in civil appeals. Mandatory appeals, appeals the court is required to hear, comprise the vast bulk of the workload of an intermediate appellate court.

Q **415. What factors influence the caseload of intermediate appellate courts?**

A Many factors influence the caseload of intermediate appellate courts, including the opportunity for indigent criminal defendants to file appeals with the support of public defenders; economic trends, such as a recession that may depress some kinds of litigation while stimulating others; and changes in state laws that shift caseload from the state court of last resort to the intermediate appellate courts.

Q **416. What is the most common action taken by an intermediate appellate court?**

A National statistics are in short supply but, clearly, the vast majority of appeals are rejected at the outset or denied after the court has reviewed the merits of the case. Minnesota's intermediate appellate court, for example, upheld a lower court's ruling in 1,114 cases in 1997, reversed a lower court's judgment in 123 cases, and reversed and remanded (ordered a new trial) in 133 cases. Intermediate appellate courts can reverse or overrule the decision of a lower court, remand the case or send it back to the lower court for reconsideration, modify the judgment, or affirm the decision of the trial court.

Q **417. Which state intermediate appellate court issued the most and fewest published opinions in 1996?**

A Among thirty state intermediate appellate courts that reported dispositions in 1996, Louisiana's intermediate appellate court issued the highest number of full written published opinions, 3,743. The court disposed of a total of 9,797 appeals. An estimated 72 percent of Louisiana's discretionary appeals in 1996 were from prisoners representing themselves.

The fewest decisions were reported by Mississippi's intermediate appellate court, which disposed of 840 cases but issued no full written published opinions. The Mississippi court did issue 645 memorandums of decisions in 1996. These are abbreviated opinions that are sufficient to inform the parties of the court's decision but which generally are not published.

Q 418. How long does it take intermediate appellate courts to clear their cases?

A A study of clearance rates of mandatory appeals in thirty-eight intermediate appellate courts from 1994 to 1996 found that twenty-three such courts cleared fewer cases than were filed, resulting in a backlog. Thirteen states had clearance rates of between 95 percent and 100 percent; six states, rates of between 90 percent and 95 percent; and four states, rates of between 90 percent and 70 percent.

Only fifteen states cleared more cases than were filed. Michigan's intermediate appellate court had the highest clearance rate. It cleared 169 percent of the mandatory appeals filed with the court, which means it removed a significant number of cases from its backlog of cases. The state used a number of innovative techniques, including increasing the number of central staff attorneys, using visiting trial court judges or retired appellate judges, and amending the state constitution to restrict appeals by defendants who pled guilty.

The worst clearance rate was posted in Hawaii's intermediate appellate court, which cleared only 70 percent of the mandatory appeals filed with the court between 1994 and 1996, contributing to a significant growing backlog.

Clearance rates are not solely an indicator of the court's efficiency. The caseload of intermediate appellate courts is closely linked to legislative initiatives, such as new laws providing a right of appeal or legislation shifting jurisdiction from the state court of last resort to the intermediate appellate court. Since the number of appellate court judges in a state remains relatively stable, a sharp increase in appeals may lead to a caseload logjam.

Personnel

JUDGES

Q 419. What do state intermediate appellate court judges do?

A Intermediate appellate court judges generally sit in rotating three- and four-judge panels rather than with the full court sitting *en banc,* or in its entirety. These panels often sit in different locales within the state. The panel considers the written record of the proceedings of the case before the lower court, including the trial transcript. It also reviews written arguments filed by the parties with respect to the legal issue in dispute and, occasionally, hears oral arguments by attorneys in the case. A majority of the panel must agree before the panel's decision is binding on other state courts.

Q 420. How are judges on state intermediate appellate courts selected?

A Most are selected and retained in the same manner as are justices on the court of last resort in their state, through merit selection, partisan or nonpartisan election, or appointment by the governor and/or legislature. They also are subject to the same procedures and conditions for discipline and removal from office. Generally, state intermediate appellate court judges are subject to the same eligibility requirements for appointment to office or election as are justices on the state's court of last resort.

See 348 What is merit selection of judges? 349 What methods of judicial selection, besides the merit system, are used by states?

Q 421. How are chief appellate judges selected?

A The most popular method of selecting a chief judge on a court of appeals is by a vote of the judges' peers. Other methods include appointment by the chief justice of the court of last resort or the court collectively, appointment by the state governor, or appointment by seniority. The chief judge of Texas's court of criminal appeals and court of appeals is selected by partisan election, while South Carolina's legislature appoints the chief judge of its court of appeals.

See 348 What is merit selection of judges? 349 What methods of judicial selection, besides the merit system, are used by states?

Q 422. What is the average salary of a state appellate judge?

A As of January 1, 1997, the salaries of judges of intermediate appellate courts ranged from $79,413 to $124,200, with an average salary of $100,406.

Q **423. What do the support staff of the state intermediate appellate court do?**

A Most intermediate appellate courts have their own clerk, who receives and manages all documents filed with the court and releases orders and opinions of the court to the public. The clerk of the state court of last resort also serves as the clerk of the intermediate appellate court in many states. In most states the clerk is not required to be a lawyer.

Intermediate appellate court judges are permitted to hire at least one law clerk to provide direct legal assistance to the judge by, for example, researching the law and drafting legal opinions and memorandums. Many intermediate appellate courts also have a central staff, which include administrative personnel and, in some cases, lawyers on a career track in the court who serve as law clerks.

STATE COURTS OF GENERAL JURISDICTION

IN GENERAL

Q **424. What is a state court of general jurisdiction?**

A All states have at least one court of general jurisdiction, the highest trial court in the state, where the most serious criminal and civil cases are processed. These courts typically have unlimited trial jurisdiction in all cases except when exclusive jurisdiction is conferred on another court by the legislature or state constitution.

State courts of general jurisdiction typically handle all felony offenses, or those involving violent, property, and drug crime that are punishable by incarceration in state prison. They also handle the dissolution or annulment of marriages, cases involving title to real property (land and buildings), and civil cases in which the monetary damages exceed a certain level. They may also handle matters concerning probate, or the estates of deceased persons, and cases in which nonmonetary relief is sought, such as a request for an injunction. Finally, courts of general jurisdiction may hear appeals from administrative agencies and appeals from lower courts.

Most courts of general jurisdiction hold trials in both criminal and civil cases, but in some areas, especially large, urban communities, they may create separate divisions that specialize in civil, criminal, juvenile, or family law.

The dividing line between the jurisdiction of a state court of general jurisdiction and that of a lesser court is established by the state's constitution or the state legislature. In some instances, courts of general jurisdiction and those of limited jurisdiction hold judicial authority concurrently in the same territory. States are generally divided into judicial districts or circuits to facilitate the administration of the courts and the election of court officials, including judges, clerks, and prosecutors.

State courts reported the filing of 89.2 million new cases in 1997. Filings in general jurisdiction courts accounted for almost 26 percent of the state court caseload, for a total of 23.2 million cases.

Q 425. How many state trial courts are there in the United States?

A In 1997 there were 16,293 state trial courts in the nation, including 2,496 courts of general jurisdiction and 13,797 courts of limited jurisdiction, which typically handle lesser criminal and civil cases.

Q 426. What are state courts of general jurisdiction called?

A These courts have many names, including circuit court in Indiana, district court in Massachusetts, supreme court in New York, superior court in California, and court of common pleas in Pennsylvania.

Q 427. What is the typical caseload of state courts of general jurisdiction?

A The following type and number of cases were filed in state courts of general jurisdiction in 1997:

- Traffic, 8.2 million
- Civil, 6.2 million
- Criminal, 4 million
- Domestic, 3.6 million
- Juvenile, 1.2 million

Q 428. How has the caseload of state courts of general jurisdiction changed over time?

A Significant increases occurred in every major category of cases but one from 1984 to 1997:

- Juvenile, 68 percent increase
- Domestic relations, 77 percent increase
- Criminal, 45 percent increase
- Civil, 34 percent increase
- Traffic, 14 percent decrease

As a result of increases in caseload, about two-thirds of all state court systems could not keep up with the flow of criminal and civil filings between 1994 and 1997. When more cases are filed than are disposed of, a backlog results.

Q 429. Why have traffic filings declined in courts of general jurisdiction?

A Most of the downturn is attributed to the decriminalization of less serious traffic offenses—parking violations. In 1989 a total of 20.6 million parking cases were filed in state courts. That total compares with 6.2 million parking filings in 1997. Does that mean that meter readers aren't writing tickets anymore? No. In some states the traffic caseload has been shifted to an executive branch agency, where the offender pays a fine to a traffic bureau or office rather than going to court. In other states the judiciary has retained authority over traffic offenses but has reclassified them as civil rather than criminal infractions. Traffic filings accounted for more than half of the caseload in state courts of general jurisdiction in 1984. In 1997 traffic filings represented 35 percent of the caseload in those courts. A total of 52,580,727 traffic cases were filed in all state courts in 1997, including 8.2 million filings in state courts of general jurisdiction and 44.4 million in state courts of limited jurisdiction.

Q 430. What state still has a court of equity?

A For centuries the English legal system had two types of courts, common law courts and equity courts. The latter, also called courts of chancery, applied equitable principles when common law courts would not or could not act, or reached results that resulted in an injustice. American state court systems have largely abolished the distinction between law and equity, giving jurisdiction over both matters to state courts of general jurisdiction. However, Delaware continues to operate a court of chancery that deals largely with corporate issues. The court was originally authorized by the Constitution of Delaware of 1792. It decides cases concerning commercial and contractual matters, trusts, estates, and other fiduciary matters and disputes involving the purchase of land and questions of title to real estate.

Delaware's Court of Chancery consists of one chancellor and four vice chancellors who are nominated by the governor and confirmed by the state senate. Appeals from the court of chancery are taken to the state supreme court.

See 13 What is equity?

TRIALS

Q 431. What is a trial?

A A trial is a criminal or civil proceeding in a court of law that has jurisdiction over both the subject matter of the case and the parties. An issue of law or fact is examined in accordance with the rule of law, leading to a decision by a judge or a jury impaneled by the court. A trial is a means of resolving a dispute by providing a fair and impartial hearing to both sides.

Q 432. What is the origin of America's jury system?

A American colonists brought the jury system from England. Until the late eighteenth century the colonists viewed themselves as English subjects living in a foreign land. They regarded themselves as heirs to the individual rights and liberties guaranteed under English constitutional law dating back to the Magna Carta in 1215.

As the New World evolved, the system of judge and jury increasingly was viewed as an important counterweight to the power of the English royal officials. For example, an American jury in 1735 refused to convict John Peter Zenger, publisher of the *New York Weekly Journal,* on a charge of seditious libel for printing harsh criticisms about the governor of the Province of New York.

The right to a trial by jury was incorporated into the U.S. Constitution (Article III) and the Bill of Rights (Sixth and Seventh Amendments). The jury system itself dates back to the ancient Greeks, who met in assemblages of five hundred or more persons called dicasteries to decide disputes by majority vote.

Q 433. How were questions of fact resolved before the jury system?

A Between the ninth and twelfth centuries, trial by ordeal, or *Judicium Dei* (judgment of God), was common in England. Ordeals were appeals to the supernatural to determine the guilt or innocence of the accused. There were four forms of ordeal: hot water, cold water, hot iron, and morsel.

The ordeal of hot water required the accused to plunge his arm into a cauldron of scalding water to retrieve a stone suspended by a cord. The more serious the crime, the deeper the stone. The accused's arm was then bandaged. If after three days the arm was not scalded, the accused was declared innocent.

The ordeal of cold water required the accused to be bound around the knees and lowered into a pool. If the accused sank, he or she was considered innocent and was pulled out of the water. The underlying theory was that one who seeks to hide the truth with a lie cannot be submerged.

The ordeal of the hot iron required the accused to hold a red-hot iron and carry it nine feet. The wound on accused's hand was then bandaged. If festering blood was found in the wound after three days, the accused was judged guilty. If the wound was clean, he or she was declared innocent.

The ordeal of the morsel was for the clergy who, when accused of a crime, were required to swallow a morsel of bread or cheese with a feather in it. If the clergyman gagged, he was found guilty.

Other methods of truth-finding in early England included trial by battle, used when one party accused another of committing a felony against him or his family, and, in civil cases, "wager of law," a medieval-era process by which eleven "oath-helpers" swore on a Bible that the defendant was truthful.

Q 434. How many trials are held nationwide each year?

A State courts of general jurisdiction held 169,065 criminal trials in 1996. The most recent fifty-state estimate indicates that state courts of general jurisdiction held more than 55,000 general civil (tort, contract, and real property) trials in 1992.

Q 435. What percentage of all cases go to trial?

A A small percentage. About 4 percent of criminal cases and 3 percent of civil cases were disposed of by trial in 1997.

Q 436. What is a petit jury?

A A petit jury is a panel of ordinary citizens selected at random from lists of official governmental records, usually voter registration and driver's license lists, to hear evidence and render a decision about the facts in a civil or criminal case. The right to a jury trial is set forth in Article III , Section 2, of the U.S. Constitution. Adopted in 1787, the article states: "The Trial of all Crimes, except in Cases of Impeachment, shall be by Jury, and such Trial shall be held in the State where the said Crimes shall have been committed."

In 1791 the Sixth Amendment to the Constitution further guaranteed defendants in "all criminal prosecutions" the right to a speedy and public trial by an impartial jury. The amendment has been interpreted to mean a defendant has a right to trial in all but petty cases, in which the penalty of imprisonment does not exceed six months.

The Seventh Amendment to the Constitution provides a right to a jury trial in civil cases "where the value in controversy shall exceed twenty dollars." Today, state courts of general jurisdiction require the amount in controversy to be considerably higher, usually at least $5,000.

A petit jury is smaller than a grand jury, an accusatory body that determines whether there is probable cause to charge a citizen with a crime.

See 496 What is a grand jury?

Q 437. What is an "impartial" jury?

A The Sixth Amendment to the U.S. Constitution guarantees criminal defendants the right to a "speedy and public trial, by an impartial jury of the State and district wherein the crime shall have been committed." By "impartial jury" the amendment means a jury must not favor one side over the other. For example, a juror who is a friend or relative of the defendant would likely be prejudiced to acquit the defendant.

Impartial jurors do not have to be completely unaware of a specific case but cannot have formed prejudices based on their knowledge of the case. Mark Twain wrote in 1872 about the futility of trying to find uninformed jurors: "[I]n our day of telegraphs and newspapers," Twain wrote, "the jury system compels us to swear in juries composed of fools and rascals, because the system rigidly excludes honest men and men of brains."

Q 438. How does the court ensure that a jury is truly impartial?

A Two features of jury selection are intended to ensure that jurors are impartial: the *voir dire* of prospective jurors and the exercise of challenges to eliminate a juror for a specific reason (for cause) or for no stated reason (peremptory challenges).

In *voir dire* ("speak the truth") the judge and/or the attorneys question potential jurors in open court about their competency to serve on the jury. Attorneys can file an unlimited number challenges "for cause" to keep potential jurors off a jury panel. An example of a valid cause might be if a juror was obviously biased, could not understand English, or was being asked to serve in a death penalty case and expressed firm opposition to the death penalty under any circumstances.

A peremptory challenge gives the attorney the right to remove or "strike" a potential juror from the jury panel without stating any reason for doing so. A peremptory challenge might be filed if a defense attorney has a gut feeling that a potential juror does not believe the defendant is innocent until proven guilty. Peremptory challenges are controversial because they can be filed for no or any reason, except an illegal one, such as to exclude jurors on the basis of race or gender.

Proponents of peremptory challenges say they achieve impartiality by allowing lawyers to eliminate biased jurors, but opponents say such challenges themselves are a source of racial bias. Some jurisdictions are considering eliminating peremptory challenges altogether or sharply reducing the number that can be lodged.

States allow varying numbers of peremptory challenges, depending on whether the case involves the death penalty, a felony or a misdemeanor, or a civil action. Typically, the highest number of peremptory challenges are given in death penalty cases. Sometimes the prosecutor gets fewer peremptory challenges than does the defense attorney.

Q 439. How many potential jurors are summoned but never serve?

A A 1998 study in the District of Columbia found that four jurors are summoned for every one who actually serves as a juror in the district. Forty-three percent of jury notices never reach the intended people; 19 percent are ignored; and 13 percent reach people who are not qualified to be jurors.

Q 440. Do any states allow jurors to question the witnesses during a trial?

A Only Arizona state courts allow jurors to submit questions for witnesses to the presiding judge in a trial. Arizona made a rule change in 1995 to allow this practice as part of an effort to reform the jury system. Other states are considering similar measures in an attempt to empower jurors and encourage participation in the court system. Another exception to the general rule occurred in 1999 when U.S. senators serving as jurors in President Bill Clinton's impeachment trial were allowed to submit questions to the presiding judge, Chief Justice William Rehnquist, who relayed the questions to witnesses.

441. How large must juries be?

Most states require juries in criminal trials to have twelve jurors. However, the U.S. Constitution does not require this, and an increasing number of states are attempting to maximize their use of jurors by permitting smaller juries, usually composed of six members.

In 1970 the U.S. Supreme Court, in *Williams v. Florida,* ruled that Florida's practice of impaneling six-member juries is constitutional. In 1993 Arizona and Utah used eight-member juries for noncapital felony cases, and Connecticut and Florida used six-member juries for such cases. Some states, including Colorado, Indiana, Ohio, and Virginia, required twelve-member juries for felony cases but allowed smaller juries for misdemeanor cases.

Although most states in 1993 required twelve-member juries in civil trials, about a dozen allowed six- to eight-member juries.

Q **442. Must a jury's verdict be unanimous?**

A Most states follow the federal model and require unanimity for jury verdicts in criminal trials, but at least half of the states do not require unanimity in civil trials.

The U.S. Constitution does not contain any explicit requirement that a jury verdict be unanimous. In 1972 the U.S. Supreme Court upheld the use of nonunanimous verdicts in *Johnson v. Louisiana* and *Apodaca v. Oregon.* The Court concluded that lack of unanimity on the question of guilt is not by itself evidence of reasonable doubt concerning guilt. The Court permitted votes in criminal trials of 10–2 in Oregon and 9–3 in Louisiana.

By 1993 Oregon, Louisiana, and Puerto Rico were the only jurisdictions that did not require a unanimous verdict in trials involving serious crimes or felonies, with the exception of trials involving the death penalty. Oklahoma allowed nonunanimous verdicts in trials concerning less serious crimes or misdemeanors. Many states allow juries to decide civil cases, in which the parties do not face a threat of imprisonment, by a less-than-unanimous vote.

In 1993 the following thirty-three states did not require unanimous verdicts in civil cases:

Alaska	Idaho	Maine
Arizona	Iowa	Massachusetts
Arkansas	Kansas	Michigan
California	Kentucky	Minnesota
Hawaii	Louisiana	Mississippi

Missouri	New York	South Dakota
Montana	Ohio	Texas
Nebraska	Oklahoma	Utah
Nevada	Oregon	Washington
New Jersey	Pennsylvania	Wisconsin
New Mexico	Rhode Island	Wyoming

The following seventeen states and the District of Columbia required unanimous verdicts in civil cases:

Alabama	Illinois	South Carolina
Colorado	Indiana	Tennessee
Connecticut	Maryland	Vermont
Delaware	New Hampshire	Virginia
Florida	North Carolina	West Virginia
Georgia	North Dakota	

Proponents of jury unanimity say it requires the majority to seriously consider the arguments of the minority, who tend to be marginalized when less-than-unanimous verdicts are permitted. Opponents say unanimous verdicts allow one or two aberrant jurors to prevent a panel from reaching a decision. England moved to allow nonunanimous verdicts in 1967.

Q 443. What is a "dynamite instruction"?

A A judge delivers a "dynamite instruction" when a jury reports that it is so divided that it cannot agree on a verdict in a criminal case. In a dynamite instruction the judge reminds the jurors of their obligation to consider the opinions of their fellow jurors and to yield their own views when possible. This type of instruction, prohibited in some states, also is called an "Allen charge," a "shotgun instruction," and a "third-degree instruction." If dynamite instructions fail, the judge is forced to declare a "hung" jury, or a jury that has reached a hopeless impasse.

Q 444. Is there a science to jury selection?

A Prosecutors traditionally tried to keep minorities off juries, especially when the defendant was a minority group member. This practice was a factor in the passage of the federal Jury Selection Act in 1968, which prohibits discrimination in picking federal jurors on the basis of race, color, religion, sex, national origin, or economic status.

Nevertheless, in recent years, a new $200-million-a-year industry, jury consulting, has developed to help lawyers on both sides of the criminal and civil divide select jurors with characteristics favorable to their clients. Consultants hold mock trials and hire surrogate jurors to evaluate the effectiveness of lawyers' strategy. Does it work? In 1972, in what is believed to be the first case in which a jury consultant was used, the jury deadlocked, 10–2, to acquit Catholic priests Daniel and Philip Berrigan of charges that they conspired to commit illegal acts in protesting the war in Vietnam. Critics of jury selection note, however, that the two jurors who voted to convict the Berrigans had been rated prodefense by the jury consultant. Nevertheless, jury consultants claim to have a success rate of at least 90 percent.

Q **445. Does the public have a right to attend a trial?**

A Yes. The U.S. Supreme Court ruled in *Richmond Newspapers Inc. v. Virginia* (1980) that the right of the public to attend a trial is "implicit" in the First Amendment of the Constitution. The First Amendment encompasses not only the right to speak but also the freedom to listen and to receive information and ideas. It also guarantees the right of assembly in public places such as courthouses.

The Supreme Court has ruled that a court may close a proceeding to the public but only after showing that closure is needed to serve a "compelling government interest and is narrowly tailored to serve that interest." This is a very high standard.

In *Globe Newspaper Co. v. Superior Court* (1982), the Court said Massachusetts had violated the First Amendment by conducting a closed trial in a case involving a male accused of raping three minors. The Court ruled that protecting the psychological well-being of a minor, while "arguably a compelling interest," did not justify Massachusetts's mandatory closure law. Furthermore, it stated that "there was no convincing empirical or logical evidence to prove that victims would be more likely to come forward if the press and the public were excluded from trials of this nature."

Just as the public has a right to attend a trial, criminal defendants, according to the Constitution, have a right to receive an open trial. The Framers of the Constitution wanted to discourage secret trials, in which a defendant can be quickly convicted and banished to prison without the public's knowledge.

Q 446. What are the seven phases of a jury trial?

A *Phase one:* The prosecution (criminal case) or the plaintiff (civil case) presents its case to the jury.

Phase two: The defense presents its case to the jury.

Phase three: Both sides offer evidence and testimony to support their cases.

Phase four: Each side gives a closing argument.

Phase five: The prosecution or plaintiff delivers the final, concluding argument.

Phase six: The judge gives instructions to the jury on the meaning of pertinent law in the case.

Phase seven: The jury deliberates and then submits its final verdict to the judge.

Q 447. What is the difference between oath and affirmation?

A An oath is a form of attestation in which a person signifies that he or she is bound by an immediate sense of responsibility to God. A solemn affirmation may be accepted by the court in lieu of an oath. An affirmation is a formal declaration that a statement is true or that the witness will tell the truth. Witnesses at a trial are asked to swear an oath or affirm that they will "tell the truth, the whole truth and nothing but the truth." The phrase "Oath or affirmation" appears in the Fourth Amendment of the U.S. Constitution, which requires that "no Warrants shall issue, but on probable cause, supported by Oath or affirmation."

Q 448. Where do the parties sit in a court proceeding?

A It is customary that the plaintiff, who has the burden of proof, sits closest to the jury and witness boxes.

Q 449. What is evidence?

A Evidence is proof presented at a trial, either by the parties or through the testimony of witnesses, that tends to confirm or deny a fact of consequence to the outcome of the case. Most states have adopted evidentiary rules patterned after the Federal Rules of Evidence, which became effective in 1975 after being enacted by Congress to govern all trials in federal courts. Only relevant evidence is admissible. Evidence is relevant if it makes any fact in dispute more probable or less probable. Evidence may be excluded by the court if it causes prejudice or confusion, or wastes the court's time.

There are many kinds of evidence, including real, demonstrative, direct, and circumstantial. Real evidence is a tangible object that played a role in the event giving rise to the litigation, such as a murder weapon. Demonstrative evidence illustrates a matter of importance in the litigation. An example of demonstrative evidence is a map or diagram prepared by a party in a civil case to show the path of a vehicle involved in an accident.

Direct evidence is evidence that, if believed, resolves a matter in issue, such as eyewitness testimony of a crime. Circumstantial evidence, even if believed, does not by itself resolve a matter in issue. A man seen fleeing from a scene of a crime, for example, did not necessarily commit the crime but may be seeking safety or attempting to alert police.

Q **450. What is hearsay?**

A Hearsay is testimony by a witness who repeats an out-of-court statement made by someone else. For example, a witness might testify that someone else told the witness that the accused stole her purse. Hearsay generally is not admissible as evidence if it is offered to prove the truth of the statement—that the accused stole the purse. The problem with hearsay is that the person who made the statement is not on the witness stand and is unavailable for cross-examination. Hearsay also can be a written statement or an account of nonverbal conduct.

To determine whether the out-of-court statement is admissible, the court must ascertain the reason the testimony was elicited from the witness. The court may permit the testimony if it is used to explain why the witness behaved in a certain way, and not to prove that the accused committed the crime. For example, having heard the third party's out-of-court statement "He stole the purse" may explain why the witness shouted, "Stop, thief!"

There are many exceptions to the rule against hearsay. These are instances when hearsay is admissible as evidence because it has a high degree of reliability. Exceptions to the hearsay rule include

- business records kept in the ordinary course of business
- spontaneous, excited, or contemporaneous utterances
- dying declarations
- declarations by a party that are against his or her own interests
- prior inconsistent statements of an available witness
- admissions made by a coconspirator in the furtherance of a crime.

Q 451. What is discovery?

A Discovery is a process that requires the production of evidence in a civil or criminal case prior to trial to prevent surprise at trial and to encourage settlement. Discovery includes interrogatories, written questions that require answers, and depositions, in which the testimony of a witness is taken under oath.

Q 452. What is the major difference between an expert witness and any other kind of witness?

A An expert witness is entitled to state his or her opinion in a matter that the court has determined is within the expert's area of expertise. Ordinary witnesses may not express opinions.

Q 453. Can a witness refuse to appear at a trial?

A A witness may be compelled to appear in court by a writ or process called a sub-poena (Latin: *sub*, under; *poena*, penalty). The witness must appear at the time specified in the subpoena to give testimony on behalf of the plaintiff or defendant. If a witness is being asked to bring documents, a clause is inserted in the subpoena describing the documents and directing the witness to produce them at trial. In that case the writ is called *subpoena duces tecum* (Latin: You bring with you). An attorney, who is an officer of the court, may obtain the writ from a court clerk and direct the sheriff or another court-appointed employee to serve it to the witness. If the witness fails to appear and has no proper excuse, the court can issue a bench warrant for the witness's arrest, and the witness is subject to a possible fine and imprisonment for "contempt of court."

Q 454. Can a witness refuse to testify at a trial?

A A witness can assert his or her Fifth Amendment privilege against self-incrimination. According to the Fifth Amendment, no one "shall be compelled in any criminal case to be a witness against himself." However, this is a limited privilege. If the court grants the witness immunity from prosecution, the witness is required to testify as long as the testimony cannot be the basis of a later criminal prosecution. Continued refusal to testify under these circumstances could result in a fine or imprisonment for contempt of court.

The Fifth Amendment generally offers no protection to a defendant who is asked to give a blood sample; submit to fingerprinting, photographing, or measurements; write or speak for identification purposes; appear in court; or stand, walk, or make a particular gesture.

Q 455. What is spousal immunity?

A Spousal immunity protects a current spouse from being forced to offer adverse testimony about the other spouse. It is generally available only in criminal proceedings.

In federal courts the privilege belongs to the testifying spouse of a defendant in a criminal case. That is, only the witness spouse can assert the privilege not to testify against the defendant spouse. The defendant cannot block his or her spouse's testimony.

A majority of states recognize the spousal immunity privilege but disagree about who may exercise it. About half of the states follow the federal rule that vests the privilege in the witness spouse, while the other half allow the defendant to prevent the nonparty spouse's testimony.

Q 456. Does any state allow lie detector tests in criminal trials?

A New Mexico was the only state in 1998 to routinely allow lie detector tests in criminal trials. Every other state prohibits or restricts the use of lie detector or polygraph evidence.

A federal appeals court in Washington, D.C., first barred lie detector testimony in 1923 on the grounds that it was not "generally accepted as a reliable technique among the scientific community." The U.S. Supreme Court reiterated that view in 1998 when it ruled that a criminal defendant has no constitutional right to present evidence at trial of having passed a lie-detector test because there is no scientific consensus on the reliability of polygraphs.

Q 457. What is genetic fingerprinting?

A DNA (deoxyribonucleic acid) are molecules in a person's blood cells that contain that person's unique genetic code. DNA typing, sometimes called genetic "fingerprinting," enables police to compare blood, hair, or semen samples found at a crime scene with samples taken from a suspect. In this way police can either make a positive identification or rule out a suspect. The process was introduced in U.S. courts in 1987 and is now generally accepted. The National Research Council, an arm of the National Academy of Sciences, concluded in 1992 that DNA typing was a reliable technique.

Q 458. What is a default judgment?

A A default judgment is entered when a party against whom a judgment for relief is sought has failed to answer or defend the complaint. A default judgment may be entered by a judge or court clerk. Nearly 14 percent of cases ended in default judgment in a 1992 study of civil cases disposed of in state general jurisdiction trial courts. The study covered forty-five of the seventy-five largest counties in the United States.

Q 459. What is a summary judgment?

A A summary judgment is a decision entered by the judge in a civil case when there is no genuine dispute about the facts in the case and one party is entitled to judgment as a matter of law. A summary judgment may be entered for all or part of a case. It is based on the pleadings, statements, and evidence entered into the record without a trial.

Q 460. What is a directed verdict?

A Often, when all of the evidence is in, one of the parties files a motion for a directed verdict. If successful, this motion results in the judge's directing the jury on the verdict it should render. If the plaintiff files the motion, the plaintiff typically argues that the facts established by the plaintiff are both undisputed and sufficient in law to justify a directed verdict. If the defendant files the motion, the defendant usually argues the facts in evidence are both undisputed and require a verdict for the defendant as a matter of law. A motion for a directed verdict can be made at various stages in the trial.

Q 461. What exactly does a judge charge a jury with?

A After both sides have presented their evidence and closing statements, the judge delivers his or her charge to the jury. The judge sums up the evidence in the case and instructs the jury on the law applicable to the case. The judge is the final arbiter of all questions of law. The jury must apply the law in accordance with the judge's charge.

Q 462. Does the jury's verdict end the case?

A No. A verdict represents the jury's finding of the facts in the case, but the judge must accept the verdict. A party may ask for a judgment that is different from the verdict reached by the jury or may move for a new trial. If the judge does accept the verdict, each side may file an appeal to a higher court.

Q 463. What is the doctrine of jury "nullification"?

It is a controversial doctrine holding that in some circumstances juries may acquit a criminal defendant even if there is sufficient evidence of the defendant's guilt. Generally, the doctrine of jury nullification is invoked when the jury believes a law to be unjust or a defendant to be unjustly accused. A modern-day example of the application of this doctrine is the O. J. Simpson trial, in which a predominately black jury in 1995 acquitted the former professional athlete of murdering his ex-wife, Nicole Browne Simpson, and her friend, Ronald Goldman, despite overwhelming evidence of Simpson's guilt. The defense urged the jury to acquit because alleged police racism tainted the investigation of the case. It is not the first time that race apparently played a role in jury deliberations. In 1955 an all-white jury refused to convict white defendants for the murder of a black Chicago teenager, Emmett Till, despite considerable evidence of their guilt.

Q 464. Can a prosecutor file an appeal if an obviously guilty defendant is acquitted by a jury?

A The double jeopardy clause of the Sixth Amendment to the U.S. Constitution prohibits the government from putting a defendant "twice in jeopardy of life and limb" for the same crime. The "clock" for determining whether double jeopardy has occurred starts when a jury has been impaneled and sworn or, in bench trials, when the first witness has been sworn. The double jeopardy privilege is not absolute. For example, a second trial may be permissible if a judge grants a mistrial at the request of the defense, unless the defense was pressured to seek a new trial by the prosecutor or judge.

CIVIL LAW

Q 465. What does civil law encompass?

A Traditionally, civil law was private law. The aim of civil law was not to punish wrongdoers but to compensate victims of intentional or negligent harm. Civil law did not prohibit anything but held persons or corporations responsible for their actions. By contrast, criminal law was public law. It was intended to regulate social behavior and to punish violators, not to compensate the victim.

These categories are still largely accurate, but the dividing line between them has blurred somewhat in modern times. Today, for example, the government enforces noncriminal statutes, such as civil and voting rights laws, while courts routinely order criminal defendants to make restitution to their victims.

Civil law encompasses a broad range of legal areas, including contracts and commerce, consumer fraud, the validity of wills and estates, auto and personal injury accidents, and landlord/tenant relations. The person filing a civil suit is known as the plaintiff, and the person being sued is called the respondent or defendant.

See 11 What is civil law?

Q 466. What is the standard of proof in a civil trial?

A A civil trial is a proceeding to resolve a dispute between two or more parties that involves property or personal rights. These parties may be private citizens, business entities, governmental units, or other organizations. The party who brings the case, the plaintiff, must show by a preponderance of the evidence that the defendant wrongfully caused his or her loss or injury. That means the plaintiff must show it is more probable than not that the defendant is responsible for the harm that occurred. There must be sufficient evidence to overcome a doubt or speculation. If the plaintiff prevails, the defendant is required to pay damages or make restitution but does not face imprisonment. The standard of proof is lower in a civil trial than in a criminal trial because stakes are generally lower. That is, in a civil trial, the defendant does not face loss of freedom.

Q 467. What is a contract?

A A contract is a private agreement between two or more persons or entities that creates an obligation to perform or not to perform a particular act. To reach a contract, the parties must be competent and mutually agree on the same thing. In addition, the agreement must be cemented by legal consideration, or some right, interest, benefit, or profit that accrues to the party who is performing the contract from the party who is benefiting from that performance. A breach of contract occurs when one of the parties fails to live up to his or her part of the contract. Contract law is designed to restore the wronged party to the same position he or she occupied before the breach. Contract law includes commercial and bankruptcy law, creditors rights litigation, and consumer and insurance law.

Q **468. What is a tort?**

A A tort is a private wrong or a personal injury for which the law provides a remedy in the form of an action for damages. Tort claims stem from medical and professional malpractice, motor vehicle accidents, product liability issues, and libel or slander. Torts typically involve injuries to persons, property, or reputation that are caused by negligence or intentional wrongdoing. Under the doctrine of strict liability, a consumer injured by an unreasonably dangerous product does not have to show fault to hold the manufacturer liable for his or her injuries. Tort law has been used to hold corporations accountable for injuries caused by dangerous cars, flammable children's pajamas, dangerous toys, and harmful family planning products. In the twentieth century tort law has stressed compensation for injured persons, placing the cost of accidents and their prevention on businesses and those most able to bear the cost. The word *tort* is derived from the Latin *tortus,* which means twisted or crooked.

Q **469. What happens to civil cases in state courts?**

A According to a 1992 survey of general jurisdiction courts in forty-five urban centers, civil cases were disposed of in the following manner:

- Settlement/dismissal, 61.5 percent
- Default judgment, 13.5 percent
- Dismissed/lack of prosecution, 11 percent
- Transfer, 4.5 percent
- Summary judgment, 3.5 percent
- Arbitration award, 2.7 percent
- Jury trial, 1.8 percent
- Bench trial, 1.5 percent

See 458 What is a default judgment? 459 What is a summary judgment?

Q **470. What type of civil case is most likely to go to trial?**

A Generally, cases involving torts, or personal injuries, are most likely to go to trial. These include cases involving medical malpractice, automobile accidents, product liability, and libel. A total of 49.6 percent of the tort cases filed in 1996 went to trial, compared with 47.9 percent of all contract cases and 2.5 percent involving real property claims. Of all civil cases, a medical malpractice case is the most likely to go to a jury trial.

471. What type of civil jury trials are the most winnable and losable?

A A plaintiff is more likely to win a personal injury case involving "toxic tort" than any other type of case. These are often class-action cases that involve a manufacturer of allegedly dangerous products, such as asbestos. In 1992 the win rate was 73 percent for toxic tort trials in state court and 87 percent in federal court. The median time for these trials is longer than for any other type of case—1,097 days in state court and 1,526 days in federal court. (The median is the middle; half take longer and half take less time.)

The most difficult type of jury trial to win is one involving medical malpractice. In 1992 plaintiffs in malpractice cases won damages in only 30 percent of jury trials in state courts and in only 26 percent of jury trials in federal courts. However, when plaintiffs win, they frequently win big. The largest jury awards go to medical malpractice cases. In 1992 the average jury award in a medical malpractice case was $1.5 million. The median (middle) jury award was $201,000.

Q **472. Is there a tort litigation explosion that is driving up the cost of doing business?**

A According to the National Center for State Courts, no evidence exists to document an explosion in tort litigation in the United States. Between 1975 and 1997 tort filings rose 58 percent in the sixteen states for which data are available. By 1993, more than thirty states had passed some form of legislation limiting the amount of damages a plaintiff can collect. Since then, tort filings remained relatively steady and actually declined by 9 percent from 1986 to 1997 after reaching an all-time high in 1990.

Nevertheless, the rising cost of liability insurance has provoked calls by business groups for "tort reform," or legislation limiting the liability of businesses. Examples of tort reform are so-called no-fault insurance, which requires an injured party's insurer to pay damages arising from an automobile accident, caps on pain and suffering in medical malpractice suits, and comparative negligence laws, which apportion damages according to fault. The American Tort Reform Association (ATRA) reports that in recent years nine states have limited awards of noneconomic damages, and thirty-one states have modified laws governing punitive damages.

The ATRA claims that U.S. sporting goods manufacturers stopped making hockey equipment because of liability concerns and that, as a result, such equipment must be imported from foreign sources. Approximately 60 percent of tort cases filed in state courts involve automobile mishaps.

Q **473. Do plaintiffs more often win or lose jury trials in tort cases?**

A They lose slightly more often than they win. Plaintiffs won 49 percent of jury trials involving torts, or personal injuries, in state courts in 1992. The breakdown by case type and plaintiff "win rate" was:

- Toxic substances, 73 percent
- Automobile, 60 percent
- Professional malpractice, 50 percent
- Intentional, 46 percent
- Premises, 43 percent
- Slander and libel, 41 percent
- Product liability, 40 percent
- Medical malpractice, 30 percent

In federal courts plaintiffs won 55 percent of jury trials involving personal injuries.

Q **474. What is the average jury award in a tort case?**

A The average jury award in state court was estimated to be $408,000 for all personal injury cases in 1992. The median, or middle, award was $51,000. This estimate includes motor vehicle, medical malpractice, product liability, and toxic tort (asbestos) jury trial awards. Federal court jury trials generally resulted in larger awards. In 1992 the average jury award in a personal injury case in federal court was $2,288,000, while the median award was $881,000.

Q **475. What percentage of jury awards in tort cases are over $1 million?**

A Eight percent of jury awards in personal injury cases in state courts are over $1 million. The breakdown by case type is:

- Medical malpractice, 25 percent
- Product liability, 15 percent
- Professional malpractice, 14 percent
- Slander/libel, 14 percent
- Toxic substances (asbestos), 13 percent
- Other torts, 11 percent
- Intentional torts (assault, battery), 7 percent
- Premises liability, 5 percent
- Automobile, 4 percent

Some of these awards were reduced by trial or appellate judges through motions and appeals.

Q 476. What is *res ipsa loquitur*?

A The theory of *res ipsa loquitur* ("the case speaks for itself") is used in cases where the victim has no idea of what caused his or her injury. This theory is invoked when the manufacturer of a product or another defendant was in control and had knowledge of the circumstances surrounding the victim's injury. For example, if a beverage is bottled and capped with a foreign substance inside and an unknowing consumer becomes ill after drinking it, the theory of *res ipsa loquitur* places the burden on the manufacturer to show that it was not negligent.

Q 477. What is the largest damage award in legal history?

A A jury awarded Pennzoil Co. $11.12 billion from Texaco, Inc., in 1989 after finding that Texaco attempted to break up a 1984 merger between Pennzoil and Getty Oil Co. Shortly after the jury award was announced in Houston, Texas, however, the parties agreed to an out-of-court settlement of $5.5 billion. The largest damage award against an individual was a $2.1 billion judgment levied by a federal court jury in 1992 against Charles H. Keating, Jr., the former owner of a California bank, Lincoln Savings and Loan, who allegedly defrauded twenty-three thousand small investors.

Q 478. What happens when the defendant refuses to pay a damage award?

A The plaintiff can place a lien on the defendant's property. A lien is a legal claim to the property that exists until a judgment or debt is paid or the property is sold and the plaintiff is paid. The plaintiff may also petition the court clerk for an order to execute the judgment. This order entitles the sheriff to seize the defendant's property and sell it at auction to satisfy the judgment.

Q 479. What are punitive damages?

A Juries in most states are allowed to award punitive damages in civil cases in which a defendant's actions were willful, malicious, or grossly negligent. Thus in cases where there are very few real damages, a plaintiff can still win a substantial award if punitive damages are assessed. However, punitive damages are a relatively rare event. Only about 6 percent of winning plaintiffs receive punitive damages. Since plaintiffs succeed only about half of the time, punitive damages are awarded in just three percent of jury trials.

Punitive damages are more likely to be awarded in cases in which the injury is financial, rather than personal, such as disputes arising from insurance or employment contracts or from unfair business practices. Overall, 64 percent of punitive damages awarded in state courts in 1992 were distributed in contract cases and only 35 percent in tort cases.

Q 480. Do plaintiffs generally get all of the punitive damages that a jury awards to them?

A No. Punitive damage awards are often reduced by judges, lowered on appeal, or decreased in a posttrial settlement to avoid an appeal. Only about 57 percent of the punitive damages dollars awarded between 1990 and 1994 were actually paid out, according to a study by the RAND Institute for Civil Justice, a nonprofit research institute. RAND examined punitive damage awards from 1960 to 1994 in San Francisco and Cook County, Illinois.

Q 481. What type of tort case is most likely to yield punitive damages?

A The percentage of plaintiffs who won punitive damage awards in tort or personal injury cases in 1992 was:

- Slander/libel, 27 percent
- Intentional tort, 18 percent
- Professional malpractice, 14 percent
- Other tort, 8 percent
- Toxic substance, 7 percent
- Medical malpractice, 3 percent
- Motor vehicle, 3 percent
- Product liability, 2 percent
- Premises liability, 2 percent

Q 482. What other kinds of damages are available in a tort case?

A In addition to punitive damages, a victim can seek compensation for economic loss, including medical expenses, out-of-pocket expenses, and lost earnings, as well as damages for physical pain and mental distress. The victim may also seek to recover any future damages, such as the cost of additional medical treatment. In many states the spouse or children of an injured party also may recover damages, generally for the economic support they have been denied or for the monetary value of lost household services.

Q **483. What is the largest award ever in a tort case?**

A A jury in New York in 1993 awarded a woman $163,882,660 for injuries she sustained when the car in which she was traveling hit a broken-down truck in the fast lane of the New Jersey Turnpike. Shiyamala Thirunayagam was almost completely paralyzed in the 1987 accident. She later agreed to settle the case for $8.2 million for pain and suffering and a guarantee that the defendants would pay up to $55 million in future medical expenses.

The largest lump sum personal injury award to date is a Los Angeles jury verdict on July 9, 1999, ordering General Motors to pay $4.9 billion to six people who were severely burned when the fuel tank of their 1979 Chevrolet Malibu exploded after a rear-end collision. The verdict included $107.6 million in compensatory damages and $4.8 billion in punitive damages. The passengers included a five-year-old girl whose face became horribly disfigured and who lost her right hand. General Motors reported earnings of $3 billion from continuing operations in 1998.

Q **484. What is the going rate for a spilled cup o' java?**

A A jury awarded $2.7 million in punitive damages and $200,000 in compensatory damages to Stella Liebeck of Albuquerque, New Mexico, who was a passenger in her grandson's car when she was severely burned by a cup of McDonald's coffee in 1992. She suffered third-degree burns over six percent of her body and was hospitalized for eight days. McDonald's coffee was heated at between 180 and 190 degrees, higher than the temperature of coffee sold by most other establishments and considerably higher than the average temperature of 135 to 140 degrees for coffee served at home.

McDonald's produced documents showing that more than seven hundred claims had been filed by people burned by its coffee between 1982 and 1992. Liebeck had tried to settle the claim for $20,000. The jury reduced the award for compensatory damages to $160,000 after finding Liebeck to be 20 percent at fault. The trial court subsequently reduced the punitive award to $480,000.

Q **485. What type of contract case is most likely to result in punitive damages?**

A The percentage of plaintiffs who won punitive damage awards in each type of contract case in 1992 was:

- Fraud, 26 percent
- Rental/lease, 12 percent
- Buyer plaintiff, 12 percent
- Seller plaintiff, 5 percent
- Other contract cases, 3 percent

See 479 What are punitive damages?

Q 486. What other kinds of damages are available in contract cases?

A A party in a contract action is entitled to receive compensatory damages in the amount of the loss the party sustained. These are damages that place the aggrieved party in the same economic position that he or she would have been in if the contract had been performed. Traditionally, damages covered the losses caused and the gains prevented by the defendant's conduct.

If there is no monetary loss, nominal damages may be awarded. Nominal damages are usually an insignificant amount—sometimes even just six cents or a dollar—but symbolize the vindication of the wrong done to the plaintiff. In addition, the plaintiff may be entitled to the costs for the action, including attorneys' fees.

Q 487. Do plaintiffs more often win or lose jury trials involving contract disputes?

A Win. In 1992 the win rate for plaintiffs in state court jury trials involving contract disputes was 62 percent. The win rate in federal courts was 60 percent.

Q 488. What is the average jury award in a contract case in state court?

A The average jury trial award in a contract case was estimated to be $620,000 in 1992. The median award was $56,000. Awards tend to be considerably higher than that in federal court jury trials in contract cases. The average federal jury trial award in a contract case was estimated to be $1,849,000, while the median award was $237,000.

Q 489. Have the number of contract cases kept pace with the growth of the economy?

A No. From 1984 to 1997 the nation's Gross Domestic Product grew by more than 30 percent, and the country's population grew by 21 percent. Contract filings declined by 4 percent. Why the decrease? One reason might be a movement among businesses to incorporate clauses in their contracts requiring that disputes be settled by mandatory arbitration rather than in court. Debt collection cases constitute approximately 52 percent of the contract caseload in large urban courts.

Q **490. Are plaintiffs more likely to win a trial in state or federal court?**

A Plaintiffs are more likely to win a civil trial in federal court than in state court. In 1992 plaintiffs in federal court won their civil cases 56 percent of the time compared with 51 percent in state court. As these percentages suggest, there is little difference overall between the win rates in state court and those in federal court, except in a few categories of cases. These include toxic torts, or large-scale product liability cases, in which plaintiffs win 87 percent of the time in federal court compared with 73 percent in state court, and automobile negligence cases, in which plaintiffs win 68 percent of the time in federal court and 60 percent in state court.

Q **491. What is the longest jury trial on record?**

A The civil trial of *Kemner v. Monsanto Co.,* which involved an allegedly toxic chemical spill in Missouri in 1979, was the longest jury trial on record. It lasted more than three years, starting on February 6, 1984, and ending on October 22, 1987. Testimony lasted 657 days. After deliberating for two months, the jury awarded residents of Sturgeon, Missouri, $1 million in compensatory damages and $16.28 million in punitive damages. The award was overturned in 1991 by an appeals court because the jury failed to find that any damage resulted from the spill.

CRIMINAL LAW

Q **492. What is a crime?**

A A crime is a voluntary act committed without justification or excuse in violation of the penal statutes of society. In the U.S. legal system, criminal law is largely statutory—that is, it is composed of laws adopted by the state and federal legislatures. A person is not guilty of a criminal offense unless he or she acted with a "guilty mind," or *mens rea.*

Under the Model Penal Code of the American Law Institute, a defendant demonstrates the requisite criminal intent if he or she acts purposefully, knowingly, or recklessly or with criminal negligence. To act purposefully is to act with a conscious objective to engage in certain conduct or cause a particular result. To act knowingly is to act voluntarily or deliberately. To act recklessly is to act with knowledge of an unjustifiable risk and with conscious disregard of that risk. Criminal negligence occurs when the defendant should have been aware of a substantial and unjustifiable risk and the defendant's failure to perceive this risk was a gross deviation from the standard of care that a reasonable person would have observed in the same situation.

In some cases the state is not required to prove criminal intent because the defendant is held to be strictly liable for the crime regardless or his or her intent. Examples are cases involving statutory rape and sale of alcohol to a minor.

See 12 What is criminal law?

Q 493. What is the source of a criminal defendant's presumption of innocence?

A It is derived from the guarantees provided to criminal defendants in the U.S. Constitution. The Fifth Amendment guarantees that a defendant in a criminal case cannot "be deprived of life, liberty or property, without due process of law." The Sixth Amendment requires that in all criminal prosecutions "the accused shall enjoy the right to a speedy and public trial, by an impartial jury of the State and district wherein the crime shall have been committed . . . and to be informed of the nature and cause of the accusation; to be confronted with the witnesses against him; to have compulsory process for obtaining witnesses in his favor, and to have the Assistance of Counsel for his defence."

Q 494. What is the standard of proof in a criminal trial?

A A criminal trial is a proceeding in a court of law in which the state attempts to prove that one or more defendants committed the crime for which they are charged. The prosecuting attorney, who represents the state, county, or city, must convince a judge or jury beyond a reasonable doubt that the crime occurred and was committed by the defendant. A reasonable doubt means a doubt that would cause a prudent person to hesitate to act in a matter of importance. The prosecutor is not required to establish guilt beyond any possibility of doubt, and the jury cannot acquit for the reason that there is a mere possibility of error. A reasonable doubt must be reasonable, not fanciful or imagined to avoid the unpleasant task of convicting a defendant.

Technically, a criminal defendant is never required to prove his or her innocence. However, in most jurisdictions a defendant has the burden of raising an affirmative defense that would excuse the accused from liability for a criminal act. Affirmative defenses include insanity, duress, necessity, and self-defense. Many states also require the defendant to prove that all requirements of the defense are met. Half of the states require a defendant who raises an insanity defense, for example, to prove that he or she was insane at the time of the crime, while half of the states require the prosecutor to prove the defendant was not insane.

The U.S. Supreme Court in *Patterson v. New York* (1977) agreed that the prosecution has the burden of proving every element of an offense, or crime. However, the Court said that placing the burden on a defendant to prove the insanity defense is not unconstitutional because the sanity of the defendant is not an element of the offense.

See 508 What is the insanity defense?

Q 495. How are crimes classified?

A Crimes are classified as misdemeanors or felonies. Misdemeanors are lesser crimes that carry a maximum penalty of a fine and/or confinement in a county or local jail, usually for not more than a year. Misdemeanors may be processed in state courts of general or limited jurisdiction and include crimes such as driving while intoxicated, selling tobacco to children, prostitution, disorderly conduct, writing bad checks, making harassing telephone calls, and most parking and traffic violations.

A felony is a crime punishable by a term of confinement at a state prison or by death. Felonies are processed in state courts of general jurisdiction and include arson, assault, burglary, murder, rape and kidnapping, and drug distribution.

Q 496. What is a grand jury?

A A grand jury is a body of citizens, numbering from seven to twenty-three members, who decide, usually by majority vote, whether there is probable cause to lodge a criminal charge against a person. It is called "grand" because it is larger than a "petit" jury, which decides a defendant's guilt or innocence. Grand juries are accusatory bodies but do not decide guilt or innocence. If the grand jury believes there is sufficient evidence to prove that a person committed a crime, it votes to issue what is called a "true bill," or indictment. A majority of the jurors must vote in favor of an indictment or the case is "no-billed," or terminated.

A prosecutor decides whether to bring a case before a grand jury, but the prosecutor has no control over the selection of the jurors, who are appointed by a judge. Like members of a petit jury, grand jurors are selected randomly from government lists, including voter registration rolls and driver's license lists. A grand jury's deliberations are secret, and only the grand jurors may be present during voting.

The Fifth Amendment to the U.S. Constitution provides that "no person shall be held to answer for a capital, or other infamous crime, unless on a presentment or indictment at a grand jury." The Supreme Court has refused to make this right binding on the states. Most states have dropped the requirement that all felony defendants be indicted by a grand jury. At least half of the states don't even use grand juries or use them only for a specific type of case. Grand jury indictments have largely been replaced in state courts by the practice of prosecutors' filing charges against criminal defendants, who then appear in court at a preliminary hearing. At the hearing a judge determines whether probable cause exists for the accused to stand trial.

See 436 What is a petit jury?

Q 497. What percentage of grand jury decisions result in a "no bill"?

A Less than 5 percent of all grand jury decisions result in "no bills," or terminations because a majority of the jury did not agree that evidence of a crime is sufficient for indictment. This statistic has led to accusations that the grand jury is a tool of the prosecutor.

Q 498. What is a criminal information?

A An information is a complaint sworn by a prosecutor charging a defendant with a crime. After an information is filed, the defendant is arrested and brought before a judge at a preliminary hearing to determine whether sufficient probable cause exists to hold the defendant in connection with the crime for which he or she is charged. The practice of filing a prosecutor's information has largely replaced the system of indictment by grand jury.

See 549 How does a case get to trial court?

Q 499. Do police need an arrest warrant to make an arrest?

A No. The vast majority of arrests are made without an arrest warrant, an order signed by a judge authorizing police to arrest a defendant. The Fourth Amendment of the U.S. Constitution provides that no warrant can be issued except on probable cause. However, it does not prohibit arrests without warrants. Police can arrest a person without a warrant if the crime is committed in the officer's presence or if the officer has probable cause to believe that someone has or is about to commit a crime. In these cases defendants have a right to a preliminary hearing before a judge, who determines whether there is probable cause for the accused to stand trial.

Q **500. What is probable cause?**

A Probable cause means that the facts being considered would make a reasonably intelligent and prudent person believe the defendant committed the crime of which he or she is accused. If a grand jury or a judge finds there is probable cause to charge a defendant with a crime, the defendant is required to enter a plea in the case. Otherwise, the charge is dismissed.

Q **501. What is an arraignment?**

A An arraignment is a proceeding in which a criminal defendant is presented to a judge or magistrate to enter a plea. The defendant has a right to an arraignment within a specified period of time after his or her arrest, usually forty-eight hours. The judge explains the defendant's constitutional rights and the charge(s) pending against him or her. The judge may also consider the defendant's request to be released on bail or to be released without paying bail based solely on his or her promise to reappear in court again.

Q **502. What is bail?**

A Bail is collateral or property paid or pledged by the defendant to ensure the defendant's future court appearances. The Eighth Amendment to the U.S. Constitution prohibits the imposition of "excessive bail" in criminal cases but does not grant an absolute right to bail to all defendants. In 1952, for example, the Supreme Court voted 5 to 4 to uphold the attorney general's denial of bail to certain foreign Communists who were detained pending deportation proceedings. The Court has also denied bail to dangerous juveniles and organized crime figures.

Q **503. What type of plea can a criminal defendant enter?**

A Most criminal defendants enter one of the following four pleas:

1. *Not Guilty.* This means that you deny guilt and require the state prosecutor to prove the charge against you beyond a reasonable doubt.

2. *Guilty.* You admit that you committed the act charged in the complaint(s), that the act is prohibited by law, and that you have no legal defense for your act.

3. *Not guilty by reason of insanity.* You claim that by reason of mental disease or defect you could not form the intent required to be considered guilty of committing the offense.

4. Nolo contendere, *or "no contest."* This means that you do not wish to contest the charge against you. This plea can be entered only with the consent of the judge. A plea of no contest is an implied admission of guilt but has no effect beyond the particular case (in other words, it can't be used against you in a subsequent civil proceeding.).

Less common pleas include a "plea to the jurisdiction" of the court, which raises an issue of law or questions regarding the authority of the court to try the case. For example, the defendant can argue the offense was not committed within the territorial jurisdiction of the court. Defendants may also plead that they were already acquitted of the offense for which they are charged or that they were tried for the same conduct at an earlier time.

See 508 What is the insanity defense?

Q 504. Must a judge accept a guilty plea?

A No. In fact, the due process clause of the U.S. Constitution prohibits the court from accepting a guilty plea not given knowingly and voluntarily. For this reason, the judge typically questions a defendant to ascertain that the plea was not induced by threats or misrepresentations. The judge explains the charges against the defendant and the burden on the prosecution in the case. The judge also asks if the defendant is fully aware of the consequences of the plea and understands that the court is not bound by any agreements made by the prosecutor.

Q 505. What is a diversion program?

A For some first offenses, such as shoplifting, domestic violence, and certain traffic offenses, the prosecutor may offer the defendant an alternative to the traditional criminal justice process. Charges are dismissed if the defendant successfully completes the diversion program.

Q **506. What is a pardon?**

A A pardon is an "act of grace" that exempts a criminal from the full punishment allowed by the law that he or she has broken. State governors generally have the power to pardon for state crimes, while the president has the power to pardon for federal offenses.

The most famous pardon in U.S. history was President Gerald Ford's pardon of former president Richard M. Nixon on August 9, 1974. Ford became the nation's thirty-eight president when Nixon resigned after the House Judiciary Committee adopted three articles of impeachment in connection with the 1972 break-in of Democratic party headquarters at the Watergate complex in Washington, D.C. A month later Ford granted Nixon an unconditional presidential pardon, sparing the nation a possibly lengthy and perhaps divisive criminal trial but also preventing Nixon from being forced to provide the nation with a full accounting of his alleged misdeeds.

Q **507. When is a defendant competent to stand trial?**

A Generally, defendants are competent to stand trial when they understand the proceedings against them and can assist counsel in their own defense. Defendants who are incompetent to stand trial are committed to a mental institution if there is any chance that they will regain their fitness to stand trial. If not, they are released and subject to civil commitment proceedings that allow the state to indefinitely commit them to a mental institution.

Q **508. What is the insanity defense?**

A Generally, a person who was insane at the time of the crime cannot form the requisite criminal intent to be guilty of the crime. All states have adopted an "insanity defense" that either requires the defendant to produce evidence showing that he or she was insane or requires the prosecutor to prove the defendant was not insane. States have different legal tests for determining whether a defendant was insane.

At least half of the states apply the so-called M'naghten rule, which requires a defendant to show that he or she had a disease of the mind at the time the act was committed that made it impossible for him or her to understand the nature and quality of the act or that it was wrong. This rule was first set forth in England in 1843 in the case of a defendant who was found not guilty after he shot and killed the prime minister's private secretary, believing him to be the prime minister.

The "irresistible impulse" defense allows a finding of insanity if the defendant understood the difference between right and wrong but was unable to control his or her conduct. The Model Penal Code of the American Law Institute requires the defendant to show that, at the time of the act, the defendant lacked the capacity to appreciate the wrongfulness of the act or to conform his or her conduct to the requirements of the law.

On being found not guilty by reason of insanity, a defendant in some states is immediately committed to a mental institution without even a hearing as to whether he or she is still insane. In some states a hearing is automatically conducted by the trial judge or jury to determine if the defendant is still insane. In a few states it is up to the prosecutor to seek the defendant's civil commitment.

Q 509. Is intoxication an excuse for a crime?

A Voluntary, self-induced, or pathological intoxication from drugs or alcohol is not a justification for a crime, but involuntary intoxication may be. The defendant must show that he or she was forced to consume an intoxicating substance against his or her will, or did so by mistake and was unable to form the intent necessary to be considered guilty of committing a crime.

Q 510. Is every defendant entitled to a lawyer?

A No. In *Gideon v. Wainwright* (1963) and in later cases, the U.S. Supreme Court has held that competent counsel and the "basic tools" of the adversary system must be provided to "any person haled into court, who is too poor to hire a lawyer." Some states have taken the position that a court-appointed lawyer is not required in misdemeanor cases or those involving "petty" offenses. However, the Supreme Court ruled in *Scott v. Illinois* (1979) that the Sixth Amendment of the Constitution prohibits the state from sentencing an indigent defendant to a term of imprisonment unless the state affords the defendant the right to assistance of appointed counsel. Thus any indigent defendant facing a possible jail sentence must be afforded a court-appointed lawyer.

Q 511. What are the Miranda warnings?

A In *Miranda v. Arizona* (1966) the U.S. Supreme Court established procedural safeguards that police must meet when interrogating a suspect to protect the suspect's Fifth Amendment privilege against self-incrimination. Ernesto A. Miranda, a suspect in a kidnapping and rape, was arrested at his home and interrogated by police for two hours until he signed a confession. He was never advised of his right to counsel. The Court ruled that suspects held in police custody for questioning must be clearly informed of their right to remain silent, to consult with a lawyer, and to have a lawyer with them during the interrogation. In addition, they must be told that anything they say may be used against them in a court of law. If a defendant is interrogated without an attorney being present, the prosecutor faces a heavy burden to demonstrate the defendant knowingly and intelligently waived his or her right to counsel. If a suspect wants an attorney but is unable to afford one, one must be appointed for him or her before any questioning.

Q 512. What is the exclusionary rule?

A The exclusionary rule is a judge-made doctrine providing that a prosecutor may not use evidence obtained in violation of the U.S. Constitution's prohibition against unreasonable searches and seizures to prove the defendant's guilt. The Fourth Amendment ensures the "right of the people to be secure in their persons, houses, papers, and effects, against unreasonable searches and seizures." The rule, intended to discourage over-reaching by police and prosecutors, has eroded in recent years. The Supreme Court in *U.S. v. Leon* (1984) ruled that prosecutors may use illegally obtained evidence if police seized it in good faith and with a warrant, even if that warrant later was found to be unsupported by probable cause.

Q 513. How many criminal cases are dropped or dismissed before trial?

A About one criminal case in five is resolved by a decision by the prosecutor not to prosecute at this time *(nolle prosequi)* or by the court to drop all charges (dismissal). A prosecutor may decide not to prosecute or to dismiss a case because witnesses are not available or because certain evidence is lacking and the court has refused a postponement. If a *nolle prosequi* is entered before the jury is sworn, it is not a bar to subsequent prosecution of the defendant for the same offense at a later time.

Q 514. What is a plea bargain?

A A plea bargain is an agreement between the prosecutor, representing the state, and the defendant and his or her attorney. Most guilty pleas are the result of a plea bargain. Typically, the defendant agrees to plead guilty to a reduced charge that carries a lesser sentence, or the prosecutor agrees to drop other charges or to recommend a lighter sentence if the defendant pleads guilty. A plea bargain avoids the necessity of a trial, which would be costly to the state and result in an uncertain outcome for the defendant. A judge is not bound by a prosecutor's sentencing recommendation and may impose any punishment within the range authorized by law.

A study of twenty-eight jurisdictions in 1997 determined that the percentage of cases settled by plea bargains ranged from a high of 88.9 percent in California to a low of 36.8 percent in the District of Columbia. Many factors determine whether a jurisdiction encourages plea bargains, including available court resources, prison overcrowding, and the impact of mandatory sentencing laws.

Q 515. What is the median time from arrest to sentencing?

A The median time from arrest to sentencing for all offenses was 143 days in 1994. Jury trial cases took the most time, 251 days. Cases disposed of by guilty plea took the least time, 136 days.

Q 516. What is the likelihood that an arrest for a serious crime will lead to conviction?

A The type of felony arrest and the percentage of defendants who were convicted of this category of felony in 1994 were:

- Murder, 65 percent
- Drug trafficking, 52 percent
- Robbery, 39 percent
- Burglary, 39 percent
- Aggravated assault, 14 percent

Of the total number of convicted felons in 1994, 89 percent pleaded guilty, and 11 percent were found guilty at trial.

Q 517. What percentage of felons plead guilty?

A Eighty-nine percent of convicted felons in 1994 entered guilty pleas, which is a slight decrease since 1988, when guilty pleas accounted for 91 percent of all felony convictions. Six percent of felony defendants were convicted after a jury trial, and 5 percent were convicted after a bench trial.

518. What crimes lead to a felony conviction in state court?

A Property offenses comprised the single largest category of felony convictions in state courts in 1994. The breakdown of the 872,217 felony convictions in state courts was:

- Property offenses, 275,198
- Drug offenses, 274,245
- Violent offenses, 164,584
- Other, 127,180

Q **519. What is the profile of a convicted felon?**

A Eighty-five percent of convicted felons in 1994 were men, despite the fact that men represent only 48 percent of the adult population in the United States. Fifty-one percent of convicted felons were white, and 48 percent were black. Seventy-four percent of convicted felons were in their twenties and thirties. The median age of convicted felons in 1994 was twenty-nine, which represents a slight increase from the median age in 1988, when it was twenty-seven. Seventy-one percent of convicted felons were sentenced to jail or prison in 1994, and 29 percent were sentenced to probation.

Q **520. Who in the adult population is least likely to commit a murder?**

A A very old woman. Only 125 of the 12,359 murders in 1996 were committed by people seventy-five or older, and, of these, only three murders were committed by women.

Q **521. Which states have the least and greatest numbers of felony filings per one hundred thousand people?**

A Of forty-two states reporting statistics, those with the most felony filings per one hundred thousand people in 1997 were:

- District of Columbia, 2,529
- Arkansas, 1,560
- Florida, 1,362
- Virginia, 1,311
- Oklahoma, 1,289

The states with the fewest felony filings per one hundred thousand people in 1997 were:

Q 522. At what point can a child be convicted of a crime?

A Children become criminally responsible for their actions when they are old enough to understand the nature of their actions and the difference between right and wrong. Children under the age of fourteen are presumed to lack this capacity. However, the state may introduce evidence to rebut this presumption in the case of children between the ages of seven and fourteen.

Q 523. Can a person be convicted for doing nothing?

A Yes. A failure to act may constitute a crime if a statute explicitly makes it a crime to omit the act in question or if other factors give rise to a distinct legal duty to act. For example, a taxpayer must file an income tax return, and a caregiver may not neglect a child.

Q 524. What is an "attempted" crime?

A An attempted crime is conduct that goes beyond mere preparation for a crime but falls short of the actual commission of the intended offense. Generally, the prosecution is required to show that the defendant intended to commit the crime and took a step toward its commission.

Q 525. Can one person be a conspiracy?

A Traditionally, a conspiracy occurs when two or more persons agree either to perform a criminal act or to do a lawful act by unlawful means. Under the American Law Institute's Model Penal Code, however, an individual is liable for conspiracy if he or she agrees with another person or persons to commit a crime. Under this formulation, the other person does not have to be part of the conspiracy. Technically, one person can be convicted of conspiracy. In the case of lesser crimes, the state generally must show the defendants acted in furtherance of the conspiracy.

Q **526. Is ignorance of the law ever a defense?**

A There is an old maxim: "Ignorance of the law excuses nobody." However, in many jurisdictions today, ignorance or mistake may be a defense if it prevents the defendant from forming the intent necessary to be considered guilty of violating the law or if the law itself provides that ignorance or mistake is a defense. For example, some courts have held that a reasonable belief that a consenting girl is over the age of eighteen negates a charge of statutory rape.

Q **527. What is "civil disobedience"?**

A Civil disobedience is a deliberate violation of a law that the actor believes to be unfair or unjust for the purpose of demonstrating the law's unfairness or injustice.

Q **528. Can a corporation be convicted of a crime?**

A Yes, but the punishment is limited to a fine, since a corporation obviously cannot be jailed. A corporation can be convicted of a crime when the criminal conduct was performed by an agent acting on the corporation's behalf within the scope of his or her employment or when the offense constituted neglect of a specific duty imposed on the corporation by law. Corporate crimes include failing to file tax returns and bribing public officials.

Q **529. What are the goals of sentencing in the criminal justice system?**

A It is no coincidence that prisons are called "penitentiaries." In the late 1700s, American prisons, such as the Walnut Street prison in Philadelphia, contained solitary cells, approximately eight feet long and six feet wide, designed to encourage prisoners to rethink the course of their lives. Unlike the punitive English system, in which even minor criminals were sometimes executed, the American system attempted to correct criminal behavior by separating criminals from society so that they could reflect and work. In the early 1800s, indeterminate sentences, time off for good behavior, probation, and parole were introduced to give criminals a second chance.

Today, society places much more emphasis on deterring crime, protecting society, and punishing the criminal. The federal government in 1988 passed sentencing guidelines for federal judges and abolished parole. State legislatures began adopting mandatory sentencing laws to eliminate judicial discretion in sentencing. As a result, criminals are spending more time in prison, and state and federal prisons are overcrowded. The average sentence for drug offenders increased 51 percent from 1982 to 1992, to 82.2 months in prison. Between 1990 and 1996 the number of prisoners with sentences of more than one year rose by 54 percent.

Q 530. What are concurrent and consecutive sentences?

A If a defendant receives multiple prison sentences, the court must decide whether the convicted felon will serve the sentences at the same time, or concurrently, with the total time being the period of the largest sentence, or consecutively, one after another, with the total time served being the sum of all of the sentences.

Q 531. What are determinate and indeterminate sentences?

A A determinate sentence is a fixed sentence that reflects the real time that a convicted felon will serve in prison. In effect, the sentence imposed is the sentence served.

An indeterminate sentence is not a fixed sentence. It is a sentence or a sentence range that allows the possibility of the defendant's release into the community after serving less than the maximum sentence.

Beginning in the 1980s, many states and Congress enacted determinate sentencing schemes as a result of public outcry over crime that questioned the legitimacy of indeterminate sentences, time off for good behavior, and the ability of parole boards to identify offenders ready for release. Opponents of indeterminate sentencing believed that criminal laws would better control crime if sentences were certain, less disparate, and more punitive.

An indeterminate sentence for a serious crime such as murder can range from fifteen years to twenty-five years to life in prison, with a release date set by the state parole board after a hearing. In 1993 inmates released from prison had served an average of 38 percent of their sentence, from a high of 54 percent for a rape conviction to a low of 32 percent for drug trafficking.

Q 532. What are intermediate sanctions?

A Intermediate sanctions are virtually any sentence other than incarceration or traditional probation. In 1994 about 41 percent of convicted felons were given a sentence that included intermediate sanctions, such as orders to pay a fine, pay victim restitution, undergo treatment, perform community service, or comply with some other additional penalty (for example, house arrest or drug testing).

Q **533. What is a "three-strikes" law?**

A The federal government and more than a dozen states have adopted "three-strikes" laws for habitual offenders. These laws require judges to levy a sentence of twenty-five years to life in prison for a third serious felony offense.

The first three-strikes law was passed by Washington State in 1993. Other states began adopting these laws in 1994 after Richard Allen Davis, a paroled child kidnapper, abducted twelve-year-old Polly Klaas from her California home and murdered her. California's three-strikes law, passed in 1994, is among the toughest in the nation. Penalties are doubled for a second felony, and a mandatory penalty of twenty-five years to life in prison is imposed for the third felony. The first two felonies must involve violent crimes, but the third is counted regardless of how minor it may be. In addition, defendants convicted under the law must serve at least 80 percent of their sentence before release, compared with 50 percent for almost all other convicted offenders. Get-tough sentencing laws generally result in many more cases going to trial, rather than their being settled in a plea bargain, and they create a demand for more prisons.

Q **534. What percentage of murderers are sentenced to life in prison?**

A About a quarter of defendants convicted of murder or nonnegligent manslaughter are sentenced to life in prison. The average prison sentence for these crimes is 22.5 years.

Life sentences are rare. Only about 0.5 percent of all sentences imposed for all crimes in 1994 were life sentences.

Q **535. How many persons are incarcerated in state and federal prisons and in local jails?**

A As of June 30, 1997, there were 1,158,763 inmates incarcerated in state and federal prisons and 567,079 prisoners incarcerated in local jails. State prisons were operating at between 15 percent and 24 percent above capacity, while federal prisons were operating at 19 percent above capacity. California reported operating at over twice its highest reported capacity (206 percent) and had the most crowded system.

Nearly one of every 150 people in the United States is in a prison or jail. The number is expected to reach 2 million by the millennium, almost double the number of a decade ago. A major factor in the increase is an influx of drug offenders into the prison system beginning in the mid-1980s.

536. How has the total number of inmates changed over time?

A From 1990 through June 1997, the nation's incarcerated population rose by more than a half a million inmates, increasing at an average annual rate of 6.5 percent. The total number of prisoners per year as follows:

Year	Total U.S. prisoners	Year	Total U.S. prisoners
1997	1,725,842	1993	1,369,185
1996	1,646,030	1992	1,295,150
1995	1,585,589	1991	1,219,014
1994	1,476,621	1990	1,148,702

Source: U.S. Department of Justice, Bureau of Justice Statistics, *Bulletin, Prisoners in 1997* (Washington, D.C.: GPO, 1998).

Q **537. How does prison population break down by race?**

A Racial composition of the prison population is as follows:

• White, 544,700 prisoners
• Black, 562,100 prisoners

About 200,400 of the 1,138,984 prisoners who were under state and federal jurisdiction in 1996 identified themselves as Hispanics, who may be of any race. A subsequent 1997 study revealed that most Hispanic prisoners identify their race as white. The study found that 79.8 percent of Hispanic inmates identify themselves as white, while 8.6 percent identify themselves as black and 11.6 percent identify themselves as "other."

Q **538. What is probation?**

A Probation is a system whereby a person convicted of a crime is given a suspended sentence in lieu of a jail term but is subject to supervision by a probation officer for a specified period of time. If the defendant violates the conditions of his or her probation, the defendant's probation can be revoked and the defendant imprisoned for the remainder of his or her sentence. Probation is a substitute for a prison sentence and is contingent on good behavior.

An estimated 29 percent of convicted felons were sentenced to straight probation in 1994, with no jail (county or local) or prison (state or federal) time to serve.

Q 539. What is parole?

A Parole is a convict's conditional release from prison after serving only part of a court-imposed sentence. Prisoners who are paroled are generally supervised by parole officers, to whom they must periodically report, and their parole can be revoked if they violate the conditions of their release.

In 1993 all but about a half-dozen states had parole boards or correctional boards with discretionary authority to release inmates or to supervise prisoners released in accordance with their court-imposed sentence. Maine abolished parole in 1976 but continues to have a parole board to supervise pre-1976 cases.

Q 540. Is the death penalty cruel and unusual punishment?

A According to the U.S. Supreme Court, the death penalty itself does not violate the Eighth Amendment's prohibition against cruel and unusual punishment, but it would if it were applied arbitrarily.

In 1972 the Court, in *Furman v. Georgia,* voted 5–4 to nullify all existing death penalty statutes in the United States because of objections over how the death penalty was applied. The Court held that the arbitrary imposition of the death penalty was cruel and unusual punishment and violated the equal protection clause of the Fourteenth Amendment. The Court also said that penal laws cannot be enforced selectively against unpopular groups.

The federal government and at least thirty-five states subsequently enacted new death penalty statutes that attempt to address the Court's concerns by, among other things, listing specific and aggravating circumstances that warrant the death penalty.

The Court revisited the subject in 1976 and, in a 7–2 vote, approved the reinstatement of discretionary death penalty laws provided that judges and juries are guided by the laws in their application of the death penalty.

In *Gregg v. Georgia* (1976) the Court said the adoption of death penalty statutes by elected state legislatures reflects the public's perception of societal standards of decency, leading the Court to conclude that the death penalty "is not unconstitutionally severe." However, the Court stressed that criminal sanctions must accord with the "basic dignity of man," cannot involve the "unnecessary and wanton infliction of pain," and must not be "grossly out of proportion to the severity of the crime."

The Court subsequently ruled that mandatory death penalty laws are unconstitutional because individual consideration must be given to a defendant's character and to the circumstances surrounding the offense or conviction. The Court also has barred the death penalty in cases of rape.

Q 541. How many states have the death penalty?

A All but twelve states had the death penalty in 1998, as did the U.S. government and military. Those states that did not impose the death penalty were Alaska, Hawaii, Iowa, Maine, Massachusetts, Michigan, Minnesota, North Dakota, Rhode Island, Vermont, West Virginia, and Wisconsin. The death penalty also did not exist in the District of Columbia.

Q 542. How frequently is the death penalty imposed?

A Only about 2 percent of felons who were convicted of murder or nonnegligent manslaughter were sentenced to death in 1994. From 1976 to 1998, a total of five hundred defendants were executed nationwide.

Q 543. How long do prisoners spend on death row?

A For prisoners executed between 1977 and 1996, the average time spent on death row was almost nine years. The forty-five prisoners executed in 1996 spent an average of ten years and five months on death row.

Q 544. What method of execution is most often employed by states?

A Thirty-four states use lethal injection as their primary means of execution. Of the five hundred defendants executed since 1976, more than two-thirds were killed by lethal injection.

The following states permit lethal injection:

Arizona	Idaho	Maryland
Arkansas	Illinois	Mississippi
California	Indiana	Missouri
Colorado	Kansas	Montana
Connecticut	Kentucky	Nevada
Delaware	Louisiana	New Hampshire

New Jersey
New Mexico
New York
North Carolina
Ohio
Oklahoma

Oregon
Pennsylvania
South Carolina
South Dakota
Tennessee

Texas
Utah
Virginia
Washington
Wyoming

The following states continue to permit death by electrocution:

Alabama
Florida
Georgia
Nebraska

Ohio
Oklahoma
South Carolina
Virginia

The following states permit the use of the gas chamber:

Arizona
California
Maryland

Missouri
Wyoming

Three states—Delaware, New Hampshire, and Washington—permit execution by hanging, and two states, Idaho and Oklahoma, permit firing squads under some circumstances.

Q 545. What is the "Execution Capital of the World"?

A Huntsville, Texas, has been dubbed the "Execution Capital of the World." From 1976, when the death penalty was reintroduced in the United States, through 1998, Texas executed 165 defendants. The runner-up in terms of the number of executions is Virginia, which has executed 59 defendants.

Q 546. Is there a minimum age for the death penalty?

A No minimum age is specified in eight states, including Arizona, Idaho, Louisiana, Montana, Pennsylvania, South Carolina, South Dakota, and Utah.

In Mississippi the minimum age by statute is thirteen, and in Virginia the minimum age by statute is fourteen, though in both states the effective minimum age is sixteen. In the remaining states the minimum age at which a defendant can be executed is from sixteen to eighteen. The minimum age is the age of the defendant at the time the crime was committed.

According to human rights group Amnesty International, eight people were executed in the United States from 1990 to 1998 for crimes committed when they were under the age of eighteen. The group reported that in 1998 more than sixty-five people were on death row for crimes committed while they were under eighteen.

The U.S. Supreme Court in a 5–4 decision in *Stanford v. Kentucky* (1989) ruled that imposing the death penalty on a defendant for a capital crime committed when he or she was sixteen or seventeen does not violate the Eighth Amendment ban on "cruel and unusual punishments." The Court pointed to the lack of a consensus in American society regarding the imposition of capital punishment on seventeen- or sixteen-year-olds and said the decision regarding capital punishment for these juveniles must be made locally by the states.

Earlier, in *Thompson v. Oklahoma* (1988), the Court had ruled that executing a person under the age of sixteen is unconstitutional. The Court explained that such an act would violate the "evolving standards of decency that mark the progress of a maturing society." In *Thompson* a plurality of the Court recognized that most other nations sharing the United States' Anglo-American heritage ban the execution of juveniles and that three major human rights treaties explicitly prohibit juvenile death penalties.

Q **547. What did the *New York Times* refer to as the most amazing court scene in Anglo-Saxon history?**

A In *State v. John Scopes*, also known as "The Scopes Monkey Trial," a Tennessee school teacher was charged with teaching Charles Darwin's theory of evolution in violation of a state law. In the first jury trial brought to the public by live radio broadcasts, defense attorney Clarence Darrow called as his sole witness the chief prosecuting attorney, William Jennings Bryan, a three-time presidential candidate who had not practiced law in thirty-six years.

Bryan, who had waged a Fundamentalist crusade to banish Darwin's theory from America's classrooms, said he had studied the Bible for about fifty years. Darrow proceeded to put Bryan's literalist interpretation of the Bible on trial. Did Bryan believe that a big fish had swallowed Jonah whole, that the first woman had been made from Adam's rib, that Joshua had made the sun stand still, that Noah and his ark had been the only survivors of a flood, that all languages dated from the Tower of Babel . . . that the world had been created in six days?

At one point the exasperated Bryan said, "I do not think about things I don't think about." Darrow asked, "Do you think about the things you do think about?" Bryan finally conceded that not every word in the Bible should be taken literally.

Darrow asked the jury to return a verdict of guilty so he could appeal the case. The court fined Scopes $100. Bryan died suddenly five days later of a cerebral hemorrhage. The Tennessee Supreme Court reversed Scopes's conviction on a technicality—because the court, not the jury, had set the fine.

Q 548. Besides the Scopes trial, what are (arguably) the nine most famous trials in American history?

A *Salem witch trials.* The most notorious criminal trial in colonial America occurred in the summer of 1692 when over 150 men and women in Salem, Massachusetts, were accused of witchcraft. The episode began when a group of teenage girls experienced fits that included barking, thrashing about, and shrieking. Under repeated questioning they identified a circle of local residents as wizards and witches. Twenty-seven people were put on trial in Massachusetts General Court. Nineteen people were hanged, including a former minister, and one man was pressed to death for refusing to enter a plea. The trials came to an abrupt halt after the girls named Lady Mary Phips, the wife of the governor, as a witch.

Trial of John Brown. In 1859 Brown and twenty-one abolitionist followers attempted unsuccessfully to seize the federal arsenal at Harpers Ferry, Virginia (now West Virginia). He hoped to kidnap and hold prisoner leading citizens of the town until an equal number of slaves were freed. Brown was charged with murder, treason, and conspiring with "Negroes" to foment an insurrection. Seriously wounded after being bayoneted by his captors, Brown lay on a pallet during the proceedings. His only defense was his assertion that he was an instrument of Divine Providence, a claim that many saw as evidence of insanity. Brown said he would gladly "mingle my blood . . . with the blood of millions in this slave country whose rights are disregarded by wicked, cruel, and unjust enactments." He was convicted by a jury of twelve slave owners and hanged from a gallows surrounded by soldiers to prevent last-minute rescue attempts.

Impeachment trial of Democratic president Andrew Johnson in the U.S. Senate. Johnson appeared to violate the Tenure of Office Act in 1868 when he removed from office Secretary of War Edwin M. Stanton. He was charged with eleven articles of impeachment, including making undignified "utterances, declarations, threats and harangues" against Congress and its members. The underlying reason for the impeachment effort was that Johnson had defied Congress by opposing Reconstruction. Johnson's defense team exposed technical ambiguities in the Tenure of Office Act, prompting seven moderate Republicans to voted for acquittal. The final vote count fell one vote short of the two-thirds majority required for impeachment.

Scottsboro cases. Nine black youths and men known as the Scottsboro Boys, ages thirteen to twenty-one, were convicted in 1931 of raping two white girls, one of whom later recanted the charge. All of them but the thirteen-year-old were sentenced to die in the electric chair. The U.S. Supreme Court in *Powell v. Alabama* held the defendants, represented only at the last minute by a local lawyer, had been denied their constitutional right to adequate representation. They were retried and convicted again. In 1935 the Court in *Norris v. Alabama* ruled the defendants had been denied their right to trial by a fairly chosen jury because blacks had been excluded from the jury pool. From 1936 to 1937 five of the defendants were tried again, were convicted, and served prison sentences in excess of twenty years. Charges against the remaining four were dismissed. One of the defendants, Clarence Norris, received a pardon from Alabama governor George Wallace in 1976.

Sacco-Vanzetti case. Two Italian immigrants, Nicola Sacco and Bartolomeo Vanzetti, self-proclaimed anarchists, were found guilty in 1921 in the murder of a paymaster and guard employed by a shoe company in South Braintree, Massachusetts. Sacco testified, and a witness corroborated, that he had been at the Italian consulate inquiring about a passport when the murders took place. The defendants' radicalism was an issue at the trial. Their execution in 1927 stirred protests around the world.

Rosenberg case. Communists Julius and Ethel Rosenberg, a machine shop owner and his wife, were executed in 1953 for providing secrets about the atomic and hydrogen bombs to the Soviet Union during the cold war. They were allegedly go-betweens for Ethel Rosenberg's brother, David Greenglass, a machinist who was stationed near the atomic testing site at Los Alamos, New Mexico, during World War II. Greenglass, who identified the Rosenbergs as his spymasters, received a sentence of fifteen years in prison in exchange for his cooperation. The Rosenbergs, who denied everything, were the first Americans to be sentenced to death for espionage in peacetime.

Leopold and Loeb case. The "perfect murder" by two brilliant and wealthy teenagers, Nathan Leopold, nineteen, and Richard Loeb, eighteen, went awry when one of them forgot his prescription glasses at the scene. The boys, then the youngest people ever to graduate from college in Illinois, thought they belonged to German philosopher Friedrich Nietzsche's race of "supermen." They murdered Loeb's fourteen-year-old cousin with a chisel and sexually assaulted him. They escaped the gallows by virtue of a passionate defense by death penalty opponent Clarence Darrow and instead were sentenced to life in prison.

Trial of the Chicago Seven. Eight defendants were accused of conspiring to incite the riots at the Democratic National Convention in Chicago in 1968. Radicals Abbie Hoffman and Jerry Rubin, self-described Yippies, rejected the law and traditional legal strategies, taunted the judge, and generally created a circus atmosphere. A mistrial was declared in the case of defendant Bobby Seale, a militant Black Panther whom the judge ordered bound and gagged for three days in the courtroom. Five defendants were found guilty, but their convictions were overturned by an appeals court, which cited the judge's overt hostility toward the defendants.

O. J. Simpson case. Despite what seemed to be overwhelming evidence of his guilt, a jury acquitted Simpson, a famous African American former football player, in the murders of his white ex-wife, Nicole Simpson, and her friend, Ronald Goldman. This 1995 "trial of the century" was a media spectacle that highlighted racial tensions in the country when the defense focused on the issue of racist conduct by members of the Los Angeles Police Department. Simpson was subsequently found liable for the murders in a civil trial for monetary damages. Between January 24 and October 3, 1995, a daily average of 5.5 million people watched live coverage of the trial, the largest number to watch any trial in history.

GETTING THERE

Q 549. How does a case get to a trial court?

A In the case of a felony, a grand jury files a bill of indictment charging a defendant with a crime, or a prosecutor files a criminal information charging the defendant with a crime. Arraignment before a judge precedes a hearing in trial court.

In the case of a civil suit, the plaintiff files a complaint in the court clerk's office. Notice is served on the defendant, who must answer the complaint, and the dispute is decided in a trial court.

Q 550. What is the avenue of appeal from a trial court?

A An appeal from trial court proceeds to an intermediate appellate court. A second appeal may be made to a state court of last resort.

See 501 What is an arraignment?

Q 551. What do judges on courts of general jurisdiction do?

A Judges on courts of general jurisdiction are primarily trial judges. They determine all questions of law and enforce established rules of procedure and evidence. Even before a case is ready for a trial, the judge has typically ruled on numerous pretrial motions and, in civil cases, has presided over a settlement conference. In a case that is tried before a jury, the judge oversees the jury selection process and impanels the jury. When all the evidence is in and the parties have completed their final arguments, the judge sums up the evidence and explains important legal principles to the jury, which must apply those principles to the facts of the case.

The judge ensures that the proceedings are not tainted with improper contact between jurors and the parties or between the parties and the judge. If a plaintiff in a civil case or a criminal defendant waives the right to a jury trial, the judge serves as both the sole judge of the facts in the case and the final arbiter of the law. A trial judge makes many rulings during the course of a trial with respect to the way in which attorneys question witnesses and present their case. These rulings are subject to appeal to a higher court, which, in the event of an egregious error, could order a new trial in the case.

In 1997 there were 10,007 judges serving in state courts of general jurisdiction and 18,553 in courts of limited or special jurisdiction.

Q 552. Must a judge on a state court of general jurisdiction be a lawyer?

A The qualifications of judges on courts of general jurisdiction are established by state statute or in the state's constitution. In virtually every state a law degree is a prerequisite. Delaware and Maine are exceptions to this rule, requiring judges only to be "learned in the law." Many states also require judges to be within a certain age range (eighteen to seventy-five), to have practiced law for a certain number of years, and to be residents of the appointing state.

Q 553. How has the number of judges on state courts of general jurisdiction changed over time?

A After climbing steadily from 1990 to 1996, the number of judges and quasi-judicial officers on state courts of general jurisdiction dropped slightly in 1997. The year and number of judicial officers employed were as follows:

Year	Judges on state courts of general jurisdiction	Year	Judges on state courts of general jurisdiction
1997	10,007	1993	8,859
1996	10,114	1992	8,700
1995	9,214	1991	8,649
1994	8,877	1990	8,586

Q **554. Which states have the largest and smallest number of judges on state courts of general jurisdiction?**

A The states with the largest number of authorized judges on their general jurisdiction courts in 1997 are California, with 990; Illinois, 865; New York, 524; Florida, 461; and Texas, 396.

The states with the smallest number of authorized judges on their general jurisdiction courts in 1997 are Maine, with 16; Wyoming, 17; Delaware, 22; Rhode Island, 25; and Vermont, 34.

Q **555. What is a trial judge paid?**

A As of January 1, 1997, salaries of judges of general jurisdiction trial courts ranged from $67,513 to $115,000. The average salary was $91,018.

New Jersey pays the highest salaries in the nation to judges on its trial and intermediate appellate courts. As of January 1, 1997, state trial judges in New Jersey earned a salary of $115,000, and judges on the state's intermediate appellate courts earned $124,200. The highest-paid judges on a state court of last resort worked in Florida, however, where they earned $133,600.

Montana paid the lowest salaries in the nation to judges on its state trial courts and to justices on its court of last resort. As of January 1, 1997, state trial court judges in Montana earned a salary of $67,513, and a justice on Montana's court of last resort earned $68,874. The lowest-paid intermediate appellate court judge in the nation worked in New Mexico, for a salary of $79,413.

Q 556. Who was the first woman chief justice in the nation?

A Susie M. Sharp became the first woman to be elected to the post of chief justice of a state supreme court in 1974. She was appointed to North Carolina Superior Court in 1949 and to the Supreme Court of North Carolina in 1962. She was elected chief justice in 1974 and served until 1979, when she reached the mandatory retirement age of seventy-two. Not a feminist, she lobbied against the proposed Equal Rights Amendment for women.

Clerks and Court Administrators

Q 557. What does the clerk of court do?

A In the state court system the clerk of court, sometimes called the court administrator, is elected at the county level to administer the operation of trial courts. The clerk is responsible for scheduling and docketing cases; collecting and managing court fees; overseeing jury selection; issuing summonses, subpoenas, passports, and marriage licenses; and ensuring that official court records are properly compiled and kept secure.

Partisan elections are used to select the clerk of court in twenty-six states, and nonpartisan elections are used in four states. In sixteen states clerks are appointed, usually by the chief judge or the bench.

Each judge also has a court clerk who performs administrative functions, including managing the court files, maintaining exhibits during the trial, and keeping track of all court documents. The clerk also administers oaths to witnesses who testify in a trial.

Q 558. What does a jury commissioner do?

A In some large jurisdictions an office of jury commissioner oversees the selection and management of all jurors. The office maintains lists of state residents who are qualified by being U.S. citizens to serve as members of a jury, and it mails notices to these persons as they are needed by the court system. In smaller jurisdictions the duties of the office are performed by the clerk of courts. The office of jury commissioner may be elected or appointed.

Q 559. What is a prosecutor?

A A prosecutor is the attorney who advocates on behalf of the state, county, or city in a felony criminal proceeding. The prosecutor ensures that justice is done on behalf of the public in criminal cases. Prosecutors also assist police agencies by providing advice on the legal aspects of criminal investigations, and they present evidence to grand juries to secure indictments in felony cases.

A prosecutor is usually assigned to a case from the time it is filed in court until it is disposed of by plea of guilty, by trial, or by dismissal. The prosecutor often negotiates with a defendant to reach an agreed-on disposition in a case, called a plea bargain. In a small percentage of cases the prosecutor represents the government at a trial at which he or she must prove beyond a reasonable doubt that a crime was committed by the defendant.

There were 2,343 state court prosecutors' offices in 1994, which employed about 65,000 attorneys, investigators, and support staff and had a median annual office budget of $226,000.

Q 560. How is a chief prosecutor selected?

A The chief prosecutor directs the prosecutor's office, including a staff of assistant attorneys. Titles for a chief prosecutor include district attorney, county attorney, prosecuting attorney, commonwealth attorney, and state's attorney. State law determines the number of prosecutors in a state and whether they are elected or appointed. Over 95 percent of chief prosecutors are elected locally. About 70 percent of them work full-time and 30 percent part-time.

Q 561. What percentage of prosecutors experience a work-related threat or assault?

A In more than half of all prosecutors' offices in 1994, a staff member experienced a work-related threat or assault. Threatened staff members included the following: chief prosecutors, 31 percent; assistant prosecutors, 28 percent; and investigators, 8 percent.

Prosecutors also face the possibility of being named in a civil suit as a result of the performance of their duties. In 1994 about 37 percent of prosecutors' offices defended against civil actions filed in connection with the discharge of prosecutorial responsibility. Sixty-eight percent of chief prosecutors in larger jurisdictions had civil suits filed against them.

Q 562. How often do prosecutors get convictions?

A About 87 percent of cases closed by prosecutors result in a felony or misdemeanor conviction.

Q 563. What is vertical prosecution?

A In a vertical prosecution, the same prosecutor stays with a case from the beginning to the end. Two-thirds of prosecutors' offices used vertical prosecution in 1994.

Q 564. What types of services do prosecutors' offices provide to victims?

A Eighty-six percent of prosecutors' offices provided services to victims in 1994. These services included notifying victims of the disposition of felony cases of concern to them and assisting them with restitution and compensation procedures. Seventy-five percent of prosecutors' offices in 1995 provided security or assistance for felony case victims or witnesses who had been threatened.

Public Defenders

Q 565. What is a public defender?

A A public defender is appointed by the court to represent a defendant in a criminal proceeding. A public defender is responsible for protecting the defendant's rights and providing the defendant with vigorous representation that includes the presentation of any available defenses. A jurisdiction may fulfill its obligation to provide counsel to indigent defendants by establishing an office of the public defender, to which attorneys are appointed by judges in the district. Alternatively, a jurisdiction may meet its obligation to provide counsel to indigent defendants by hiring private attorneys or by contracting with private law firms or the local bar association to represent indigent defendants.

A 1994 survey of state legal systems found that 68 percent of districts primarily used a public defender, 20 percent assigned private counsel, and 12 percent contracted with law firms or local bar associations to represent indigent defendants.

Q 566. What is an attorney's obligation to his or her client?

A An attorney is an officer of the court who is hired by a party to conduct that party's legal affairs. Attorneys have a duty to their clients but also to the court. Ethical rules require attorneys to aid the court in the pursuit of justice. Attorneys cannot, for example, present as truthful testimony that which they know to be false. Attorneys must provide their clients with skillful and zealous representation, keep client information confidential, and avoid incurring any obligation that would place them in a position where their interests conflict with those of their clients.

Q 567. What country has the world record for having the most lawyers?

A According to the *Guinness Book of World Records, 1998,* that country is the United States of America, which had 946,499 lawyers in 1996, or one lawyer for every 276 people.

Q 568. Is there any difference between a lawyer and an attorney?

A Technically, lawyers cannot represent themselves to be attorneys-at-law unless they are admitted to the practice of law in a state and authorized to perform civil and criminal legal functions for clients. A law license is issued by the state supreme court to individuals who have passed a comprehensive examination regarding their knowledge of the law and who have met other state requirements. A similar document is issued by federal courts to attorneys who have been admitted to practice law by state courts.

Q 569. What is the magic cigar trick?

A Clarence Darrow, the famous labor and criminal lawyer, allegedly put a strand of wire down the length of his cigar that caused the ashes to remain on the lit cigar in defiance of the laws of gravity. This stunt fascinated jurors and drew their attention away from Darrow's opposing counsel.

A A *bailiff* calls the courtroom into order, announces the judge's entry into the courtroom, and keeps order in the court. The bailiff also is responsible for the custody of the jury, ensuring that no one talks to the jurors or attempts to influence them in any way.

The *court reporter* compiles a verbatim account of the proceedings in a courtroom, including the testimony of witnesses, legal arguments, court orders, judgments, and the judge's instructions to the jury. The court reporter logs all objections filed by counsel and rulings made by the judge and records the judge's instructions to the jury. The accuracy of the transcript of the proceedings is vital as it forms the basis for an appeal to a higher court.

STATE COURTS OF SPECIAL JURISDICTION

IN GENERAL

Q **571. What is a state court of special jurisdiction?**

A Many states have found it necessary or expedient to establish courts of specialized jurisdiction, especially in densely populated urban areas. These courts hear cases pertaining to a specific subject. They generally operate as a division of the state court of general jurisdiction but in some states are classified as state courts of limited jurisdiction. Courts of special jurisdiction handle cases involving juveniles, families, drug offenses, probate disputes, domestic violence, and environmental issues.

JUVENILE COURT

Q **572. What is a juvenile court?**

A The first juvenile court was founded a hundred years ago in Chicago. Until 1899, juveniles were prosecuted and jailed like adults. Juvenile courts were designed to treat an offender who is eighteen or younger not as a common criminal but as a ward of the court who needs special corrective action. With the advent of drug and gang violence, sympathy for juveniles has waned in recent years, and many more youths are being treated like adults.

A total of 2,030,346 juvenile cases were filed in state courts in 1997. That figure represents an increase of 68 percent since 1984. Property-related crime has declined among juveniles in recent years, while person-related crime has increased.

Juvenile courts handle two types of cases: criminal and dependency. Criminal cases arise when a juvenile is accused of being delinquent or of having committed an act that would be a crime if committed by an adult. About 68 percent of juvenile cases involve some type of delinquent act. About 28 percent of them involve "status" offenses, which are not crimes if committed by adults, such as truancy and alcohol consumption, and child-victim offenses, including neglect and physical abuse.

Juvenile courts are committed to both protecting the public and rehabilitating juveniles. Therefore, unlike other courts, juvenile courts safeguard the confidentiality and privacy of juveniles accused of crimes and may close certain proceedings to the general public. The records of a juvenile found guilty of a crime (excluding certain felonies) are expunged. Juvenile court cases are generally heard by a judge, not a jury.

Juvenile courts protect children who become court dependents because of allegations of abuse or neglect by their parents or who, because of their behavior or condition, pose a threat to their own well-being or physical safety. A dependency case is closed when the child is returned home, adopted, emancipated, or has achieved a permanent placement that does not require court supervision.

Finally, the court provides supervision to juveniles who are habitually absent from school without justification, repeatedly run away from home, or are the victims of child abuse and neglect. Child abuse and neglect involve the improper care or violent handling of juveniles.

Juvenile court judges are surrounded by a variety of support personnel, some of whom are referred to as intake or probation officers. These officers review complaints and determine whether there are enough facts to warrant the court's involvement. If so, the officer may authorize the filing of a petition to bring the matter before the judge. Officers also conduct a thorough background investigation of the juvenile, including a review of his or her social and educational history. Probation officers supervise delinquent juveniles who are held in detention and children in need of services who are released to a home. Representatives of welfare and social service agencies frequently perform the initial investigation in abuse and neglect cases and provide other services as ordered by the court.

Juveniles have a right to be represented by counsel. The court appoints a lawyer, known as a *guardian ad litem,* to represent a juvenile's best interests in cases in which the juvenile is alleged to have been abandoned, neglected, or abused and in proceedings that may result in termination of parental rights. A lawyer also is appointed in some circumstances for adults who cannot afford legal counsel.

573. What criminal sanctions do juveniles face?

A Juveniles convicted of crimes may be sent to an institution for juveniles, placed on probation, ordered to perform community service, or directed to pay a fine. Some courts are experimenting with alternative dispositions, including bootcamps, wilderness programs, house arrest, and restitution. Most delinquency cases end in dismissals or probation sanctions, often after the juvenile has successfully completed a court program.

Q **574. When does a juvenile "grow up"?**

A In 1997 most states, as well as the District of Columbia and Puerto Rico, transferred jurisdiction over juveniles to adult courts when they reached the age of eighteen. These states included the following:

Alabama	Kentucky	Ohio
Alaska	Maine	Oklahoma
Arizona	Maryland	Oregon
Arkansas	Minnesota	Pennsylvania
California	Mississippi	Rhode Island
Colorado	Montana	South Dakota
Delaware	Nebraska	Tennessee
Florida	Nevada	Utah
Idaho	New Hampshire	Virginia
Indiana	New Jersey	Washington
Iowa	New Mexico	West Virginia
Kansas	North Dakota	

The cut-off age for juveniles was seventeen in Georgia, Illinois, Louisiana, Massachusetts, Michigan, Missouri, South Carolina, Texas, and Wisconsin, and it was sixteen in Connecticut, Hawaii, New York, North Carolina, and Vermont. In Wyoming the cut-off age was nineteen.

In several states a case involving a juvenile accused of a felony who is above a certain minimum age, often thirteen or fourteen, may be certified, or transferred, to adult court. In Vermont a child may be transferred to adult court at the age of ten under certain circumstances.

Q **575. How is the decision made to send a juvenile to adult court, where a juvenile can be sentenced to an adult prison?**

A Less than one percent of juvenile cases are transferred to adult courts. The total was 12,300 cases in 1994. The decision whether to try a juvenile as an adult is made by a judge or state prosecutor based on the seriousness of the juvenile's crime, his or her past criminal record, and, in some cases, the age of the juvenile.

FAMILY COURT

Q **576. What is a family court?**

A A family court is typically a division of the state court of general jurisdiction that hears matters pertaining to children and the family, including cases involving the dissolution of marriage, child custody, child and spouse support, paternity establishment, child abuse and neglect, adoptions, terminations of parental rights, juvenile delinquency, orders of protection from abuse, and intrafamily misdemeanor crimes. In some states family court is seen as offering an alternative to the traditional adversarial model of the court system. Family courts do not have jurisdiction over adults charged with felonies or juveniles charged with serious crimes, such as murder, rape, and kidnapping.

Many family courts emphasize alternative dispute resolution for divorcing couples, including mediation of disputes to reach a mutually acceptable agreement on child support and child custody issues. Many of these courts mandate parenting education programs for divorcing parents to raise awareness of the problems associated with divorce, custody, and visitation and to assist parents in helping their children cope with the divorce.

Some states have consolidated their family and juvenile courts under one umbrella so that a single family court judge handles all aspects of the problems relating to a family, from divorce and substance abuse issues to child neglect and juvenile delinquency matters.

Meanwhile, some states have formed separate "domestic violence" courts that handle the unique problems of family violence. In recent years domestic violence cases have become the fastest-growing segment of the "domestic relations" caseload, having increased 99 percent between 1989 and 1995. A total of 5,009,044 domestic relations cases were filed in all state courts in 1997.

In addition to specialized family court judges, family courts frequently use a variety of hearing examiners, referees, masters, and commissioners to hear certain types of cases, such as support or paternity cases. These officials are usually attorneys. Their decisions generally can be appealed to the family court judge.

Several types of attorneys may be assigned to family court. Attorneys from the city and/or state prosecutor's office may prosecute certain juvenile delinquency cases. An attorney from the local department of social services may prosecute child abuse and neglect cases and termination of parental rights cases, and may also present support cases involving children who are receiving public assistance.

The court appoints a *guardian ad litem* to safeguard the interests of certain parties. A guardian ad litem is assigned by the judge to act in place of a parent for a child whose parents are required to appear in court but are not available to appear, or is assigned for an adult who is mentally or physically unable to speak for himself or herself in court.

Other family court personnel may include social service agency caseworkers who are assigned to work with families, bring case records to court, and testify at hearings; probation officers who prepare background reports for judges about the parties; and case managers who coordinate court services and refer litigants to social service agencies when needed. A court clerk or court assistant often sits near the judge or hearing examiner and prepares court orders for his or her signature.

Q **577. What is the domestic relations caseload in state courts?**

A Domestic relations cases include divorce, support/custody, domestic violence, paternity, interstate child support, and adoption suits. About five million domestic relations cases were filed in 1997, 65 percent more than were filed in 1985. Case types and the contribution of each type to total domestic relations filings (in twenty states in 1997) were as follows:

- Divorce, 36.4 percent
- Custody, 19 percent
- Domestic violence, 15.8 percent
- Paternity, 12.6 percent
- Miscellaneous, 10.3 percent
- Adoption, 3.1 percent
- Interstate support, 2.8 percent

The most rapid growth in domestic relations cases has occurred in the area of domestic violence, which increased about 239 percent from 1985 to 1997.

DRUG COURTS

Q 578. What is a drug court?

A Drug courts were developed in Florida in the 1990s as an alternative to the traditional approach to prosecuting drug-related offenses. Drug courts combine the coercive power of the judicial system with resources available through alcohol- and drug-treatment services. The goal of the drug court movement is to reduce recidivism through closely supervised treatment. Drug courts (including Native American tribal courts) now operate in at least forty-eight states and the District of Columbia.

The prosecutor offers eligible defendants the opportunity to enter the drug court program as part of a pre-plea, pre-trial diversion program. Criminal charges are dismissed if the defendant successfully completes the program.

Defendants in felony drug cases often must agree to multiple probation conditions to participate in drug court programs. These conditions include limited jail time, regular drug testing, treatment program attendance, employment counseling, compliance with child support orders, payment of fines and costs, and periodic follow-up appearances before the judge to review individual progress. Some research indicates that drug courts are more effective than traditional prosecution methods at reducing crime—and also cheaper, with the average cost of a treatment component in drug court ranging from $900 to $1,600 per participant, compared with an average cost of $5,000 per defendant for a minimal period of incarceration. In addition to judicial staff, a social service coordinator is frequently assigned to drug court to refer defendants to the proper treatment facilities.

Q 579. What percentage of serious crime is related to drugs?

A Of the 872,217 felony convictions in state courts in 1994, 19 percent, or 165,430, were for felony drug trafficking, including the sale and manufacture of drugs, or drug possession. This is the largest category of crime. The breakdown of all felony convictions in 1994 was:

Felony	Number of convictions	Felony	Number of convictions
Drug trafficking	165,430	Aggravated assault	65,174
Larceny	113,026	Fraud/forgery	64,063
Drug possession	108,815	Robbery	46,028
Burglary	98,109	Weapons	31,010
			(continued)

(continued)

Felony	Number of convictions	Felony	Number of convictions
Other violent crimes	21,307	Murder/	
Rape	20,068	manslaughter	12,007

Source: Bureau of Justice Statistics, U.S. Department of Justice, *Felony Sentences in State Courts, 1994* (Washington, D.C.: GPO, 1995).

Q **580. What percentage of drug offenders plead guilty?**

A Approximately 94 percent of defendants charged with drug possession and 90 percent of defendants charged with drug trafficking plead guilty. Those figures compare with 89 percent for all offenses.

PROBATE/ORPHAN/SURROGATE COURT

Q **581. What is a probate court?**

A Probate is the judicial procedure that transfers the legal ownership of a person's property after that person dies. The court that handles these matters is called probate court. Probate courts handle disputes over and settlement of the estates of deceased persons; the appointment of guardians, conservators, and administrators of estates; the processing of adoptions; and the authorization of mental health commitments. Probate courts are also known as orphan or surrogate courts in some jurisdictions.

Some estates are administered in formal proceedings that involve court supervision. The personal representative of a decedent's estate or any interested person may request instructions from the court or ask the court to resolve conflicts among parties. Some estates require litigation to determine the validity of wills, the identity of the decedent's heirs, paternity, or the amount of the fee payable to fiduciaries, attorneys, and accountants. They may also require legal proceedings to resolve common law or putative spouse claims or creditors' claims against the decedent or the estate. These conflicts can be complex, involve multiple parties, and require considerable pretrial and trial time.

The probate court supervises trusts and makes transfers to or from trusts on behalf of persons unable to act for themselves due to disability. A trust is a right of property held by one party for the benefit of another. These cases include claims for improper investments, distributions to beneficiaries, and complex litigation involving trustees' duties and obligations to trust beneficiaries.

The probate court may be called on to appoint a conservator to oversee the settlement of a personal injury claim for a minor or for an individual who, because of illness, accident, or other circumstances, has lost the ability to make responsible decisions about his or her own living arrangements and medical needs. A conservator is an individual or institution appointed to supervise the financial affairs of an impaired person.

The probate court may review the treatment of mentally ill persons, including petitions to administer medications or electroconvulsive therapy to a certified mentally ill person against his or her wishes. And the court may consider requests to commit persons for involuntary alcohol or drug treatment.

In some states probate court judges are elected, and in others they are appointed by the legislature or the chief judge of the district court. Other probate court staff members may include a division clerk, law clerk, bailiff, registrar, and court reporter.

Q 582. How do cases get to probate court?

A The person who has possession of a decedent's will must file it with the state court of general jurisdiction in the county in which the decedent lived. The probate judge ensures that it is the decedent's last will, appoints the executor named in the will (or appoints an administrator), and supervises the executor's administration of the estate. If no will exists, the court will distribute the decedent's estate in accordance with the provisions of state law.

Q 583. Which will had the largest number of codicils, or supplemental provisions modifying the will?

A The will of oil magnate J. Paul Getty, who died on June 6, 1965, had twenty-one codicils, which, according to the *Guinness Book of World Records,* is the largest number in recorded history. These codicils were added from September 1958 through March 1976.

STATE COURTS OF LIMITED JURISDICTION

IN GENERAL

Q 584. What are state courts of limited jurisdiction?

A State courts of limited jurisdiction are the courts with which the average citizen has the most contact—traffic, magistrate, municipal, justice of the peace, and small claims courts. Sixty-six percent of the 89.2 million cases filed in state courts in 1997 were filed in the 13,797 state courts of limited jurisdiction around the nation. These courts have limited criminal and/or civil jurisdiction and sometimes share jurisdiction with each other. They are authorized by state law to handle a narrower range of matters than do state courts of general jurisdiction. Procedures are more relaxed, with the emphasis on moving criminal cases through the system. Parties in civil cases often represent themselves without the assistance of a lawyer.

There are wide variances among the states with respect to the financing and organization of state courts of limited jurisdiction. In most states these courts exercise jurisdiction within the geographic boundaries of a governmental unit, such as a city, county, or township. In some states they exercise jurisdiction along geographic lines, such as within a single county.

The criminal jurisdiction of these courts is limited to lesser offenses, including misdemeanors and traffic violations. Sentences imposed by judges cannot exceed a certain maximum fine and/or a short jail term, usually less than a year. Courts of limited jurisdiction may also handle preliminary hearings in felony cases or felony cases in which the defendant has entered a guilty plea.

Many courts of limited jurisdiction do not use juries or keep a verbatim record of court proceedings. Criminal defendants who wish to exercise their right to a jury trial may opt to have their case heard in a state court of general jurisdiction. Appeals from judgments generally take the form of a trial *de novo* (in other words, the case is tried over again) in a higher court.

State courts of limited jurisdiction also hear civil cases in which the monetary damages sought do not exceed a maximum amount, often $5,000 or less. In 1997, 4.1 million small claims cases were filed in limited jurisdiction courts. Some limited jurisdiction courts also handle probate and domestic relations cases.

Most courts of limited jurisdiction have a clerk, who performs administrative duties, and a single judge, who either works part-time or splits his or her time with other districts. Historically, courts of limited jurisdiction occupied the bottom rung of the judicial ladder, neglected by bar associations, state supreme courts, and the press. Former New Jersey chief justice Arthur T. Vanderbilt in 1956 called the neglect of these courts "incomprehensible" in view of their critical importance to society. In these courts, said Vanderbilt, "rests the primary responsibility for the maintenance of peace in the various communities of the states, for the safety on our streets and highways and, most important of all, for the development of respect for law on the part of our citizenry, on which, in the last analysis, all of our democratic institutions depend."

Q **585. How many states have courts of limited jurisdiction?**

A In 1997 forty-six states had courts of limited jurisdiction. The four states that did not have such courts were Illinois, Iowa, Minnesota, and South Dakota. Puerto Rico and the District of Columbia also lack limited jurisdiction courts.

Q **586. What type of case is filed most often in courts of limited jurisdiction?**

A Traffic filings accounted for 44.4 million, or 67 percent, of the 66 million cases filed in state courts of limited jurisdiction in 1997. This category represents the single largest segment of the caseload of courts of limited jurisdiction.

In addition to traffic cases, the following types of proceedings, listed by number of cases filed, were processed in state courts of limited jurisdiction in 1997:

- Criminal, 10.1 million
- Civil, 9.2 million
- Domestic, 1.5 million
- Juvenile, 0.8 million

Q **587. How have the number of judges on state courts of limited jurisdiction changed over time?**

A Surprisingly little. The year and number of judicial officers serving on state courts of limited jurisdiction from 1990 to 1997 were as follows:

Year	Judges on state courts of limited jurisdiction	Year	Judges on state courts of limited jurisdiction
1997	18,553	1993	18,316
1996	18,301	1992	18,272
1995	17,974	1991	18,279
1994	18,317	1990	18,234

Q **588. Who staffs state courts of limited jurisdiction?**

A Typically, a single judge staffs a court of limited jurisdiction, often on a part-time basis. Depending on the type of court of limited jurisdiction, the judge may be appointed or elected. Most courts of limited jurisdiction also employ court clerks, who perform largely administrative and clerical functions. In many jurisdictions these clerks are employed on a part-time basis.

TYPES OF COURTS OF LIMITED JURISDICTION

Q 589. What are magistrate courts?

A Magistrate courts handle misdemeanors, traffic offenses, felony preliminary hearings, and civil cases in which monetary damages are limited to an amount set by the state legislature. Magistrates issue subpoenas and arrest and search warrants, authorize bail or commit a defendant to custody, administer oaths, and issue emergency custody and protective orders as well as civil and criminal medical emergency temporary detention orders. In large urban areas magistrate court is often open twenty-four hours a day. Magistrates have no power to take any action unless authority has been expressly conferred by statute. Magistrates are typically appointed to fixed terms by the chief judge of the state court of general jurisdiction. Many magistrates are not lawyers; however, they are specially trained to perform such duties as setting bail and issuing search warrants, subpoenas, arrest warrants, and summonses.

The office of magistrate traces its development through centuries of English and American history. Many of the duties now performed by magistrates were once carried out by justices of the peace. In Virginia, for example, the office of justice of the peace was phased out in 1974, and the Virginia magistrate system was established as part of a statewide court reorganization plan.

Q 590. What is a municipal court?

A The municipal court is the judicial branch of a city or county government and has jurisdiction over parking and traffic violations and violations of local ordinances, including fire safety, zoning, public health, juvenile curfew, and sanitation ordinances. Municipal courts may also issue orders of protection and injunctions prohibiting harassment. These courts may have concurrent jurisdiction with other courts over misdemeanor criminal cases that occur within their boundaries, such as those involving driving under the influence of alcohol, hit-and-run accidents, and reckless driving that does not result in serious injuries.

In some jurisdictions municipal judges act as magistrates and issue search and arrest warrants, in addition to presiding over hearings to determine whether there is probable cause to hold a defendant for further court proceedings. Municipal court judges may be appointed by the governing authority of the jurisdiction in which they operate, such as the city or town council, or they may seek election in their districts. These judges often work part-time and may not be required to be lawyers.

Q 591. What is a community court?

A Many cities are forming community courts to handle misdemeanor "quality-of-life" crimes on the premise that, if left unaddressed, these low-level offenses erode communal order, lead to disinvestment and neighborhood decay, and create an atmosphere where more serious crime can flourish. New York City created one of the first community courts, Midtown Community Court, in 1993. The city had replaced its network of neighborhood courts with centralized borough courts that increasingly focused on serious crimes at the expense of lesser, so-called quality-of-life offenses, such as prostitution, illegal vending, shoplifting, and graffiti vandalizing. Midtown Community Court refocuses attention on misdemeanor crimes that erode the morale of neighborhood residents.

Built on the model of community policing, community courts emphasize "restorative justice" that benefits the community. Judges often impose alternative sentences that require defendants to pay back the community they have harmed by sweeping parks, cleaning up graffiti, or volunteering for nonprofit groups. Community courts also emphasize treatment and rehabilitation of offenders. Educational and social services agencies are invited to assign personnel to the courthouse itself, so that their representatives can meet with defendants upon sentencing. A community advisory board gives residents an institutional mechanism to interact with judges and the court, and allows the community to have input on the success of alternative sentencing programs.

Community courts require a broader array of staffing than traditional courts, and private funding is actively encouraged. The Midtown Community Court, for example, is operated as a public/private partnership among the New York State Unified Court System, the City of New York, and the Fund for the City of New York. In addition to judges, security personnel, and clerks, community courts employ a resource coordinator, who links defendants with an array of community educational and social service resources.

Q 592. What is a traffic court?

A The most serious traffic jam in many states is in the court system. More traffic cases are filed in state courts than are any other type of case. About 52.6 million traffic cases were filed in 1997, including 8.2 million cases in courts of general jurisdiction and 44.4 million in courts of limited jurisdiction. To alleviate the congestion, many jurisdictions have established a separate court to handle all but the most serious traffic offenses. Traffic courts frequently share jurisdiction over traffic offenses with other courts, including justice of the peace courts.

Traffic courts typically handle infractions, minor offenses punishable by a fine only, and misdemeanors, which carry a maximum penalty of a fine and up to a year in a city or county jail. Violations of speed laws and other moving violations, such as running a stoplight, are generally infractions. Driving under the influence of alcohol or drugs and driving without a valid license are often charged as misdemeanors.

Felonies, or more serious crimes that carry a possible term of incarceration at a state prison for a year or more, may be referred to the state court of general jurisdiction. Felonies include such crimes as vehicular homicide. Increasingly, legislatures are removing the responsibility for enforcement of parking ordinances from the courts to the agency that issues the notice of violation.

Q **593. What is a small claims court?**

A Small claims courts are courts of limited jurisdiction that hear civil cases involving claims for monetary damages or those for recovery of property that do not exceed a limited amount, from typically $3,000 to $5,000. These claims stem from breach of contract, consumer complaints, minor injuries sustained in automobile accidents, landlord/tenants suits, and property disputes.

Generally, these cases are prosecuted and defended by individuals without the assistance of an attorney. A handful of states prohibit litigants from being represented by a lawyer in small claims court. An aggrieved party goes to the clerk's office, fills out a form, and pays a filing fee, which is usually under $100. Trials are informal, though witnesses are sworn to tell the truth. A judgment for the plaintiff is essentially an official statement in the court's records that the defendant, the judgment debtor, owes the plaintiff, the judgment creditor, a certain amount of money with interest. The judgment must be enforced out of the assets of the defendant.

In some states a small claims court decision cannot be appealed. In other states dissatisfied litigants may file an appeal to the next-highest court in the system. Small claims courts are not courts of record, and no transcript of the proceeding is prepared. Therefore, an appeal results in a retrial of the claim, or a "trial de novo." Judges on small claims courts are elected by voters in the circuit or district where the court is located. The vast majority of small claims cases are disposed of in limited jurisdiction courts. In 1997 4.1 million small claims cases were filed in limited jurisdiction courts.

Q **594. What is justice of the peace court?**

A Justice of the peace court is the base of the pyramid of the state court system, the place where most people enter the system. In some states, such as Delaware, more than half of all cases are disposed of at the justice of the peace court without any further impact on the state's judicial system.

The office of justice of the peace dates back to the 1600s, when prominent members of the community were commissioned to handle minor civil and criminal cases. In the seventeenth and eighteenth centuries, justices of the peace administered local government on behalf of the English crown.

In recent years, many U.S. jurisdictions have sought to reduce the role played by justices of the peace in local government. They have eliminated their office as state court systems have become unified and as court functions have been consolidated into one or two trial courts.

Established by state law, justice of the peace courts have jurisdiction over traffic cases, except felonies, and over certain lesser criminal cases and civil cases in which the monetary damages do not exceed a certain level. A justice of the peace is often a nonlawyer who works part-time. Generally, the jurisdiction of the justice of the peace court is not exclusive but is concurrent with that of other courts. Justices of the peace also act as the committing authority for all crimes (conducting arraignments, accepting pleas, and "binding over" the defendant for trial), issue warrants, and conduct preliminary hearings. In jurisdictions that have no medical examiners, the justice of the peace also may serve as the coroner.

Criminal defendants may elect to transfer their case from justice of the peace court to a higher state court. No transcript is made of the proceedings in justice of the peace court. Therefore, an appeal of a decision of a justice of the peace requires a retrial of the claim, or a "trial de novo," in a state court of general jurisdiction.

Justice of the peace courts may employ one or more court clerks to provide clerical assistance and maintain court records. Justice of the peace courts in some busy urban precincts also have a court administrator.

Q **595. Why were justices of the peace sometimes referred to as "justices for the plaintiff"?**

A Traditionally, the office of justice of the peace was financed entirely by fees assessed and collected by the justice of the peace. Therefore, a justice of the peace was paid more if a defendant was found guilty and fined. An acquittal meant the justice didn't get paid. This system understandably led to complaints of conflict of interest. The U.S. Supreme Court declared the fee collection system to be unconstitutional in *Tumey v. Ohio* (1927). In many states justice of the peace court is being discontinued as state courts consolidate their trial courts into a single general jurisdiction court.

REFERENCE MATERIALS

CONSTITUTION OF THE UNITED STATES

We the People of the United States, in Order to form a more perfect Union, establish Justice, insure domestic Tranquility, provide for the common defence, promote the general Welfare, and secure the Blessings of Liberty to ourselves and our Posterity, do ordain and establish this Constitution for the United States of America.

ARTICLE I

SECTION 1. All legislative Powers herein granted shall be vested in a Congress of the United States, which shall consist of a Senate and House of Representatives.

SECTION 2. The House of Representatives shall be composed of Members chosen every second Year by the People of the several States, and the Electors in each State shall have the Qualifications requisite for Electors of the most numerous Branch of the State Legislature.

No Person shall be a Representative who shall not have attained to the age of twenty five Years, and been seven Years a Citizen of the United States, and who shall not, when elected, be an Inhabitant of that State in which he shall be chosen.

[Representatives and direct Taxes shall be apportioned among the several States which may be included within this Union, according to their respective Numbers, which shall be determined by adding to the whole Number of free Persons, including those bound to Service for a Term of Years, and excluding Indians not taxed, three fifths of all other Persons.][1] The actual Enumeration shall be made within three Years after the first Meeting of the Congress of the United States, and within every subsequent Term of ten Years, in such Manner as they shall by Law direct. The Number of Representatives shall not exceed one for every thirty Thousand, but each State shall have at Least one Representative; and until such enumeration shall be made, the State of New Hampshire shall be entitled to chuse three, Massachusetts eight, Rhode-Island and Providence Plantations one, Connecticut five, New-York six, New Jersey four, Pennsylvania eight, Delaware one, Maryland six, Virginia ten, North Carolina five, South Carolina five, and Georgia three.

When vacancies happen in the Representation from any State, the Executive Authority thereof shall issue Writs of Election to fill such Vacancies.

The House of Representatives shall chuse their Speaker and other Officers; and shall have the sole Power of Impeachment.

SECTION 3. The Senate of the United States shall be composed of two Senators from each State, [chosen by the Legislature thereof,][2] for six Years; and each Senator shall have one Vote.

Immediately after they shall be assembled in Consequence of the first Election, they shall be divided as equally as may be into three Classes. The Seats of the Senators of the first Class shall be vacated at the Expiration of the second Year, of the second Class at the Expiration of the fourth Year, and of the third Class at the Expiration of the sixth Year, so that one third may be chosen every second Year; [and if Vacancies happen by Resignation, or otherwise, during the Recess of the

Legislature of any State, the Executive thereof may make temporary Appointments until the next Meeting of the Legislature, which shall then fill such Vacancies.][3]

No Person shall be a Senator who shall not have attained to the Age of thirty Years, and been nine Years a Citizen of the United States, and who shall not, when elected, be an Inhabitant of that State for which he shall be chosen.

The Vice President of the United States shall be President of the Senate, but shall have no Vote, unless they be equally divided.

The Senate shall chuse their other Officers, and also a President pro tempore, in the Absence of the Vice President, or when he shall exercise the Office of President of the United States.

The Senate shall have the sole Power to try all Impeachments. When sitting for that Purpose, they shall be on Oath or Affirmation. When the President of the United States is tried, the Chief Justice shall preside: And no Person shall be convicted without the Concurrence of two thirds of the Members present.

Judgment in Cases of Impeachment shall not extend further than to removal from Office, and disqualification to hold and enjoy any Office of honor, Trust or Profit under the United States: but the Party convicted shall nevertheless be liable and subject to Indictment, Trial, Judgment and Punishment, according to Law.

SECTION 4. The Times, Places and Manner of holding Elections for Senators and Representatives, shall be prescribed in each State by the Legislature thereof; but the Congress may at any time by Law make or alter such Regulations, except as to the Places of chusing Senators.

The Congress shall assemble at least once in every Year, and such Meeting shall [be on the first Monday in December],[4] unless they shall by Law appoint a different Day.

SECTION 5. Each House shall be the Judge of the Elections, Returns and Qualifications of its own Members, and a Majority of each shall constitute a Quorum to do Business; but a smaller Number may adjourn from day to day, and may be authorized to compel the Attendance of absent Members, in such Manner, and under such Penalties as each House may provide.

Each House may determine the Rules of its Proceedings, punish its Members for disorderly Behaviour, and, with the Concurrence of two thirds, expel a Member.

Each House shall keep a Journal of its Proceedings, and from time to time publish the same, excepting such Parts as may in their Judgment require Secrecy; and the Yeas and Nays of the Members of either House on any question shall, at the Desire of one fifth of those Present, be entered on the Journal.

Neither House, during the Session of Congress, shall, without the Consent of the other, adjourn for more than three days, nor to any other Place than that in which the two Houses shall be sitting.

SECTION 6. The Senators and Representatives shall receive a Compensation for their Services, to be ascertained by Law, and paid out of the Treasury of the United States. They shall in all Cases, except Treason, Felony and Breach of the Peace, be privileged from Arrest during their Attendance at the Session of their respective Houses, and in going to and returning from the same; and for any Speech or Debate in either House, they shall not be questioned in any other Place.

No Senator or Representative shall, during the Time for which he was elected, be appointed to any civil Office under the Authority of the United States, which shall have been created, or the Emoluments whereof shall have been encreased during such time; and no Person holding any Office under the United States, shall be a Member of either House during his Continuance in Office.

SECTION 7. All Bills for raising Revenue shall originate in the House of Representatives; but the Senate may propose or concur with Amendments as on other Bills.

Every Bill which shall have passed the House of Representatives and the Senate, shall, before it become a Law, be presented to the President of the United States; If he approve he shall sign it, but if not he shall return it, with his Objections to that House in which it shall have originated, who shall enter the Objections at large on their Journal, and proceed to reconsider it. If after such Reconsideration two thirds of that House shall agree to pass the Bill, it shall be sent, together with the Objections, to the other House, by which it shall likewise be reconsidered, and if approved by two thirds of that House, it shall become a Law. But in all such Cases the Votes of both Houses shall be determined by yeas and Nays, and the Names of the Persons voting for and against the Bill shall be entered on the Journal of each House respectively. If any Bill shall not be returned by the President within ten Days (Sundays excepted) after it shall have been presented to him, the Same shall be a Law, in like Manner as if he had signed it, unless the Congress by their Adjournment prevent its Return, in which Case it shall not be a Law.

Every Order, Resolution, or Vote to which the Concurrence of the Senate and House of Representatives may be necessary (except on a question of Adjournment) shall be presented to the President of the United States; and before the Same shall take Effect, shall be approved by him, or being disapproved by him, shall be repassed by two thirds of the Senate and House of Representatives, according to the Rules and Limitations prescribed in the Case of a Bill.

SECTION 8. The Congress shall have Power To lay and collect Taxes, Duties, Imposts and Excises, to pay the Debts and provide for the common Defence and general Welfare of the United States; but all Duties, Imposts and Excises shall be uniform throughout the United States;

To borrow Money on the credit of the United States;

To regulate Commerce with foreign Nations, and among the several States, and with the Indian Tribes;

To establish an uniform Rule of Naturalization, and uniform Laws on the subject of Bankruptcies throughout the United States;

To coin Money, regulate the Value thereof, and of foreign Coin, and fix the Standard of Weights and Measures;

To provide for the Punishment of counterfeiting the Securities and current Coin of the United States;

To establish Post Offices and post Roads;

To promote the Progress of Science and useful Arts, by securing for limited Times to Authors and Inventors the exclusive Right to their respective Writings and Discoveries;

To constitute Tribunals inferior to the supreme Court;

To define and punish Piracies and Felonies committed on the high Seas, and Offences against the Law of Nations;

To declare War, grant Letters of Marque and Reprisal, and make Rules concerning Captures on Land and Water;

To raise and support Armies, but no Appropriation of Money to that Use shall be for a longer Term than two Years;

To provide and maintain a Navy;

To make Rules for the Government and Regulation of the land and naval Forces;

To provide for calling forth the Militia to execute the Laws of the Union, suppress Insurrections and repel Invasions;

To provide for organizing, arming, and disciplining, the Militia, and for governing such Part of them as may be employed in the Service of the United States, reserving to the States respectively, the Appointment of the Officers, and the Authority of training the Militia according to the discipline prescribed by Congress;

To exercise exclusive Legislation in all Cases whatso-ever, over such District (not exceeding ten Miles square) as may, by Cession of particular States, and the Acceptance of Congress, become the Seat of the Government of the United States, and to exercise like Authority over all Places purchased by the Consent of the Legislature of the State in which the Same shall be, for the Erection of Forts, Magazines, Arsenals, dock-Yards, and other needful Buildings;—And

To make all Laws which shall be necessary and proper for carrying into Execution the foregoing Powers, and all other Powers vested by this Constitution in the Government of the United States, or in any Department or Officer thereof.

SECTION 9. The Migration or Importation of such Persons as any of the States now existing shall think proper to admit, shall not be prohibited by the Congress prior to the Year one thousand eight hundred and eight, but a Tax or duty may be imposed on such Importation, not exceeding ten dollars for each Person.

The Privilege of the Writ of Habeas Corpus shall not be suspended, unless when in Cases of Rebellion or Invasion the public Safety may require it.

No Bill of Attainder or ex post facto Law shall be passed.

No Capitation, or other direct, Tax shall be laid, unless in Proportion to the Census or Enumeration herein before directed to be taken.[5]

No Tax or Duty shall be laid on Articles exported from any State.

No Preference shall be given by any Regulation of Commerce or Revenue to the Ports of one State over those of another; nor shall Vessels bound to, or from, one State, be obliged to enter, clear, or pay Duties in another.

No Money shall be drawn from the Treasury, but in Consequence of Appropriations made by Law; and a regular Statement and Account of the Receipts and Expenditures of all public Money shall be published from time to time.

No Title of Nobility shall be granted by the United States: And no Person holding any Office of Profit or Trust under them, shall, without the Consent of the Congress, accept of any present, Emolument, Office, or Title, of any kind whatever, from any King, Prince, or foreign State.

SECTION 10. No State shall enter into any Treaty, Alliance, or Confederation; grant Letters of Marque and Reprisal; coin Money; emit Bills of Credit; make any Thing but gold and silver Coin a Tender in Payment of Debts; pass any Bill of Attainder, ex post facto Law, or Law impairing the Obligation of Contracts, or grant any Title of Nobility.

No State shall, without the Consent of the Congress, lay any Imposts or Duties on Imports or Exports, except what may be absolutely necessary for executing it's inspection Laws: and the net Produce of all Duties and Imposts, laid by any State on Imports or Exports, shall be for the Use of the Treasury of the United States; and all such Laws shall be subject to the Revision and Controul of the Congress.

No State shall, without the Consent of Congress, lay any Duty of Tonnage, keep Troops, or Ships of War in time of Peace, enter into any Agreement or Compact with another State, or with a foreign Power, or engage in War, unless actually invaded, or in such imminent Danger as will not admit of delay.

ARTICLE II

SECTION 1. The executive Power shall be vested in a President of the United States of America. He shall hold his Office during the Term of four Years, and, together with the Vice President, chosen for the same Term, be elected, as follows

Each State shall appoint, in such Manner as the Legislature thereof may direct, a Number of Electors, equal to the whole Number of Senators and Representatives to which the State may be entitled in the Congress: but no Senator or Representative, or Person holding an Office of Trust or Profit under the United States, shall be appointed an Elector.

[The Electors shall meet in their respective States, and vote by Ballot for two Persons, of whom one at least shall not be an Inhabitant of the same State with themselves. And they shall make a List of all the Persons voted for, and of the Number of Votes for each; which List they shall sign and certify, and transmit sealed to the Seat of the Government of the United States, directed to the President of the Senate. The President of the Senate shall, in the Presence of the Senate and House of Representatives, open all the Certificates, and the Votes shall then be counted. The Person having the greatest Number of Votes shall be the President, if such Number be a Majority of the whole Number of Electors appointed; and if there be more than one who have such Majority, and have an equal Number of Votes, then the House of Representatives shall immediately chuse by Ballot one of them for President; and if no Person have a Majority, then from the five highest on the list the said House shall in like Manner chuse the President. But in chusing the President, the Votes shall be taken by States, the Representation from each State having one Vote; A quorum for this Purpose shall consist of a Member or Members from two thirds of the States, and a Majority of all the States shall be necessary to a Choice. In every Case, after the Choice of the President, the Person having the greatest Number of Votes of the Electors shall be the Vice President. But if there should remain two or more who have equal Votes, the Senate shall chuse from them by Ballot the Vice President.][6]

The Congress may determine the Time of chusing the Electors, and the Day on which they shall give their Votes; which Day shall be the same throughout the United States.

No Person except a natural born Citizen, or a Citizen of the United States, at the time of the Adoption of this Constitution, shall be eligible to the Office of President; neither shall any Person be eligible to that Office who shall not have attained to the Age of thirty five Years, and been fourteen Years a Resident within the United States.

In Case of the Removal of the President from Office, or of his Death, Resignation, or Inability to discharge the Powers and Duties of the said Office,[7] the Same shall devolve on the Vice President, and the Congress may by Law provide for the Case of Removal, Death, Resignation or Inability, both of the President and Vice President, declaring what Officer shall then act as President, and such Officer shall act accordingly, until the Disability be removed, or a President shall be elected.

The President shall, at stated Times, receive for his Services, a Compensation, which shall neither be encreased nor diminished during the Period for which he shall have been elected, and he shall not receive within that Period any other Emolument from the United States, or any of them.

Before he enter on the Execution of his Office, he shall take the following Oath or Affirmation:—"I do solemnly swear (or affirm) that I will faithfully execute the Office of President of the United States, and will to the best of my Ability, preserve, protect and defend the Constitution of the United States."

SECTION 2. The President shall be Commander in Chief of the Army and Navy of the United States, and of the Militia of the several States, when called into the actual Service of the United States; he may require the Opinion, in writing, of the principal Officer in each of the executive Departments, upon any Subject relating to the Duties of their respective Offices, and he shall have Power to grant Reprieves and Pardons for Offences against the United States, except in Cases of Impeachment.

He shall have Power, by and with the Advice and Consent of the Senate, to make Treaties, provided two thirds of the Senators present concur; and he shall nominate, and by and with the Advice and Consent of the Senate, shall appoint Ambassadors, other public Ministers and Consuls, Judges of the supreme Court, and all other Officers of the United States, whose Appointments are not herein otherwise provided for, and which shall be established by Law: but the Congress may by Law vest the Appointment of such inferior Officers, as they think proper, in the President alone, in the Courts of Law, or in the Heads of Departments.

The President shall have Power to fill up all Vacancies that may happen during the Recess of the Senate, by granting Commissions which shall expire at the End of their next Session.

SECTION 3. He shall from time to time give to the Congress Information of the State of the Union, and recommend to their Consideration such Measures as he shall judge necessary and expedient; he may, on extraordinary Occasions, convene both Houses, or either of them, and in Case of Disagreement between them, with Respect to the Time of Adjournment, he may adjourn them to such Time as he shall think proper; he shall receive Ambassadors and other public Ministers; he shall take Care that the Laws be faithfully executed, and shall Commission all the Officers of the United States.

SECTION 4. The President, Vice President and all civil Officers of the United States, shall be removed from Office on Impeachment for, and Conviction of, Treason, Bribery, or other high Crimes and Misdemeanors.

ARTICLE III

SECTION 1. The judicial Power of the United States, shall be vested in one supreme Court, and in such inferior Courts as the Congress may from time to time ordain and establish. The Judges, both of the supreme and inferior Courts, shall hold their Offices during good Behaviour, and shall, at stated Times, receive for their Services, a Compensation, which shall not be diminished during their Continuance in Office.

SECTION 2. The judicial Power shall extend to all Cases, in Law and Equity, arising under this Constitution, the Laws of the United States, and Treaties made, or which shall be made, under their Authority; — to all Cases affecting Ambassadors, other public Ministers and Consuls; —to all Cases of admiralty and maritime Jurisdiction; —to Controversies to which the United States shall be a Party; —to Controversies between two or more States; —between a State and Citizens of another State;[8] —between Citizens of different States; —between Citizens of the same State claiming Lands under Grants of different States, and between a State, or the Citizens thereof, and foreign States, Citizens or Subjects.[8]

In all Cases affecting Ambassadors, other public Ministers and Consuls, and those in which a State shall be Party, the supreme Court shall have original Jurisdiction. In all the other Cases before mentioned, the supreme Court shall have appellate Jurisdiction, both as to Law and Fact, with such Exceptions, and under such Regulations as the Congress shall make.

The Trial of all Crimes, except in Cases of Impeachment, shall be by Jury; and such Trial shall be held in the State where the said Crimes shall have been committed; but when not committed within any State, the Trial shall be at such Place or Places as the Congress may by Law have directed.

SECTION 3. Treason against the United States, shall consist only in levying War against them, or in adhering to their Enemies, giving them Aid and Comfort. No Person shall be convicted of Treason unless on the Testimony of two Witnesses to the same overt Act, or on Confession in open Court.

The Congress shall have Power to declare the Punishment of Treason, but no Attainder of Treason shall work Corruption of Blood, or Forfeiture except during the Life of the Person attainted.

ARTICLE IV

SECTION 1. Full Faith and Credit shall be given in each State to the public Acts, Records, and judicial Proceedings of every other State. And the Congress may by general Laws prescribe the Manner in which such Acts, Records and Proceedings shall be proved, and the Effect thereof.

SECTION 2. The Citizens of each State shall be entitled to all Privileges and Immunities of Citizens in the several States.

A Person charged in any State with Treason, Felony, or other Crime, who shall flee from Justice, and be found in another State, shall on Demand of the executive Authority of the State from which he fled, be delivered up, to be removed to the State having Jurisdiction of the Crime.

[No Person held to Service or Labour in one State, under the Laws thereof, escaping into another, shall, in Consequence of any Law or Regulation therein, be discharged from such Service or Labour, but shall be delivered up on Claim of the Party to whom such Service or Labour may be due.][9]

SECTION 3. New States may be admitted by the Congress into this Union; but no new State shall be formed or erected within the Jurisdiction of any other State; nor any State be formed by the Junction of two or more States, or Parts of States, without the Consent of the Legislatures of the States concerned as well as of the Congress.

The Congress shall have Power to dispose of and make all needful Rules and Regulations respecting the Territory or other Property belonging to the United States; and nothing in this Constitution shall be so construed as to Prejudice any Claims of the United States, or of any particular State.

SECTION 4. The United States shall guarantee to every State in this Union a Republican Form of Government, and shall protect each of them against Invasion; and on Application of the Legislature, or of the Executive (when the Legislature cannot be convened) against domestic Violence.

ARTICLE V

The Congress, whenever two thirds of both Houses shall deem it necessary, shall propose Amendments to this Constitution, or, on the Application of the Legislatures of two thirds of the several States, shall call a Convention for proposing Amendments, which, in either Case, shall be valid to all Intents and Purposes, as Part of this Constitution, when ratified by the Legislatures of three fourths of the several States, or by Conventions in three fourths thereof, as the one or the other Mode of Ratification may be proposed by the Congress; Provided [that no Amendment which may be made prior to the Year One thousand eight hundred and eight shall in any Manner affect the first and fourth Clauses in the Ninth section of the first Article; and][10] that no State, without its Consent, shall be deprived of its equal Suffrage in the Senate.

ARTICLE VI

All Debts contracted and Engagements entered into, before the Adoption of this Constitution, shall be as valid against the United States under this Constitution, as under the Confederation.

This Constitution, and the Laws of the United States which shall be made in Pursuance thereof; and all Treaties made, or which shall be made, under the Authority of the United States, shall be the supreme Law of the Land; and the Judges in every State shall be bound thereby, any Thing in the Constitution or Laws of any State to the Contrary notwithstanding.

The Senators and Representatives before mentioned, and the Members of the several State Legislatures, and all executive and judicial Officers, both of the United States and of the several States, shall be bound by Oath or Affirmation, to support this Constitution; but no religious Test shall ever be required as a Qualification to any Office or public Trust under the United States.

ARTICLE VII

The Ratification of the Conventions of nine States, shall be sufficient for the Establishment of this Constitution between the States so ratifying the Same.

Done in Convention by the Unanimous Consent of the States present the Seventeenth Day of September in the Year of our Lord one thousand seven hundred and Eighty seven and of the Independence of the United States of America the Twelfth. IN WITNESS whereof We have hereunto subscribed our Names,

George Washington,
President and deputy from Virginia.

New Hampshire:

John Langdon,
Nicholas Gilman.

Massachusetts:

Nathaniel Gorham,
Rufus King.

Connecticut:

William Samuel Johnson,
Roger Sherman.

New York:

Alexander Hamilton.

New Jersey:

William Livingston,
David Brearley,
William Paterson,
Jonathan Dayton.

Pennsylvania:

Benjamin Franklin,
Thomas Mifflin,
Robert Morris,
George Clymer,
Thomas FitzSimons,
Jared Ingersoll,
James Wilson,
Gouverneur Morris.

Delaware:

George Read,
Gunning Bedford Jr.,
John Dickinson,
Richard Bassett,
Jacob Broom.

Maryland:	James McHenry, Daniel of St. Thomas Jenifer, Daniel Carroll.
Virginia:	John Blair, James Madison Jr.
North Carolina:	William Blount, Richard Dobbs Spaight, Hugh Williamson.
South Carolina:	John Rutledge, Charles Cotesworth Pinckney, Charles Pinckney, Pierce Butler.
Georgia:	William Few, Abraham Baldwin.

[The language of the original Constitution, not including the Amendments, was adopted by a convention of the states on September 17, 1787, and was subsequently ratified by the states on the following dates: Delaware, December 7, 1787; Pennsylvania, December 12, 1787; New Jersey, December 18, 1787; Georgia, January 2, 1788; Connecticut, January 9, 1788; Massachusetts, February 6, 1788; Maryland, April 28, 1788; South Carolina, May 23, 1788; New Hampshire, June 21, 1788.

Ratification was completed on June 21, 1788.

The Constitution subsequently was ratified by Virginia, June 25, 1788; New York, July 26, 1788; North Carolina, November 21, 1789; Rhode Island, May 29, 1790; and Vermont, January 10, 1791.]

AMENDMENTS

Amendment I

(First ten amendments ratified December 15, 1791.)
Congress shall make no law respecting an establishment of religion, or prohibiting the free exercise thereof; or abridging the freedom of speech, or of the press; or the right of the people peaceably to assemble, and to petition the Government for a redress of grievances.

Amendment II

A well regulated Militia, being necessary to the security of a free State, the right of the people to keep and bear Arms, shall not be infringed.

Amendment III

No Soldier shall, in time of peace be quartered in any house, without the consent of the Owner, nor in time of war, but in a manner to be prescribed by law.

Amendment IV

The right of the people to be secure in their persons, houses, papers, and effects, against unreasonable searches and seizures, shall not be violated, and no Warrants shall issue, but upon probable cause, supported by Oath or affirmation, and particularly describing the place to be searched, and the persons or things to be seized.

Amendment V

No person shall be held to answer for a capital, or otherwise infamous crime, unless on a presentment or indictment of a Grand Jury, except in cases arising in the land or naval forces, or in the Militia, when in actual service in time of War or public danger; nor shall any person be subject for the same offence to be twice put in jeopardy of life or limb; nor shall be compelled in any criminal case to be a witness against himself, nor be deprived of life, liberty, or property, without due process of law; nor shall private property be taken for public use, without just compensation.

Amendment VI

In all criminal prosecutions, the accused shall enjoy the right to a speedy and public trial, by an impartial jury of the State and district wherein the crime shall have been committed, which district shall have been previously ascertained by law, and to be informed of the nature and cause of the accusation; to be confronted with the witnesses against him; to have compulsory process for obtaining witnesses in his favor, and to have the Assistance of Counsel for his defence.

Amendment VII

In Suits at common law, where the value in controversy shall exceed twenty dollars, the right of trial by jury shall be preserved, and no fact tried by a jury, shall be otherwise re-examined in any Court of the United States, than according to the rules of the common law.

Amendment VIII

Excessive bail shall not be required, nor excessive fines imposed, nor cruel and unusual punishments inflicted.

Amendment IX

The enumeration in the Constitution, of certain rights, shall not be construed to deny or disparage others retained by the people.

Amendment X

The powers not delegated to the United States by the Constitution, nor prohibited by it to the States, are reserved to the States respectively, or to the people.

Amendment XI (Ratified February 7, 1795)

The Judicial power of the United States shall not be construed to extend to any suit in law or equity, commenced or prosecuted against one of the United States by Citizens of another State, or by Citizens or Subjects of any Foreign State.

Amendment XII (Ratified June 15, 1804)

The Electors shall meet in their respective states and vote by ballot for President and Vice-President, one of whom, at least, shall not be an inhabitant of the same state with themselves; they shall name in their ballots the person voted for as President, and in distinct ballots the person voted for as Vice-President, and they shall make distinct lists of all persons voted for as President, and of all persons voted for as Vice-President, and of the number of votes for each, which lists they shall sign and certify, and transmit sealed to the seat of the government of the United States, directed to the President of the Senate; — The President of the Senate shall, in the presence of the Senate and House of Representatives, open all the certificates and the votes shall then be counted; — The person having the greatest number of votes for President, shall be the President, if such number be a majority of the whole number of Electors appointed; and if no person have such majority, then from the persons having the highest numbers not exceeding three on the list of those voted for as President, the House of Representatives shall choose immediately, by ballot, the President. But in choosing the President, the votes shall be taken by states, the representation from each state having one vote; a quorum for this purpose shall consist of a member or members from two-thirds of the states, and a majority of all the states shall be necessary to a choice. [And if the House of Representatives shall not choose a President whenever the right of choice shall devolve upon them, before the fourth day of March next following, then the Vice-President shall act as President, as in the case of the death or other constitutional disability of the President. —][11] The person having the greatest number of votes as Vice-President, shall be the Vice-President, if such number be a majority of the whole number of Electors appointed, and if no person have a majority, then from the two highest numbers on the list, the Senate shall choose the Vice-President; a quorum for the purpose shall consist of two-thirds of the whole number of Senators, and a majority of the whole number shall be necessary to a choice. But no person constitutionally ineligible to the office of President shall be eligible to that of Vice-President of the United States.

Amendment XIII (Ratified December 6, 1865)

SECTION 1. Neither slavery nor involuntary servitude, except as a punishment for crime whereof the party shall have been duly convicted, shall exist within the United States, or any place subject to their jurisdiction.

SECTION 2. Congress shall have power to enforce this article by appropriate legislation.

Amendment XIV (Ratified July 9, 1868)

SECTION 1. All persons born or naturalized in the United States, and subject to the jurisdiction thereof, are citizens of the United States and of the State wherein they reside. No State shall make or enforce any law which shall abridge the privileges or immunities of citizens of the United States; nor shall any State deprive any person of life, liberty, or property, without due process of law; nor deny to any person within its jurisdiction the equal protection of the laws.

SECTION 2. Representatives shall be apportioned among the several States according to their respective numbers, counting the whole number of persons in each State, excluding Indians not taxed. But when the right to vote at any election for the choice of electors for President and Vice President of the United States, Representatives in Congress, the Executive and Judicial officers of a State, or the members of the Legislature thereof, is denied to any of the male inhabitants of such State, being twenty-one years of age,[12] and citizens of the United States, or in any way abridged, except for participation in rebellion, or other crime, the basis of representation therein shall be reduced in the proportion which the number of such male citizens shall bear to the whole number of male citizens twenty-one years of age in such State.

SECTION 3. No person shall be a Senator or Representative in Congress, or elector of President and Vice President, or hold any office, civil or military, under the United States, or under any State, who, having previously taken an oath, as a member of Congress, or as an officer of the United States, or as a member of any State legislature, or as an executive or judicial officer of any State, to support the Constitution of the United States, shall have engaged in insurrection or rebellion against the same, or given aid or comfort to the enemies thereof. But Congress may by a vote of two-thirds of each House, remove such disability.

SECTION 4. The validity of the public debt of the United States, authorized by law, including debts incurred for payment of pensions and bounties for services in suppressing insurrection or rebellion, shall not be questioned. But neither the United States nor any State shall assume or pay any debt or obligation incurred in aid of insurrection or rebellion against the United States, or any claim for the loss or emancipation of any slave; but all such debts, obligations and claims shall be held illegal and void.

SECTION 5. The Congress shall have power to enforce, by appropriate legislation, the provisions of this article.

Amendment XV (Ratified February 3, 1870)

SECTION 1. The right of citizens of the United States to vote shall not be denied or abridged by the United States or by any State on account of race, color, or previous condition of servitude.

SECTION 2. The Congress shall have power to enforce this article by appropriate legislation.

Amendment XVI (Ratified February 3, 1913)

The Congress shall have power to lay and collect taxes on incomes, from whatever source derived, without apportionment among the several States, and without regard to any census or enumeration.

Amendment XVII (Ratified April 8, 1913)

The Senate of the United States shall be composed of two Senators from each State, elected by the people thereof, for six years; and each Senator shall have one vote. The electors in each State shall have the qualifications requisite for electors of the most numerous branch of the State legislatures.

When vacancies happen in the representation of any State in the Senate, the executive authority of such State shall issue writs of election to fill such vacancies: Provided, That the legislature of any State may empower the executive thereof to make temporary appointments until the people fill the vacancies by election as the legislature may direct.

This amendment shall not be so construed as to affect the election or term of any Senator chosen before it becomes valid as part of the Constitution.

Amendment XVIII (Ratified January 16, 1919)[13]

SECTION 1. After one year from the ratification of this article the manufacture, sale, or transportation of intoxicating liquors within, the importation thereof into, or the exportation thereof from the United States and all territory subject to the jurisdiction thereof for beverage purposes is hereby prohibited.

SECTION 2. The Congress and the several States shall have concurrent power to enforce this article by appropriate legislation.

SECTION 3. This article shall be inoperative unless it shall have been ratified as an amendment to the Constitution by the legislatures of the several States, as provided in the Constitution, within seven years from the date of the submission hereof to the States by the Congress.

Amendment XIX (Ratified August 18, 1920)

The right of citizens of the United States to vote shall not be denied or abridged by the United States or by any State on account of sex.

Congress shall have power to enforce this article by appropriate legislation.

Amendment XX (Ratified January 23, 1933)

SECTION 1. The terms of the President and Vice President shall end at noon on the 20th day of January, and the terms of Senators and Representatives at noon on the 3d day of January, of the years in which such terms would have ended if this article had not been ratified; and the terms of their successors shall then begin.

SECTION 2. The Congress shall assemble at least once in every year, and such meeting shall begin at noon on the 3d day of January, unless they shall by law appoint a different day.

SECTION 3.[14] If, at the time fixed for the beginning of the term of the President, the President elect shall have died, the Vice President elect shall become President. If a President shall not have been chosen before the time fixed for the beginning of his term, or if the President elect shall have failed to qualify, then the Vice President elect shall act as President until a President shall have qualified; and the Congress may by law provide for the case wherein neither a President elect nor a Vice President elect shall have qualified, declaring who shall then act as President, or the manner in which one who is to act shall be selected, and such person shall act accordingly until a President or Vice President shall have qualified.

SECTION 4. The Congress may by law provide for the case of the death of any of the persons from whom the House of Representatives may choose a President whenever the right of choice shall have devolved upon them, and for the case of the death of any of the persons from whom the Senate may choose a Vice President whenever the right of choice shall have devolved upon them.

SECTION 5. Sections 1 and 2 shall take effect on the 15th day of October following the ratification of this article.

SECTION 6. This article shall be inoperative unless it shall have been ratified as an amendment to the Constitution by the legislatures of three-fourths of the several States within seven years from the date of its submission.

Amendment XXI (Ratified December 5, 1933)

SECTION 1. The eighteenth article of amendment to the Constitution of the United States is hereby repealed.

SECTION 2. The transportation or importation into any State, Territory, or possession of the United States for delivery or use therein of intoxicating liquors, in violation of the laws thereof, is hereby prohibited.

SECTION 3. This article shall be inoperative unless it shall have been ratified as an amendment to the Constitution by conventions in the several States, as provided in the Constitution, within seven years from the date of the submission hereof to the States by the Congress.

Amendment XXII (Ratified February 27, 1951)

SECTION 1. No person shall be elected to the office of the President more than twice, and no person who has held the office of President, or acted as President, for more than two years of a term to which some other person was elected President shall be elected to the office of the President more than once. But this Article shall not apply to any person holding the office of President when this Article was proposed by the Congress, and shall not prevent any person who may be holding the office of President, or acting as President, during the term within which this Article becomes operative from holding the office of President or acting as President during the remainder of such term.

SECTION 2. This article shall be inoperative unless it shall have been ratified as an amendment to the Constitution by the legislatures of three-fourths of the several States within seven years from the date of its submission to the States by the Congress.

Amendment XXIII (Ratified March 29, 1961)

SECTION 1. The District constituting the seat of Government of the United States shall appoint in such manner as the Congress may direct:

A number of electors of President and Vice President equal to the whole number of Senators and Representatives in Congress to which the District would be entitled if it were a State, but in no event more than the least populous State; they shall be in addition to those appointed by the States, but they shall be considered, for the purposes of the election of President and Vice President, to be electors appointed by a State; and they shall meet in the District and perform such duties as provided by the twelfth article of amendment.

SECTION 2. The Congress shall have power to enforce this article by appropriate legislation.

Amendment XXIV (Ratified January 23, 1964)

SECTION 1. The right of citizens of the United States to vote in any primary or other election for President or Vice President, for electors for President or Vice President, or for Senator or Representative in Congress, shall not be denied or abridged by the United States or any State by reason of failure to pay any poll tax or other tax.

SECTION 2. The Congress shall have power to enforce this article by appropriate legislation.

Amendment XXV (Ratified February 10, 1967)

SECTION 1. In case of the removal of the President from office or of his death or resignation, the Vice President shall become President.

SECTION 2. Whenever there is a vacancy in the office of the Vice President, the President shall nominate a Vice President who shall take office upon confirmation by a majority vote of both Houses of Congress.

SECTION 3. Whenever the President transmits to the President pro tempore of the Senate and the Speaker of the House of Representatives his written declaration that he is unable to discharge the powers and duties of his office, and until he transmits to them a written declaration to the contrary, such powers and duties shall be discharged by the Vice President as Acting President.

SECTION 4. Whenever the Vice President and a majority of either the principal officers of the executive departments or of such other body as Congress may by law provide, transmit to the President pro tempore of the Senate and the Speaker of the House of Representatives their written declaration that the President is unable to discharge the powers and duties of his office, the Vice President shall immediately assume the powers and duties of the office as Acting President.

Thereafter, when the President transmits to the President pro tempore of the Senate and the Speaker of the House of Representatives his written declaration that no inability exists, he shall resume the powers and duties of his office unless the Vice President and a majority of either the principal officers of the executive departments or of such other body as Congress may by law provide, transmit within four days to the President pro tempore of the Senate and the Speaker of the House of Representatives their written declaration that the President is unable to discharge the powers and duties of his office. Thereupon Congress shall decide the issue, assembling within forty-eight hours for that purpose if not in session. If the Congress, within twenty-one days after receipt of the latter written declaration, or, if Congress is not in session, within twenty-one days after Congress is required to assemble, determines by two-thirds vote of both Houses that the President is unable to discharge the powers and duties of his office, the Vice President shall continue to discharge the same as Acting President; otherwise, the President shall resume the powers and duties of his office.

Amendment XXVI (Ratified July 1, 1971)

SECTION 1. The right of citizens of the United States, who are eighteen years of age or older, to vote shall not be denied or abridged by the United States or by any State on account of age.

SECTION 2. The Congress shall have power to enforce this article by appropriate legislation.

Amendment XXVII (Ratified May 7, 1992)

No law varying the compensation for the services of the Senators and Representatives shall take effect, until an election of Representatives shall have intervened.

Notes

1. The part in brackets was changed by section 2 of the Fourteenth Amendment.
2. The part in brackets was changed by the first paragraph of the Seventeenth Amendment.
3. The part in brackets was changed by the second paragraph of the Seventeenth Amendment.
4. The part in brackets was changed by section 2 of the Twentieth Amendment.
5. The Sixteenth Amendment gave Congress the power to tax incomes.
6. The material in brackets was superseded by the Twelfth Amendment.
7. This provision was affected by the Twenty-fifth Amendment.
8. These clauses were affected by the Eleventh Amendment.
9. This paragraph was superseded by the Thirteenth Amendment.

10. Obsolete.
11. The part in brackets was superseded by section 3 of the Twentieth Amendment.
12. See the Nineteenth and Twenty-sixth Amendments.
13. This amendment was repealed by section 1 of the Twenty-first Amendment.
14. See the Twenty-fifth Amendment.

Source: U.S. Congress, House, Committee on the Judiciary, *The Constitution of the United States of America, as Amended,* 100th Cong., 1st sess., 1987, H Doc 100-94.

JUDICIARY ACT OF 1789

Although the Constitution created the Supreme Court, it said much less about the Court than about Congress and the president. With the Judiciary Act of 1789, Congress set up a system of lower federal courts (district courts and circuit courts with limited jurisdiction), spelled out the appellate jurisdiction of the Supreme Court, and gave the Court the power to review and reverse or affirm state court rulings.

The act also set the number of Supreme Court justices at six: a chief justice and five associates. (Subsequent statutes changed the total number of justices successively to seven, nine, ten, seven, and nine.) In addition to establishing the size and jurisdiction of the Supreme Court, the act required the justices to "ride circuit"—a burdensome duty of traveling to and sitting on circuit courts around the country.

JUDICIARY ACT OF 1789

An Act to establish the Judicial Courts of the United States.

STATUTE I
Sept. 24, 1789.

Supreme court to consist of a chief justice, and five associates.

Two sessions annually.

Precedence.

SECTION 1. *Be it enacted by the Senate and House of Representatives of the United States of America in Congress assembled,* That the supreme court of the United States shall consist of a chief justice and five associate justices, any four of whom shall be a quorum, and shall hold annually at the seat of government two sessions, the one commencing the first Monday of February, and the other the first Monday of August. That the associate justices shall have precedence according to the data of their commissions, or when the commissions of two or more of them bear date on the same day, according to the respective ages.

Thirteen districts.

Maine.

N. Hampshire.

Massachusetts.
Connecticut.

SEC. 2. *And be it further enacted,* That the United States shall be, and they hereby are divided into thirteen districts, to be limited and called as follows, to wit: one to consist of that part of the State of Massachusetts which lies easterly of the State of New Hampshire, and to be called Maine District; one to consist of the State of New Hampshire, and to be called New Hampshire District; one to consist of the remaining part of the State of Massachusetts, and to be called Massachusetts district; one to consist of the State of Connecticut, and to be called Connecticut District; one to consist of the State of New York, and to be called New York District; one to consist of the State of New Jersey, and to be called New Jersey District; one to consist of the State of Pennsylvania, and to be called Pennsylvania District; one to consist of the State of Delaware, and to be called Delaware District; one to consist of the State of Maryland, and to be called Maryland District; one to consist of the State of Virginia, except that part called the District of Kentucky, and to be called Virginia District; one to consist of the remaining part of the State of Virginia, and to be called Kentucky District; one to consist of the State of South Carolina, and to be called South Carolina District; and one to consist of the State of Georgia, and to be called Georgia District.

SEC. 3. *And be it further enacted,* That there be a court called a District Court, in each of the aforementioned districts, to consist of one judge, who shall reside in the district for which he is appointed, and shall be called a District Judge, and shall hold annually four sessions, the first of which to commence as follows, to wit: in the districts of New York and of New Jersey on the first, in the district of Pennsylvania on the second, in the district of Connecticut on the third, and in the district of Delaware on the fourth, Tuesdays of November next; in the districts of Massachusetts, of Maine, and of Maryland, on the first, in the district of Georgia on the second, and in the districts of New Hampshire, of Virginia, and of Kentucky, on the third Tuesdays of December next; and the other three sessions progressively in the respective districts on the like Tuesdays of every third calendar month afterwards, and in the district of South Carolina, on the third Monday in March and September, the first Monday in July, and the second Monday in December of each and every year, commencing in December next; and that the District Judge shall have power to hold special courts at his discretion. That the stated District Court shall be held at the places following, to wit: in the district of Maine, at Portland and Pownalsborough alternately, beginning at the first; in the district of New Hampshire, at Exeter and Portsmouth alternately, beginning at the first; in the district of Massachusetts, at Boston and Salem alternately, beginning at the first; in the district of Connecticut, alternately at Hartford and New Haven, beginning at the first; in the district of Connecticut, alternately at Hartford and New Haven, beginning at the first; in the district of New York, at New York; in the district of New Jersey, alternately at New Brunswick and Burlington, beginning at the first; in the district of Pennsylvania, at Philadelphia and York Town alternately, beginning at the first; in the district of Delaware, alternately at Newcastle and Dover, beginning at the first; in the district of Maryland, alternately at Baltimore and Easton, beginning at the first; in the district of Virginia, alternately at Richmond and Williamsburgh, beginning at the first; in the district of Kentucky, at Harrodsburgh; in the district of South Carolina, at Charleston; and in the district of Georgia, alternately at Savannah and Augusta, beginning at the first; and that the special courts shall be held at the same place in each district as the stated courts, or in districts that have two, at either of them, in the discretion of the judge, or at such other place in the district, as the nature of the business and his discretion shall direct. And that in the districts that have but one place for holding the District Court, the records thereof shall be kept at that place; and in districts that have two, at that place in each district which the judge shall appoint.

Where records kept.

SEC. 4. *And be it further enacted,* That the before mentioned districts, except those of Maine and Kentucky, shall be divided into three circuits, and be called the eastern, the middle, and the southern circuit. That the eastern circuit shall consist of the districts of New Hampshire, Massachusetts, Connecticut and New York; that the middle circuit shall consist of the districts of New Jersey, Pennsylvania, Delaware, Maryland and Virginia; and that the southern circuit shall consist of the districts of South Carolina and Georgia, and that there shall be held annually in each district of said circuits, two courts, which shall be called Circuit Courts, and shall consist of any two justices of the Supreme Court, and the district judge of such districts, any two of whom shall constitute a quorum: *Provided,* That no district judge shall give a vote in any case of appeal or error from his own decision; but may assign the reasons of such his decision.

Three circuits, and how divided.

SEC. 5. *And be it further enacted,* That the first session of the said circuit court in the several districts shall commence at the times following, to wit: in New Jersey on the second, in New York on the fourth, in Pennsylvania on the eleventh, in Connecticut on the twenty-second, and in Delaware on the twenty-seventh, days of April next; in Massachusetts on the third, in Maryland on the seventh, in South Carolina on the twelfth, in New Hampshire on the twentieth, in Virginia on the twenty-second, and in Georgia on the twenty-eighth, days of May next, and the subsequent sessions in the respective districts on the like days of every sixth calendar month afterwards, except in South Carolina, where the session of the said court shall commence on the first, and in Georgia where it shall commence on the seventeenth day of October, and except when any of those days shall happen on a Sunday, and then the session shall commence on the next day following. And the sessions of the said circuit court shall be held in the district of New Hampshire, at Portsmouth and Exeter alternately, beginning at the first; in the district of Massachusetts, at Boston; in the district of Connecticut, alternately at Hartford and New Haven, beginning at the last; in the district of New York, alternately at New York and Albany, beginning at the first; in the district of New Jersey, at Trenton; in the district of Pennsylvania, alternately at Philadelphia and Yorktown, beginning at the first; in the district of Delaware, alternately at New Castle and Dover, beginning at the first; in the district of Maryland, alternately at Annapolis and Easton, beginning at the first; in the district of Virginia, alternately at Charlottesville and Williamsburgh, beginning at the first; in the district of South Carolina, alternately at Columbia and Charleston, beginning at the first; and in the district of Georgia, alternately at Savannah and Augusta, beginning at the first. And the circuit courts shall have power to hold special sessions for the trial of criminal

First session of the circuit courts; when holden.

Where holden.

Circuit courts. Special sessions.

causes at any other time at their discretion, or at the discretion of the Supreme Court.

Supreme court adjourned by one or more justices; circuit courts adjourned.

SEC. 6. *And be it further enacted,* That the Supreme Court may, by any one or more of its justices being present, be adjourned from day to day until a quorum be convened; and that a circuit court may also be adjourned from day to day by any one of its judges, or if none are present, by the marshal of the district until a quorum be convened; and that a district court, in case of the inability of the judge to attend at the commencement of a session, may by virtue of a written order from the said judge, directed to the marshal of the district, be adjourned by the said marshal to such day, antecedent to the next stated session of the said court, as in the said order shall be appointed; and in case of the death of the said judge, and his vacancy not being supplied, all process, pleadings and proceedings of what nature soever, pending before the said court, shall be continued of course until the next stated session after the appointment and acceptance of the office by his successor.

District courts adjourned.

The courts have power to appoint clerks.

SEC. 7. *And be it [further] enacted,* That the Supreme Court, and the district courts shall have power to appoint clerks for their respective courts, and that the clerk for each district court shall be clerk also of the circuit court in such district, and each of the said clerks shall, before he enters upon the execution of his office, take the following oath or affirmation, to wit: "I, A. B., being appointed clerk of _____, do solemnly swear, or affirm, that I will truly and faithfully enter and record all the orders, decrees, judgments and proceedings of the said court, and that I will faithfully and impartially discharge and perform all the duties of my said office, according to the best of my abilities and understanding. So help me God." Which words, so help me God, shall be omitted in all cases where an affirmation is admitted instead of an oath. And the said clerks shall also severally give bond, with sufficient sureties, (to be approved of by the Supreme and district courts respectively) to the United States, in the sum of two thousand dollars, faithfully to discharge the duties of his office, and seasonably to record the decrees, judgments and determinations of the court of which he is clerk.

Their oath or affirmation.

SEC. 8. *And be it further enacted,* That the justices of the Supreme Court, and the district judges, before they proceed to execute the duties of their respective offices, shall take the following oath or affirmation, to wit: "I, A. B., do solemnly swear or affirm, that I will administer justice without respect to persons, and do equal right to the poor and to the rich, and that I will faithfully and impartially discharge and perform all the duties incumbent on me as _____, according to the best of my abilities and understanding, agreeably to the constitution and laws of the United States. So help me God."

Oath of justices of supreme court and judges of the district court.

District courts exclusive jurisdiction.

SEC. 9. *And be it further enacted,* That the district courts shall have, exclusively of the courts of the several States, cognizance of all crimes and offences that shall be cognizable under the authority of the United States, committed within their respective districts, or upon the high seas; where no other punishment than whipping, not exceeding thirty stripes, a fine not exceeding one hundred dollars, or a term of imprisonment not exceeding six months, is to be inflicted; and shall also have exclusive original cognizance of all civil causes of admiralty and maritime jurisdication, including all seizures under laws of impost, navigation or trade of the United States, where the seizures are made, on waters which are navigable from the sea by vessels of ten or more tons burthen, within their respective districts as well as upon the high seas; saving to suitors, in all cases, the right of a common law remedy, where the common law is competent to give it; and shall also have exclusive original cognizance of all seizures on land, or other waters than as aforesaid, made, and of all suits for penalties and forfeitures incurred, under the laws of the United States. And shall also have cognizance, concurrent with the courts of the several States, or the circuit courts, as the case may be, of all causes where an alien sues for a tort only in violation of the law of nations or a treaty of the United States. And shall also have cognizance, concurrent as last mentioned, of all suits at common law where the United States sue, and the matter in dispute amounts, exclusive of costs, to the sum or value of one hundred dollars. And shall also have jurisdiction exclusively of the courts of the several States, of all suits against consuls or vice-consuls, except for offences above the description aforesaid. And the trial of issues in fact, in the district courts, in all causes except civil causes of admiralty and maritime jurisdiction, shall be by jury.

Original cognizance in maritime causes and of seizure under the laws of the United States.

Concurrent jurisdiction.

Trial of fact by jury.

Kentucky district court.

Maine district court.

Circuit courts original cognizance where the matter in dispute exceeds five hundred dollars.

Exclusive cognizance of crimes and offences cognizable under the laws of the United States.

SEC. 10. *And be it further enacted,* That the district court in Kentucky district shall, besides the jurisdiction aforesaid, have jurisdiction of all other causes, except of appeals and writs of error, hereinafter made cognizable in a circuit court, and shall proceed therein in the same manner as a circuit court, and writs of error and appeals shall lie from decisions therein to the Supreme Court in the same causes, as from a circuit court to the Supreme Court, and under the same regulations. And the district court in Maine district shall, besides the jurisdiction herein before granted, have jurisdiction of all causes, except of appeals and writs of error herein after made cognizable in a circuit court, and shall proceed therein in the same manner as a circuit court: And writs of error shall lie from decisions therein to the circuit court in the district of Massachusetts in the same manner as from other district courts to their respective circuit courts.

SEC. 11. *And be it further enacted,* That the circuit courts shall have original cognizance, concurrent with the courts of the several States, of all suits of a civil nature at common law or in equity, where the matter in dispute exceeds, exclusive of costs, the sum or value of five hundred dollars, and the United States are plaintiffs, or petitioners; or an alien is a party, or the suit is between a citizen of the State where the suit is brought, and a citizen of another State. And shall have exclusive cognizance of all crimes and offences cognizable under the authority of the United States, except where this act otherwise provides, or the laws of the United States shall otherwise direct, and concurrent jurisdiction with the district courts of the crimes and offences cognizable therein. But no person shall be arrested in one district for trial in another, in any civil action before a circuit or district court. And no civil suit shall be brought before either of said courts against an inhabitant of the United States, by any original process in any other district than that whereof he is an inhabitant, or in which he shall be found at the time of serving the writ, nor shall any district or circuit court have cognizance of any suit to recover the contents of any promissory note or other chose in action in favour of an assignee, unless a suit might have been prosecuted in such court to recover the said contents if no assignment had been made, except in cases of foreign bills of exchange. And the circuit courts shall also have appellate jurisdiction from the district courts under the regulations and restrictions herein after provided.

SEC. 12. *And be it further enacted,* That if a suit be commenced in any state court against an alien, or by a citizen of the state in which the suit is brought against a citizen of another state, and the matter in dispute exceeds the aforesaid sum or value of five hundred dollars, exclusive of costs, to be made to appear to the satisfaction of the court; and the defendant shall, at the time of entering his appearance in such state court, file a petition for the removal of the cause for trial into the next circuit court, to be held in the district where the suit is pending, or if in the district of Maine to the district court next to be holden therein, or if in Kentucky district to the district court next to be holden therein, and offer good and sufficient surety for his entering in such court, on the first day of its session, copies of said process against him, and also for his there appearing and entering special bail in the cause, if special bail was originally requisite therein, it shall then be the duty of the state court to accept the surety, and proceed no further in the cause, and any bail that may have been originally taken shall be discharged and the said copies being entered as aforesaid, in such court of the United States, the cause shall there proceed in the same manner as if it had been brought there by original process. And any attachment of the goods or estate of the defendant by the original process, shall hold the goods or estate so attached, to answer the final judgment in the same manner as by the laws of such state they would have been holden to answer final judgment, had it been rendered by the court in which the suit commenced. And if in any action commenced in a state court, the title of land be concerned, and the parties are citizens of the same state, and the matter in dispute exceeds the sum or value of five hundred dollars, exclusive of costs, the sum or value being made to appear to the satisfaction of the court, either party, before the trial, shall state to the court and make affidavit if they require it, that he claims and shall rely upon a right or title to the land, under a grant from a state other than that in which the suit is pending, and produce the original grant or an exemplification of it, except where the loss of public records shall put it out of his power, and shall move that the adverse party inform the court, whether he claims a right or title to the land under a grant from the state in which the suit is pending; the said adverse

No person to be arrested in one district for trial in another on any civil suit.
Limitation as to civil suits.

Actions on promissory notes.

Circuit courts shall also have appellate jurisdiction.

Matter in dispute above 500 dollars.

Removal of causes from state courts.

Special bail.

Attachment of goods holden to final judgment.

Title of land where value exceeds 500 dollars.

[party] shall give such information, or otherwise not be allowed to plead such grant, or give it in evidence upon the trial, and if he informs that he does claim under such grant, the party claiming under the grant first mentioned may then, on motion, remove the cause for trial to the next circuit court to be holden in such district, or if in the district of Maine, to the court next to be holden therein; or if in Kentucky district, to the district court next to be holden therein; but if he is the defendant, shall do it under the same regulations as in the beforementioned case of the removal of a cause into such court by an alien; and neither party removing the cause, shall be allowed to plead or give evidence of any other title than that by him stated as aforesaid, as the ground of his claim; and the trial of issues in fact in the circuit courts shall, in all suits, except those of equity, and of admiralty, and maritime jurisdiction, be by jury.

SEC. 13. *And be it further enacted,* That the Supreme Court shall have exclusive jurisdiction of all controversies of a civil nature, where a state is a party, except between a state and its citizens; and except also between a state and citizens of other states, or aliens, in which latter case it shall have original but not exclusive jurisdiction. And shall have exclusively all such jurisdiction of suits or proceedings against ambassadors, or other public ministers, or their domestics, or domestic servants, as a court of law can have or exercise consistently with the law of nations; and original, but not exclusive jurisdiction of all suits brought by ambassadors, or other public ministers, or in which a consul, or vice consul, shall be a party. And the trial of issues in fact in the Supreme Court, in all actions at law against citizens of the United States, shall be by jury. The Supreme Court shall also have appellate jurisdiction from the circuit courts and courts of the several states, in the cases herein after specially provided for; and shall have power to issue writs of prohibition to the district courts, when proceeding as courts of admiralty and maritime jurisdiction, and writs of *mandamus,* in cases warranted by the principles and usages of law, to any courts appointed, or persons holding office, under the authority of the United States.

SEC. 14. *And be it further enacted,* That all the before-mentioned courts of the United States, shall have power to issue writs of *scire facias, habeas corpus,* and all other writs not specially provided for by statute, which may be necessary for the exercise of their respective jurisdictions, and agreeable to the principles and usages of law. And that either of the justices of the supreme court, as well as judges of the district courts, shall have power to grant writs of habeas corpus for the purpose of an inquiry into the cause of commitment — *Provided,* That writs of *habeas corpus* shall in no case extend to prisoners in gaol, unless where they are in custody, under or by colour of the authority of the United States, or are committed for trial before some court of the same, or are necessary to be brought into court to testify.

If in Maine and Kentucky, where causes are removable.

Issues in fact by jury.

Supreme court exclusive jurisdiction.

Proceedings against public ministers.

Sup. Court appellate jurisdiction.

Writs of Prohibition.

Of Mandamus.

Courts may issue writs scire facias, habeas corpus, &c.

Limitation of writs of habeas corpus.

Parties shall produce books and writings.

SEC. 15. *And be it further enacted,* That all the said courts of the United States, shall have power in the trial of actions at law, on motion and due notice thereof being given, to require the parties to produce books or writings in their possession or power, which contain evidence pertinent to the issue, in cases and under circumstances where they might be compelled to produce the same by the ordinary rules of proceeding in chancery; and if a plaintiff shall fail to comply with such order, to produce books or writings, it shall be lawful for the courts respectively, on motion, to give the like judgment for the defendant as in cases of nonsuit; and if a defendant shall fail to comply with such order, to produce books or writings, it shall be lawful for the courts respectively on motion as aforesaid, to give judgment against him or her by default.

Suits in equity limited.

SEC. 16. *And be it further enacted,* That suits in equity shall not be sustained in either of the courts of the United States, in any case where plain, adequate and complete remedy may be had at law.

Courts may grant new trials.

SEC. 17. *And be it further enacted,* That all the said courts of the United States shall have power to grant new trials, in cases where there has been a trial by jury for reasons for which new trials have usually been granted in the courts of law; and shall have power to impose and administer all necessary oaths or affirmations, and to punish by fine or imprisonment, at the discretion of said courts, all contempts of authority in any cause or hearing before the same; and to make and establish all necessary rules for the orderly conducting business in the said courts, provided such rules are not repugnant to the laws of the United States.

Execution may be stayed on conditions.

SEC. 18. *And be it further enacted,* That when in a circuit court, judgment upon a verdict in a civil action shall be entered, execution may on motion of either party, at the discretion of the court, and on such conditions for the security of the adverse party as they may judge proper, be stayed forty-two days from the time of entering judgment, to give time to file in the clerk's office of said court, a petition for a new trial. And if such petition be there filed within said term of forty-two days, with a certificate thereon from either of the judges of such court, that he allows the same to be filed, which certificate he may make or refuse at his discretion, execution shall of course be further stayed to the next session of said court. And if a new trial be granted, the former judgment shall be thereby rendered void.

Facts to appear on record.

SEC. 19. *And be it further enacted,* That it shall be the duty of circuit courts, in causes in equity and of admiralty and maritime jurisdiction, to cause the facts on which they found their sentence or decree, fully to appear upon the record of either from the pleadings and decree itself, or a state of the case agreed by the parties, or their counsel, or if they disagree by a stating of the case by the court.

SEC. 20. *And be it further enacted,* That where in a circuit court, a plaintiff in an action, originally brought there, or a petitioner in equity, other than the United States, recovers less than the sum or value of five hundred dollars, or a libellant, upon his own appeal, less than the sum or value of three hundred dollars, he shall not be allowed, but at the discretion of the court, may be adjudged to pay costs.

SEC. 21. *And be it further enacted,* That from final decrees in a district court in causes of admiralty and maritime jurisdiction, where the matter in dispute exceeds the sum or value of three hundred dollars, exclusive of costs, an appeal shall be allowed to the next circuit court, to be held in such district. *Provided nevertheless,* That all such appeals from final decrees as aforesaid, from the district court of Maine, shall be made to the circuit court, next to be holden after each appeal in the district of Massachusetts.

SEC. 22. *And be it further enacted,* That final decrees and judgments in civil actions in a district court, where the matter in dispute exceeds the sum or value of fifty dollars, exclusive of costs, may be re-examined, and reversed or affirmed in a circuit court, holden in the same distict, upon a writ of error, whereto shall be annexed and returned therewith at the day and place therein mentioned, an authenticated transcript of the record, an assignment of errors, and prayer for reversal, with a citation to the adverse party, signed by the judge of such district court, or a justice of the Supreme Court, the adverse party having at least twenty days' notice. And upon a like process, may final judgments and decrees in civil actions, and suits in equity in a circuit court, brought there by original process, or removed there from courts of the several States, or removed there by appeal from a district court where the matter in dispute exceeds the sum or value of two thousand dollars, exclusive of costs, be re-examined and reversed or affirmed in the Supreme Court, the citation being in such case signed by a judge of such circuit court, or justice of the Supreme Court, and the adverse party having at least thirty days' notice. But there shall be no reversal in either court on such writ of error for error in ruling any plea in abatement, other than a plea to the jurisdiction of the court, or such plea to a petition or bill in equity, as is in the nature of a demurrer, or for any error in fact. And writs of error shall not be brought but within five years after rendering or passing the judgment or decree complained of, or in case the person entitled to such writ of error be an infant, feme covert, non compos mentis, or imprisoned, then within five years as aforesaid, exclusive of the time of such disability. And every justice or judge signing a citation on any writ of error as aforesaid, shall take good and sufficient security, that the plaintiff in error shall prosecute his writ to effect, and answer all damages and costs if he fail to make his plea good.

SEC. 23. *And be it further enacted,* That a writ of error as aforesaid shall be a supersedeas and stay execution in cases only where the writ of error is served, by a copy thereof being lodged for the adverse party in the clerk's office

---

Costs not allowed unless 500 dollars recovered.

Appeals from the district to the circuit court where matter in dispute exceeds 300 dolls.

Final decrees re-examined above 50 dollars.

Altered by the 2d section of the act of March 3, 1803, chap. 40.

And suits in equity, exceeding 2000 dollars in value.

Writs of error limited.

Plaintiff to give security.

Writ of error a supersedeas.

where the record remains, within ten days, Sundays exclusive, after rendering the judgment or passing the decree complained of. Until the expiration of which term of ten days, executions shall not issue in any case where a writ of error may be a supersedeas; and whereupon such writ of error the Supreme or a circuit court shall affirm a judgment or decree, they shall adjudge or decree to the respondent in error just damages for his delay, and single or double costs at their discretion.

SEC. 24. *And be it further enacted,* That when a judgment or decree shall be reversed in a circuit court, such court shall proceed to render such judgment or pass such decree as the district court should have rendered or passed; and the Supreme Court shall do the same on reversals therein, except where the reversal is in favor of the plaintiff, or petitioner in the original suit, and the damages to be assessed, or matter to be decreed, are uncertain, in which case they shall remand the cause for a final decision. And the Supreme Court shall not issue execution in causes that are removed before them by writs of error, but shall send a special mandate to the circuit court to award execution thereupon.

SEC. 25. *And be it further enacted,* That a final judgment or decree in any suit, in the highest court of law or equity of a State in which a decision in the suit could be had, where is drawn in question the validity of a treaty or statute of, or an authority exercised under the United States, and the decision is against their validity; or where is drawn in question the validity of a statute of, or an authority exercised under any State, on the ground of their being repugnant to the constitution, treaties or laws of the United States, and the decision is in favour of such their validity, or where is drawn in question the construction of any clause of the constitution, or of a treaty, or statute of, or commission held under the United States, and the decision is against the title, right, privilege or exemption specially set up or claimed by either party, under such clause of the said Constitution, treaty, statute or commission, may be reexamined and reversed or affirmed in the Supreme Court of the United States upon a writ of error, the citation being signed by the chief justice, or judge or chancellor of the court rendering or passing the judgment or decree complained of, or by a justice of the Supreme Court of the United States, in the same manner and under the same regulations, and the writ shall have the same effect, as if the judgment or decree complained of had been rendered or passed in a circuit court, and the proceeding upon the reversal shall also be the same, except that the Supreme Court, instead of remanding the cause for a final decision as before provided, may at their discretion, if the cause shall have been once remanded before, proceed to a final decision of the same, and award execution. But no other error shall be assigned or regarded as a ground of reversal in any such case as aforesaid, than such as appears on the face of the record, and immediately respects the before mentioned questions of validity or construction of the said constitution, treaties, statutes, commissions, or authorities in dispute.

Margin notes:

Judgment or decree reversed.

Supreme court not to issue execution but mandate.

Cases in which judgment and decrees of the highest court of a state may be examined by the supreme court, on writ of error.

Proceedings on reversal.

No writs of error but as above mentioned.

In cases of forfeiture
the courts may give
judgment according
to equity.

SEC. 26. *And be it further enacted,* That in all causes brought before either of the courts of the United States to recover the forfeiture annexed to any articles of agreement, covenant, bond, or other speciality, where the forfeiture, breach or non-performance shall appear, by the default or confession of the defendant, or upon demurrer, the court before whom the action is, shall render judgment therein for the plaintiff to recover so much as is due according to equity. And when the sum for which judgment should be rendered is uncertain, the same shall, if either of the parties request it, be assessed by a jury.

Jury to assess
damages when the
sum is uncertain.

Marshal to be
appointed.
Duration of office.

SEC. 27. *And be it further enacted,* That a marshal shall be appointed in and for each district for the term of four years, but shall be removable from office at pleasure, whose duty it shall be to attend the district and circuit courts when sitting therein, and also the Supreme Court in the district in which that court shall sit. And to execute throughout the district, all lawful precepts directed to him, and issued under the authority of the United States, and he shall have power to command all necessary assistance in the execution of his duty, and to appoint as there shall be occasion, one or more deputies, who shall be removable from office by the judge of the district court, or the circuit court sitting within the district, at the pleasure of either; and before he enters on the duties of his office, he shall become bound for the faithful performance of the same, by himself and by his deputies before the judge of the district court to the United States, jointly and severally, with two good and sufficient sureties, inhabitants and freeholders of such district, to be approved by the district judge, in the sum of twenty thousand dollars, and shall take before said judge, as shall also his deputies, before they enter on the duties of their appointment, the following oath of office: "I, A. B., do solemnly swear or affirm, that I will faithfully execute all lawful precepts directed to the marshal of the district of _____ under the authority of the United States, and true returns make, and in all things well and truly, and without malice or partiality, perform the duties of the office of marshal (or marshal's deputy, as the case may be) of the district of _____, during my continuance in said office, and take only my lawful fees. So help me God."

Oath of marshal,
and of his
deputies.

If marshal, or his
deputy, a party to a
suit, process to be
directed to a person
selected by the court.

SEC. 28. *And be it further enacted,* That in all causes wherein the marshal or his deputy shall be a party, the writs and precepts therein shall be directed to such disinterested person as the court, or any justice or judge thereof may appoint, and the person so appointed, is hereby authorized to execute and return the same. And in case of the death of any marshal, his deputy or deputies shall continue in office, unless otherwise specially removed; and shall execute the same in the name of the deceased, until another marshal shall be appointed and sworn: And the defaults or misfeasances in office of such deputy or deputies in the mean time, as well as before, shall be adjudged a breach of the condition of the bond given, as before directed, by the marshal who appointed them; and the executor or administrator of the deceased marshal shall have like remedy for the defaults and misfeasances in office of

Deputies to
continue in office
on the death of
the marshal.

Powers of the ex-
ecutor or administra-
tor of deceased
marshals.

such deputy or deputies during such interval, as they would be entitled to if the marshal had continued in life and in the exercise of his said office, until his successor was appointed, and sworn or affirmed: And every marshal or his deputy when removed from office, or when the term for which the marshal is appointed shall expire, shall have power notwithstanding to execute all such precepts as may be in their hands respectively at the time of such removal or expiration of office; and the marshal shall be held answerable for the delivery to his successor of all prisoners which may be in his custody at the time of his removal, or when the term for which he is appointed shall expire, and for that purpose may retain such prisoners in his custody until his successor shall be appointed and qualified as the law directs.

Marshal's power after removal.

Trial of cases punishable with death to be had in county.

Jurors by lot.

SEC. 29. *And be it further enacted,* That in cases punishable with death, the trial shall be had in the county where the offence was committed, or where that cannot be done without great inconvenience, twelve petit jurors at least shall be summoned from thence. And jurors in all cases to serve in the courts of the United States shall be designated by lot or otherwise in each State respectively according to the mode of forming juries therein now practised, so far as the laws of the same shall render such designation practicable by the courts or marshals of the United States; and the jurors shall have the same qualifications as are requisite for jurors by the laws of the State of which they are citizens, to serve in the highest courts of law of such State, and shall be returned as there shall be occasion for them, from such parts of the district from time to time as the court shall direct, so as shall be most favourable to an impartial trial, and so as not to incur an unnecessary expense, or unduly to burthen the citizens of any part of the district with such services. And writs of *venire farias* when directed by the court shall issue from the clerk's office, and shall be served and returned by the marshal in his proper person, or by his deputy, or in case the marshal or his deputy is not an indifferent person, or is interested in the event of the cause, by such fit person as the court shall specially appoint for that purpose, to whom they shall administer an oath or affirmation that he will truly and impartially serve and return such writ. And when from challenges or otherwise there shall not be a jury to determine any civil or criminal cause, the marshal or his deputy shall, by order of the court where such defect of jurors shall happen, return jurymen *de talibus circumstantibus* sufficient to complete the pannel; and when the marshal or his deputy are disqualified as aforesaid, jurors may be returned by such disinterested person as the court shall appoint.

Writs of venire facias from clerk's office.

Juries de talibus, &c.

Mode of proof.

SEC. 30. *And be it further enacted,* That the mode of proof by oral testimony and examination of witnesses in open court shall be the same in all the courts of the United States, as well in the trial of causes in equity and of admiralty and maritime jurisdiction, as of actions at common law. And when the testimony of any person shall be necessary in any civil cause depending in any district in any court of the United States, who shall live at a greater distance from the place of trial than one hundred miles, or is bound on a voyage to sea, or is about to go out of the United States, or out of such district, and to a greater distance from the place of trial than as aforesaid, before the time of trial, or is ancient or very infirm, the deposition of such person may be taken *de bene esse* before any justice or judge of any of the courts of the United States, or before any chancellor, justice or judge of a supreme or superior court, mayor or chief magistrate of a city, or judge of a county court or court of common pleas of any of the United States, not being of counsel or attorney to either of the parties, or interested in the event of the cause, provided that a notification from the magistrate before whom the deposition is to be taken to the adverse party, to be present at the taking of the same, and to put interrogatories, if he think fit, be first made out and served on the adverse party or his attorney as either may be nearest, if either is within one hundred miles of the place of such caption, allowing time for their attendance after notified, not less than at the rate of one day, Sundays exclusive, for every twenty miles travel. And in causes of admiralty and maritime jurisdiction, or other cases of seizure when a libel shall be filed, in which an adverse party is not named, and depositions of persons circumstanced as aforesaid shall be taken before a claim be put in, the like notification as aforesaid shall be given to the person having the agency or possession of the property libelled at the time of the capture or seizure of the same, if known to the libellant. And every person deposing as aforesaid shall be carefully examined and cautioned, and sworn or affirmed to testify the whole truth, and shall subscribe the testimony by him or her given after the same shall be reduced to writing, which shall be done only by the magistrate taking the deposition, or by the deponent in his presence. And the depositions so taken shall be retained by such magistrate until he deliver the same with his own hand into the court for which they are taken, or shall, together with a certificate of the reasons as aforesaid of their being taken, and of the notice if any given to the adverse party, be by him the said magistrate sealed up and directed to such court, and remain under his seal until opened in court. And any person may be compelled to appear and depose as aforesaid in the same manner as to appear and testify in court. And in the trial of any cause of admiralty or maritime jurisdiction in a district court, the decree in which may be appealed from, if either party shall suggest to and satisfy the court that probably it will not be in his power to produce the witnesses there testifying before the circuit court should an appeal be had, and shall move that their testimony be taken down in writing, it shall be so done by the clerk of the court. And if an appeal be had, such testimony may be used on the trial of the same if it shall appear to the satisfaction of the court which shall try the appeal, that the witnesses are then dead or gone out of the United States, or to a greater distance than as aforesaid from the place where the court is sitting, or that by reason of age, sickness, bodily infirmity or imprisonment, they are unable to travel and appear at court, but not otherwise. And unless the same shall be made to appear on the trial of any cause, with respect to witnesses whose depositions may have been taken therein, such depositions shall not be admitted or used in the cause. *Provided,* That nothing herein shall be construed to prevent any

Depositions de bene esse.

Adverse party to be notified.

Notice in admiralty and maritime causes.

Agent notified.

Depositions retained.

Persons may be compelled to appear and testify.

Appeal allowed.

Depositions used in case of sickness, death, &c.

court of the United States from granting a *dedimus potestatem* to take depositions according to common usage, when it may be necessary to prevent a failure or delay of justice, which power they shall severally possess, nor to extend to depositions taken in *perpetuam rei memoriam,* which if they relate to matters that may be cognizable in any court of the United States, a circuit court on application thereto made as a court of equity, may, according to the usages in chancery direct to be taken.

SEC. 31. *And be it [further] enacted,* That where any suit shall be depending in any court of the United States, and either of the parties shall die before final judgment, the executor or administrator of such deceased party who was plaintiff, petitioner, or defendant, in case the cause of action doth by law survive, shall have full power to prosecute or defend any such suit or action until final judgment; and the defendant or defendants are hereby obliged to answer thereto accordingly; and the court before whom such cause may be depending, is hereby empowered and directed to hear and determine the same, and to render judgment for or against the executor or administrator, as the case may require. And if such executor or administrator having been duly served with a *scire facias* from the office of the clerk of the court where such suit is depending, twenty days beforehand, shall neglect or refuse to become a party to the suit, the court may render judgment against the estate of the deceased party, in the same manner as if the executor or administrator had voluntarily made himself a party to the suit. And the executor or administrator who shall become a party as aforesaid, shall, upon motion to the court where the suit is depending, be entitled to a continuance of the same until the next term of the said court. And if there be two or more plaintiffs or defendants, and one or more of them shall die, if the cause of action shall survive to the surviving plaintiff or plaintiffs, or against the surviving defendant or defendants, the writ or action shall not be thereby abated; but such death being suggested upon the record, the action shall proceed at the suit of the surviving plaintiff or plaintiffs against the surviving defendant or defendants.

SEC. 32. *And be it further enacted,* That no summons, writ, declaration, return, process, judgment, or other proceedings in civil causes in any of the courts of the United States, shall be abated, arrested, quashed or reversed, for any defect or want of form, but the said courts respectively shall proceed and give judgment according as the right of the cause and matter in law shall appear unto them, without regarding any imperfections, defects, or want of form in such writ, declaration, or other pleading, return, process, judgment, or course of proceeding whatsoever, except those only in cases of demurrer, which the party demurring shall specially sit down and express together with his demurrer as the cause thereof. And the said courts respectively shall and may, by virtue of this act, from time to time, amend all and every such imperfections, defects and wants of form, other than those only which the party demurring shall express as aforesaid, and may at any time permit either of the parties to amend any defect in the process or pleadings, upon such

Executor or adminis-
trator may prosecute
and defend.

Neglect of executor
or administrator to
become a party to
the suit, judgment to
be rendered.

Executor and admin-
istrator may have
continuance.
Two plaintiffs.
Surviving plaintiff
may continue suit.

Writs shall not abate
for defect of form.

Exceptions.

Courts may amend
imperfections.

conditions as the said courts respectively shall in their discretion, and by their rules prescribe.

Criminals against U.S. arrested by any justice of the peace.

SEC. 33. *And be it further enacted,* That for any crime or offence against the United States, the offender may, by any justice or judge of the United States, or by any justice of the peace, or other magistrate of any of the United States where he may be found agreeably to the usual mode of process against offenders in such state, and at the expense of the United States, be arrested, and imprisoned or bailed, as the case may be, for trial before such court of the United States as by this act has cognizance of the offence. And copies of

Recognizance to be returned to the clerk's office.

the process shall be returned as speedily as may be into the clerk's office of such court, together with the recognizances of the witnesses for their appearance to testify in the case; which recognizances the magistrate before whom the examination shall be, may require on pain of imprisonment. And if such commitment of the offender, or the witnesses shall be in a district other than

Offender may be removed by warrant.

that in which the offence is to be tried, it shall be the duty of the judge of that district where the delinquent is imprisoned, seasonably to issue, and of the marshal of the same district to execute, a warrant for the removal of the offender, and the witnesses, or either of them, as the case may be, to the district in which the trial is to be had. And upon all arrests in criminal cases, bail

Bail admitted.

shall be admitted, except where the punishment may be death, in which cases it shall not be admitted but by the supreme or a circuit court, or by a justice of the supreme court, or a judge of a district court, who shall exercise their discretion therein, regarding the nature and circumstances of the offence, and of the evidence, and the usages of law. And if a person committed by a

Bail, how taken.

justice of the supreme or a judge of a district court for an offence not punishable with death, shall afterwards procure bail, and there be no judge of the United States in the district to take the same, it may be taken by any judge of the supreme or superior court of law of such state.

Laws of States rules of decision.

SEC. 34. *And be it further enacted,* That the laws of the several states, except where the constitution, treaties or statutes of the United States shall otherwise require or provide, shall be regarded as rules of decision in trials at common law in the courts of the United States in cases where they apply.

Parties may manage their own cause.

SEC. 35. *And be it further enacted,* That in all the courts of the United States, the parties may plead and manage their own causes personally or by the assistance of such counsel or attorneys at law as by the rules of the said courts respectively shall be permitted to manage and conduct causes therein. And there shall be appointed in each district a meet person learned in the law to

Attorney of the U.S. for each district.

act as attorney for the United States in such district, who shall be sworn or affirmed to the faithful execution of his office, whose duty it shall be to pros-

His duties.

ecute in such district all delinquents for crimes and offences, cognizable under the authority of the United States, and all civil actions in which the United States shall be concerned, except before the supreme court in the district in which that court shall be holden. And he shall receive as a compensa-

Compensation.

tion for his services such fees as shall be taxed therefore in the respective courts before which the suits or prosecutions shall be. And there shall also be appointed a meet person, learned in the law, to act as attorney-general for the United States, who shall be sworn or affirmed to a faithful execution of his office; whose duty it shall be to prosecute and conduct all suits in the Supreme Court in which the United States shall be concerned, and to give his advice and opinion upon questions of law when required by the President of the United States, or when requested by the heads of any of the departments, touching any matters that may concern their departments, and shall receive

such compensation for his services as shall by law be provided.

APPROVED, September 24, 1789.

Source: Public Statutes at Large of the United States of America, Vol. I (Boston: Charles C. Little & James Brown, 1845).

ONLINE SOURCES
OF DECISIONS

Using the Internet and bulletin board systems (BBSs), it is possible to read the full text of Supreme Court decisions, listen to oral arguments from historic cases, and receive alerts when new decisions are posted online. A number of Internet sites and BBSs offer free Supreme Court information. Here are some of the best:

U.S. SUPREME COURT BBS

Access method: BBS
Data: 202-554-2570

The Supreme Court BBS provides online users with opinions, calendars, order lists, an automated docket, and a booklet about the Court.

Opinions are available dating back to 1995. Opinions from October 1997 onward are provided in ASCII text and Portable Document Format (PDF), while earlier opinions are available in Word-Perfect 5.1 and ASCII text formats.

The Supreme Court BBS posts opinions within five days after they are announced from the bench. The documents posted are the "slip" opinions, which contain page numbers so that users can cite them before they are formally published.

CORNELL LEGAL INFORMATION INSTITUTE

Access method: WWW
To access: *http://supct.law.cornell.edu/supct*

Although several Internet sites provide Supreme Court opinions, the Cornell Legal Information Institute is a popular choice because it is so easy to use.

Cornell offers the full text of all Supreme Court decisions from May 1990 to the present. Decisions are posted the same day the Court releases them and can be accessed by using the name of the first party, the name of the second party, keyword, date, and other variables.

The site also provides nearly six hundred historic Supreme Court decisions dating back to the Court's beginnings on topics such as school prayer, abortion, administrative law, copyright, patent law, and trademarks. Some of the cases include *Regents of the University of California v. Bakke, Roe v. Wade, New York Times Co. v. United States, Tinker v. Des Moines Independent Community School*

District, Miranda v. Arizona, Griswold v. Connecticut, New York Times Co. v. Sullivan, Gideon v. Wainwright, and *Brown v. Board of Education.* Cases can be accessed by topic, party name, or opinion author.

The site also has the full text of the Supreme Court Rules, the Court calendar for the current term, the schedule of oral arguments, biographical data about current and former justices, and a glossary of legal terms.

LIIBULLETIN

Access method: E-mail
To access: Send an e-mail message to *listserv@listserv.law.cornell.edu*

The liibulletin is a free mailing list that alerts subscribers when new Supreme Court decisions are placed on the Internet. The list provides syllabi of new decisions, in addition to instructions about how to obtain the full text. Cornell Law School's Legal Information Institute operates the site.

To subscribe, send an e-mail message to listserv@listserv.law.cornell.edu and leave the subject line blank. In the message area type: subscribe liibulletin *firstname lastname* where *firstname* and *lastname* are replaced by your first and last names.

OYEZ OYEZ OYEZ: A U.S. SUPREME COURT DATABASE

Access method: WWW
To access: *http://oyez.nwu.edu*

This site offers recordings of oral arguments from more than 250 historic Supreme Court cases dating back to 1956. The site is operated by Northwestern University, and the recordings are digitized from tapes in the National Archives.

Listening to the cases requires RealAudio software. Oyez offers a link to another Internet site where the software can be downloaded for free.

Some of the cases available include *Planned Parenthood v. Casey, Hustler Magazine v. Falwell, Regents of the University of California v. Bakke, Roe v. Wade, Furman v. Georgia, Griswold v. Connecticut,* and *New York Times v. Sullivan.* The database can be searched by title, citation, subject, and date. For each case, the site provides recordings of oral arguments and text listing the facts of the case, the constitutional question involved, and the Court's conclusion.

Oyez also provides brief biographies of all current and former justices and a virtual tour of the Supreme Court building.

FINDLAW

Access method: WWW
To access: *http://www.findlaw.com/casecode/supreme.html*

This site provides the full text of all Supreme Court decisions from 1893 to the present. The database can be browsed by year and *U.S. Reports* volume number, and it also can be searched by citation, case title, and keywords. The decisions are in HTML format, and many have hyperlinks to citations from previous decisions.

The site also offers the full text of the U.S. Constitution, with annotations by the Congressional Research Service, and links to cited Supreme Court cases. FindLaw, a legal publisher, operates the site.

USSC+ ONLINE

Access method: WWW

To access: *http://www.usscplus.com/online/index.htm*

The database at this site provides the full text of all Supreme Court decisions from 1945 to the present. The database can be searched by citation, name, subject, keywords, docket, and subject.

Many decisions have hyperlinks to citations from earlier cases. InfoSynthesis, a legal publisher, operates the site.

FEDWORLD/FLITE SUPREME COURT DECISIONS

Access method: WWW

To access: *http://www.fedworld.gov/supcourt/index.htm*

FedWorld's database contains the full text of all Supreme Court decisions issued between 1937 and 1975. The database was originally compiled by the U.S. Air Force, and has been placed online by the National Technical Information Service.

The more than seven thousand decisions are from volumes 300 to 422 of *U.S. Reports*. They can be searched by case name and keyword. The decisions are provided in ASCII text format.

Source: Bruce Maxwell, *How to Access the Federal Government on the Internet: Washington Online*, 3d ed. (Washington, D.C.: Congressional Quarterly, 1997).

HOW TO READ
A COURT CITATION

The official version of each Supreme Court decision and opinion is contained in a series of volumes entitled *United States Reports,* published by the U.S. Government Printing Office.

While there are several unofficial compilations of Court opinions, including *United States Law Week,* published by the Bureau of National Affairs; *Supreme Court Reporter,* published by West Publishing Company; and *United States Supreme Court Reports, Lawyers' Edition,* published by Lawyers Cooperative Publishing Company, it is the official record that is generally cited. An unofficial version or the official slip opinion might be cited if a decision has not yet been officially reported.

A citation to a case includes, in order, the name of the parties to the case, the volume of *United States Reports* in which the decision appears, the page in the volume on which the opinion begins, the page from which any quoted material is taken, and the year of the decision.

For example, *Colegrove v. Green,* 328 U.S. 549, 553 (1946) means that the Supreme Court decision in the case of Colegrove against Green can be found in volume 328 of *United States Reports* beginning on page 549. The specific quotation in question will be found on page 553. The case was decided in 1946.

Until 1875 the official reports of the Court were published under the names of the Court reporters, and it is their names, or abbreviated versions, that appear in cites for those years, although U.S. volume numbers have been assigned retroactively to them. A citation such as *Marbury v. Madison,* 1 Cranch 137 (1803) means that the opinion in the case of Marbury against Madison is in the first volume of reporter Cranch beginning on page 137. (Between 1875 and 1883 a Court reporter named William T. Otto compiled the decisions and opinions; his name appears on the volumes for those years as well as the *United States Reports* volume number, but Otto is seldom cited.)

The titles of the volumes to 1875, the full names of the reporters, and the corresponding *United States Reports* volumes are:

1–4 Dall.	Dallas	1–4 U.S.
1–9 Cranch or Cr.	Cranch	5–13 U.S.
1–12 Wheat.	Wheaton	14–25 U.S.
1–16 Pet.	Peters	26–41 U.S.
1–24 How.	Howard	42–65 U.S.
1–2 Black	Black	66–67 U.S.
1–23 Wall.	Wallace	68–90 U.S.

GLOSSARY OF COMMON LEGAL TERMS

Accessory. In criminal law, a person not present at the commission of an offense who commands, advises, instigates, or conceals the offense.

Acquittal. Discharge of a person from a charge of guilt. A person is acquitted when a jury returns a verdict of not guilty. A person may also be acquitted when a judge determines that there is insufficient evidence to convict him or that a violation of due process precludes a fair trial.

Adjudicate. To determine finally by the exercise of judicial authority to decide a case.

Affidavit. A voluntary written statement of facts or charges affirmed under oath.

A fortiori. With stronger force, with more reason.

Amicus curiae. A friend of the court, a person not a party to litigation, who volunteers or is invited by the court to give his views on a case.

Appeal. To take a case to a higher court for review. Generally, a party losing in a trial court may appeal once to an appellate court as a matter of right. If he loses in the appellate court, appeal to a higher court is within the discretion of the higher court. Most appeals to the U.S. Supreme Court are within the Court's discretion. However, when the highest court in a state rules that a U.S. statute is unconstitutional or upholds a state statute against the claim that it is unconstitutional, appeal to the Supreme Court is a matter of right.

Appellant. The party that appeals a lower court decision to a higher court.

Appellee. One who has an interest in upholding the decision of a lower court and is compelled to respond when the case is appealed to a higher court by the appellant.

Arraignment. The formal process of charging a person with a crime, reading him the charge, asking whether he pleads guilty or not guilty, and entering his plea.

Attainder, Bill of. A legislative act pronouncing a particular individual guilty of a crime without trial or conviction and imposing a sentence upon him.

Bail. The security, usually money, given as assurance of a prisoner's due appearance at a designated time and place (as in court) in order to procure in the interim his release from jail.

Bailiff. A minor officer of a court usually serving as an usher or a messenger.

Brief. A document prepared by counsel to serve as the basis for an argument in court, setting out the facts of and the legal arguments in support of his case.

Burden of proof. The need or duty of affirmatively proving a fact or facts that are disputed.

Case law. The law as defined by previously decided cases, distinct from statutes and other sources of law.

Cause. A case, suit, litigation, or action, civil or criminal.

Certiorari, Writ of. A writ issued from the Supreme Court, at its discretion, to order a lower court to prepare the record of a case and send it to the Supreme Court for review.

Civil law. Body of law dealing with the private rights of individuals, as distinguished from criminal law.

Class action. A lawsuit brought by one person or group on behalf of all persons similarly situated.

Code. A collection of laws, arranged systematically.

Comity. Courtesy, respect; usually used in the legal sense to refer to the proper relationship between state and federal courts.

Common law. Collection of principles and rules of action, particularly from unwritten English law, which derive their authority from longstanding usage and custom or from courts recognizing and enforcing these customs. Sometimes used synonymously with case law.

Consent decree. A court-sanctioned agreement settling a legal dispute and entered into by the consent of the parties.

Contempt (civil and criminal). Civil contempt consists in the failure to do something that the party is ordered by the court to do for the benefit of another party. Criminal contempt occurs when a person willfully exhibits disrespect for the court or obstructs the administration of justice.

Conviction. Final judgment or sentence that the defendant is guilty as charged.

Criminal law. That branch of law which deals with the enforcement of laws and the punishment of persons who, by breaking laws, commit crimes.

Declaratory judgment. A court pronouncement declaring a legal right or interpretation but not ordering a specific action.

De facto. In fact, in reality.

Defendant. In a civil action, the party denying or defending itself against charges brought by a plaintiff. In a criminal action, the person indicted for commission of an offense.

De jure. As a result of law, as a result of official action.

Deposition. Oral testimony from a witness taken out of court in response to written or oral questions, committed to writing, and intended to be used in the preparation of a case.

Dicta. See Obiter dictum.

Dismissal. Order disposing of a case without a trial.

Docket. See Trial docket.

Due process. Fair and regular procedure. The Fifth and Fourteenth Amendments guarantee persons that they will not be deprived of life, liberty, or property by the government until fair and usual procedures have been followed.

Error, Writ of. A writ issued from an appeals court to a lower court requiring it to send to the appeals court the record of a case in which it has entered a final judgment and which the appeals court will now review for error.

Ex parte. Only from, or on, one side. Application to a court for some ruling or action on behalf of only one party.

Ex post facto. After the fact; an ex post facto law makes an action a crime after it has already been committed, or otherwise changes the legal consequences of some past action.

Ex rel. Upon information from; usually used to describe legal proceedings begun by an official in the name of the state, but at the instigation of, and with information from, a private individual interested in the matter.

Grand jury. Group of twelve to twenty-three persons impaneled to hear in private evidence presented by the state against persons accused of crime and to issue indictments when a majority of the jurors find probable cause to believe that the accused has committed a crime. Called a "grand" jury because it comprises a greater number of persons than a "petit" jury.

Grand jury report. A public report released by a grand jury after an investigation into activities of public officials that fall short of criminal actions. Grand jury reports are often called "presentments."

Guilty. A word used by a defendant in entering a plea or by a jury in returning a verdict, indicating that the defendant is legally responsible as charged for a crime or other wrongdoing.

Habeas corpus. Literally, "you have the body"; a writ issued to inquire whether a person is lawfully imprisoned or detained. The writ demands that the persons holding the prisoner justify his detention or release him.

Immunity. A grant of exemption from prosecution in return for evidence or testimony.

In camera. "In chambers." Refers to court hearings in private without spectators.

In forma pauperis. In the manner of a pauper, without liability for court costs.

In personam. Done or directed against a particular person.

In re. In the affair of, concerning. Frequent title of judicial proceedings in which there are no adversaries, but rather where the matter itself—as a bankrupt's estate—requires judicial action.

In rem. Done or directed against the thing, not the person.

Indictment. A formal written statement based on evidence presented by the prosecutor from a grand jury decided by a majority vote, charging one or more persons with specified offenses.

Information. A written set of accusations, similar to an indictment, but filed directly by a prosecutor.

Injunction. A court order prohibiting the person to whom it is directed from performing a particular act.

Interlocutory decree. A provisional decision of the court that temporarily settles an intervening matter before completion of a legal action.

Judgment. Official decision of a court based on the rights and claims of the parties to a case that was submitted for determination.

Jurisdiction. The power of a court to hear a case in question, which exists when the proper parties are present, and when the point to be decided is within the issues authorized to be handled by the particular court.

Juries. See Grand jury and Petit jury.

Magistrate. A judicial officer having jurisdiction to try minor criminal cases and conduct preliminary examinations of persons charged with serious crimes.

Mandamus. "We command." An order issued from a superior court directing a lower court or other authority to perform a particular act.

Moot. Unsettled, undecided. A moot question is also one that is no longer material; a moot case is one that has become hypothetical.

Motion. Written or oral application to a court or a judge to obtain a rule or an order.

Nolo contendere. "I will not contest it." A plea entered by a defendant at the discretion of the judge with the same legal effect as a plea of guilty, but it may not be cited in other proceedings as an admission of guilt.

Obiter dictum. Statement by a judge or justice expressing an opinion and included with, but not essential to, an opinion resolving a case before the court. Dicta are not necessarily binding in future cases.

Parole. A conditional release from imprisonment under conditions that if the prisoner abides by the law and other restrictions that may be placed upon him, he will not have to serve the remainder of his sentence. But if he does not abide by specified rules, he will be returned to prison.

Per curiam. "By the court." An unsigned opinion of the court or an opinion written by the whole court.

Petit jury. A trial jury, originally a panel of twelve persons who tried to reach a unanimous verdict on questions of fact in criminal and civil proceedings. Since 1970 the Supreme Court has upheld the legality of state juries with fewer than twelve persons. Because it comprises fewer persons than a "grand" jury, it is called a "petit" jury.

Petitioner. One who files a petition with a court seeking action or relief, including a plaintiff or an appellant. But a petitioner is also a person who files for other court action where charges are not necessarily made; for example, a party may petition the court for an order requiring another person or party to produce documents. The opposite party is called the respondent.

When a writ of certiorari is granted by the Supreme Court, the parties to the case are called petitioner and respondent in contrast to the appellant and appellee terms used in an appeal.

Plaintiff. A party who brings a civil action or sues to obtain a remedy for injury to his rights. The party against whom action is brought is termed the defendant.

Plea bargaining. Negotiations between prosecutors and the defendant aimed at exchanging a plea of guilty from the defendant for concessions by the prosecutors, such as reduction of charges or a request for leniency.

Pleas. See Guilty and Nolo contendere.

Presentment. See Grand jury report.

Prima facie. At first sight; referring to a fact or other evidence presumably sufficient to establish a defense or a claim unless otherwise contradicted.

Probation. Process under which a person convicted of an offense, usually a first offense, receives a suspended sentence and is given his freedom, usually under the guardianship of a probation officer.

Quash. To overthrow, annul, or vacate; as to quash a subpoena.

Recognizance. An obligation entered into before a court or magistrate requiring the performance of a specified act—usually to appear in court at a later date. It is an alternative to bail for pretrial release.

Remand. To send back. In the event of a decision being remanded, it is sent back by a higher court to the court from which it came for further action.

Respondent. One who is compelled to answer the claims or questions posed in court by a petitioner. A defendant and an appellee may be called respondents, but the term also includes those parties who answer in court during actions where charges are not necessarily brought or where the Supreme Court has granted a writ of certiorari.

Seriatim. Separately, individually, one by one.

Stare decisis. "Let the decision stand." The principle of adherence to settled cases, the doctrine that principles of law established in earlier judicial decisions should be accepted as authoritative in similar subsequent cases.

Statute. A written law enacted by a legislature. A collection of statutes for a particular governmental division is called a code.

Stay. To halt or suspend further judicial proceedings.

Subpoena. An order to present one's self before a grand jury, court, or legislative hearing.

Subpoena duces tecum. An order to produce specified documents or papers.

Tort. An injury or wrong to the person or property of another.

Transactional immunity. Protects a witness from prosecution for any offense mentioned in or related to his testimony, regardless of independent evidence against him.

Trial docket. A calendar prepared by the clerks of the court listing the cases set to be tried.

Use immunity. Protects a witness against the use of his own testimony against him in prosecution.

Vacate. To make void, annul, or rescind.

Writ. A written court order commanding the designated recipient to perform or not perform acts specified in the order.

BIBLIOGRAPHY

Abraham, Henry J. *The Judiciary: The Supreme Court in the Governmental Process.* New York and London: New York University Press, 1996.

Biskupic, Joan, and Elder Witt. *The Supreme Court at Work,* 2d ed. Washington, D.C.: Congressional Quarterly, 1997.

Black, Henry Campbell. *Black's Law Dictionary,* 3d ed. St. Paul, Minn.: West Publishing, 1983.

Callender, Clarence N. *American Courts: Their Organization and Procedure.* New York: McGraw-Hill, 1927.

Carp, Robert A., and Ronald Stidham. *Judicial Process in America,* 4th ed. Washington, D.C.: CQ Press, 1998.

Carp, Robert A., and Ronald Stidham. *The Federal Courts,* 3d ed. Washington, D.C.: CQ Press, 1998.

Court Statistics Project. *State Court Caseload Statistics, 1996.* Williamsburg, Va.: National Center for State Courts, 1997.

Foner, Eric, and John A. Garraty, eds. *The Reader's Companion to American History.* Boston: Houghton Mifflin, 1991.

Friedman, Lawrence M. *A History of American Law,* 2d ed. New York: Simon & Schuster, 1985.

Gates, John B., and Charles A. Johnson. *The American Courts: A Critical Assessment.* Washington, D.C.: Congressional Quarterly, 1991.

Gilmore, Grant. *The Ages of American Law.* New Haven and London: Yale University Press, 1977.

Glick, Henry R., and Kenneth N. Vines. *State Court Systems.* Englewood Cliffs, N.J.: Prentice-Hall, 1973.

Goulden, Joseph C. *The Benchwarmers: The Private World of the Powerful Federal Judges.* New York: Ballantine Books, 1976.

Guinness Book of World Records. New York: Bantam Books, 1998.

Hall, Kermit L., William M. Wiecek, and Paul Finkelman. *American Legal History: Cases and Materials.* New York: Oxford University Press, 1991.

Henderson, Dwight F. *Congress, Courts, and Criminals: The Development of Federal Criminal Law, 1801.*

Judicial Conference of the United States. *Long-Range Plan for the Federal Courts.* Washington, D.C.: Administrative Office of the United States Courts, 1995.

Kruman, Marc W. *Between Authority & Liberty: State Constitution Making in Revolutionary America.* Chapel Hill: University of North Carolina Press, 1997.

Maddex, Robert L. *State Constitutions of the United States.* Washington, D.C.: Congressional Quarterly, 1998.

Maddex, Robert L. *The Illustrated History of Constitutional Concepts.* Washington, D.C.: Congressional Quarterly, 1996.

McLynn, Frank. *Famous Trials: Cases That Made History.* New York: Reader's Digest, 1995.

Mecham, Leonidas R. *Judicial Business of the United States Courts: 1998 Report of the Director.* Washington, D.C.: Administrative Office of the United States Courts, 1998.

Ostrom, Brian J., and Neal B. Kauder, eds. *Examining the Work of State Courts, 1996: A National Perspective from the Court Statistics Project.* Williamsburg, Va.: National Center for State Courts, 1997.

Ostrom, Brian J., and Neal B. Kauder, eds. *Examining the Work of State Courts, 1994: A National Perspective from the Court Statistics Project.* Williamsburg, Va.: National Center for State Courts, 1996.

Quigley, Charles N., and Duane E. Smith, eds. *With Liberty and Justice for All: The Story of the Bill of Rights.* Calabasas, Calif.: Center for Civic Education, 1991.

Rottman, David B., et al. *State Court Organization, 1993.* Washington, D.C.: U.S. Department of Justice, Bureau of Justice Statistics, 1995.

Smith, Patricia, ed. *The Nature and Process of Law: An Introduction to Legal Philosophy.* New York: Oxford University Press, 1993.

Tarr, G. Alan, and Mary Cornelia Aldis Porter. *State Supreme Courts in State and Nation.* New Haven: Yale University Press, 1988.

Tindall, George Brown. *America: A Narrative History, Vol. II,* 5th ed. New York: W.W. Norton, 1999.

U.S. Supreme Court. *Rules of the Supreme Court of the United States,* rev. ed. Washington, D.C.: U.S. Supreme Court, 1980.

Wheeler, Russell R., and Cynthia Harrison. *Creating the Federal Judicial System,* 2d ed. Washington, D.C.: Federal Judicial Center, 1994.

Witt, Elder, ed. *The Supreme Court A to Z: A Ready Reference Encyclopedia,* rev. ed. Washington, D.C.: Congressional Quarterly, 1994.

INDEX

NOTE: Locator references point to question numbers in the text.

NOTE: Locator references point to question numbers in the text.

NOTE: *Locator references point to question numbers in the text.*

NOTE: Locator references point to question numbers in the text.

NOTE: Locator references point to question numbers in the text.

NOTE: Locator references point to question numbers in the text.

NOTE: Locator references point to question numbers in the text.

NOTE: *Locator references point to question numbers in the text.*

NOTE: Locator references point to question numbers in the text.

NOTE: *Locator references point to question numbers in the text.*

NOTE: Locator references point to question numbers in the text.

NOTE: Locator references point to question numbers in the text.

NOTE: Locator references point to question numbers in the text.

NOTE: Locator references point to question numbers in the text.

NOTE: Locator references point to question numbers in the text.

NOTE: *Locator references point to question numbers in the text.*

Warren, Earl, 212
Washington, George, 35, 116, 160, 167, 178, 273
Washington (state)
  constitution of, 334
  court system governance of, 342
  three-strikes law in, 533
Watergate affair, executive privilege and, 18
Web site for U.S. Supreme Court decisions, 127
Webster, Daniel, 60
Webster v. Reproductive Health Services, 109 S. Ct. 3040 (1989), 130
Western District Court of Texas, drug cases in, 248
West Virginia
  cost of court system in, per capita, 366
  felony filings in, 521
Wheaton, Henry, 189
Whitehill, Robert, 47
Wickersham, James, 240

Williams, Aubrey, 391
Williams v. Florida 399 U.S. 78 (1970), 441
Wills, 582, 583
Wilson, Woodrow, 155, 195
Wisconsin, court structure in, 343
Witness(es)
  expert *versus* other, 452
  questioning by jurors, 440
  requirements for trial appearance by, 453
  requirements for trial testimony by, 454
Women
  as chief justices, 556
  as federal judges, 80, 82, 228
  state constitution suffrage clauses for, 324
  on U.S. Supreme Court Bar, 199
Woodmen of the World, 392
Worcester, Samuel, 390
Worcester v. Georgia, 6 Pet. 515 (1832), 390
Workplace discrimination, U.S. Supreme Court and, 181

Writ of certiorari, 107
  Rule of Four and, 108
  U.S. Supreme Court and, 143
  written page limit on, 128
Writ of habeas corpus, 60
  suspension of, 62
  U.S. Supreme Court cases accepted under, 111
  U.S. Supreme Court cases filed under, 110
Writ of mandamus, 102
Written opinions, U.S. Supreme Court, 126
Wyoming
  appellate filings in, 381
  general jurisdiction authorized judges of, 554
Wyoming Territory, women's suffrage in, 324

Yale Law School, 264
Yippies, 548

Zenger, John Peter, 432

NOTE: Locator references point to question numbers in the text.